Katja Schönian
Just 'A Machine for Doing Business'?

Katja Schönian gained her PhD at Europa Universität Viadrina, Frankfurt/Oder. Prior to this, she completed the three-year postgraduate programme "Sociology of Social Practices" at the Institut für Höhere Studien (IHS) in Vienna where she also worked as a junior researcher. She holds a Master's degree in "Critical and Creative Analysis" from the Sociology Department at Goldsmiths College, University of London and finished the BA-programme "Philosophy and Culture" at Universität Witten/Herdecke. Her research interests involve the study of work practices and technologies, consumer research, and methodological innovations within qualitative research.

Katja Schönian

Just 'A Machine for Doing Business'?

Sociomaterial Configurations of the Intranet in a Post-merger
Telecommunications Company

[transcript]

This publication was supported by the Viadrina Center for Graduate Studies (VCGS).

The book is based on the author's dissertation which was successfully defended on July 9, 2021 at the Faculty of Social and Cultural Sciences of the European University Viadrina, Frankfurt (Oder). The dissertation was supervised by Prof. Dr. Andreas Reckwitz.

Bibliographic information published by the Deutsche Nationalbibliothek
The Deutsche Nationalbibliothek lists this publication in the Deutsche Nationalbibliografie; detailed bibliographic data are available in the Internet at http://dnb.d-nb.de

Cover layout: Maria Arndt, Bielefeld
Cover illustration: Martinelle / Pixabay

Print-ISBN 978-3-8376-6187-3
PDF-ISBN 978-3-8394-6187-7
https://doi.org/10.14361/9783839461877
ISSN of series: 2702-7910
eISSN of series: 2703-0326

Contents

*"System design [...] must include not only
the design of innovative artifacts,
but their artful integration with the rest
of the social and material world."*

Lucy Suchman (1997)

Acknowledgements

This dissertation was made possible because of the support and involvement of many people. To begin, I would like to offer my sincere thanks to those who participated in my research, who agreed to be interviewed and whom I was able to visit at their workplace. It is impossible to imagine this dissertation without you – you all contributed to its development! Many thanks also to those who supported my dissertation financially; I received stipends from the Institute for Advanced Studies (IHS), the German Academic Exchange Service (DAAD), and the Family Affairs Office at the European University Viadrina.

My theoretical and empirical interest in organisations started as an undergraduate student at Witten/Herdecke University. I would like to thank Dirk Baecker who encouraged this interest which laid the foundation for my academic pathway. I also want to thank Athanasios Karafillidis who was central to my undergraduate study by providing feedback on my Bachelor thesis. I also owe a special thank you to Vikki Bell of Goldsmiths College, University of London; you were not only important to my Master programme but also when my PhD got caught up in the administrative pitfalls of undertaking an international education. This dissertation was accomplished because of your immediate response and intervention – thank you! Many thanks also to my supervisor, Andreas Reckwitz, and to Hilmar Schäfer who gave me advice and encouraged me at various times.

During my dissertation research, I was fortunate to be affiliated with two research communities; first of all, I was part of the postgraduate training programme "Sociology of Social Practices" in the Sociology Department at the Institute for Advanced Studies (IHS) in Vienna. Secondly, as a Visiting Student at Lancaster University, I was lucky to join the vibrant research community at the Department of Sociology. My work greatly benefitted from the conversations and exchange there for which I am very grateful. I also owe a great thanks to a number of colleagues at these two places who supported me by reading and commenting on my work.

Above all, this dissertation is indebted to my dear friends and colleagues who stuck by me through it all. A special thank you to Stefan Laube and Alexandra Vinson, I am forever grateful for your unwavering feedback and support. Stefan, you always encouraged me to believe in my work; Alex, you kept me on track by settling my doubts and reassuring me to continue this process. Without you both, this dissertation would not have been possible. I also owe a great thanks to Sarah Richards who commented on the text, proof-read my English and supported me with her optimistic thinking. I would also like to thank Anna Pichelstorfer for sharing experiences throughout the different phases of doing a PhD and Julia Wildeis for her good company during these years. I am also very grateful for the immediate and precise work of my editor, Jan Leichsenring.

This work could not have been completed without the love and support of my family – my parents and my sister. You did not give up on me, even when I could not always provide very convincing explanations of what I actually did all day and why my dissertation was not finished yet. Thank you for accompanying me in this endeavour.

List of Figures and Tables

1 Introduction: Intranet technologies

Relying on the promise to connect employees despite their physical separation, intranets have gained increasing popularity in recent years; almost every organisation, be it in the private or the public sector, has a version of intranet software in order to organise their internal information and communication processes in the company. Intranets are defined as "internal closed network[s] based on Internet technology designed to foster communication and collaboration within a single enterprise" (Bayles Kalman, 2003: 683). Indeed, the emergence of intranets in the 1990s started in close association with the World Wide Web since both the Internet and intranets rely on hypertext transfer protocol (so-called "http"). Such protocols allow to transfer and download data in a web browser. But while the main characteristic of the Internet is its global scope and availability, intranets are limited to an organisation and stored on private servers, offering access to employees and registered users only, usually through personal username and password (Callaghan, 2002: 3–4). Hence, one of the central characteristics of an intranet is its dedication to the whole of a company, (theoretically) meant to connect all employees across different departments and work settings. Within the formal organisational structure of a company, intranets are most often maintained in the Internal Communications department.

Early versions of intranets were set up like an archive or database enabling access to files and documents. More elaborated features were added through individual programming, making the development of these sites rather costly. As a response, the development of large packages encompassing software for entire companies increased, usually including applications for distinct departments and work processes. A prominent example of such an enterprise resource planning system, as they are called, is SAP (the name stands for "Systems, Analysis and Products in Data Processing") which started as a standard software package (Jacobs and Weston, 2007). By now, SAP comprises different packages serving individual business processes, such as accounting, purchasing and inventory management. Other enterprise application software address specific industries only, such as financial or telecommunication businesses. From a managerial perspective, enterprise software packages serve well the idea of governing and planning business operations and objectives. But they prove themselves to be somewhat static when aiming to adapt to a company's individual work processes (cf. Farhoomand, 2007; see also Leimbach, 2008; Conrad, 2017).

The next phase of intranets brought about so-called 'portals' which were based on the idea to easily add and remove specific features and applications. Thus, intranets became more like a loose 'grid', allowing to integrate individual elements which can easily be relocated. With the emergence of Web 2.0 technologies, the focus oriented towards more interactive software in order to share and generate content and thereby enable collaboration. Especially so-called "Wikis" became popular since these websites assist shared content generation, usually among a smaller group of people (Trkman and Trkman, 2009). Today, intranets mostly integrate text, graphics, sounds and videos as well as characteristics of Web 2.0 technologies, that is, social media features such as buttons and commentary functions. Also, with greater technological adaptability, the increasing personalisation of features and content on the intranet has become an important characteristic.

In this manner, intranets assemble static but also interactive content and applications. They are often built around the formal structure of a company, mapping the hierarchical as well as labour-divisional set up of an organisation. A central feature is the presentation of internal and external company news in the form of a newsfeed on the starting page. Furthermore, an organisational chart and the company's benefit scheme is usually stored and ready for inspection. Also, intranets document and proceed various work processes; for example, travel expenses may be submitted or new software ordered in a pre-set application on the intranet. On top of that, a variety of communication instruments such as instant or mobile text messaging applications or a video channel are often accessible through the intranet. Another important function on the intranet is the option to search its database for specific content or applications.

1.1   Just "a machine for doing business"?[1]

Looking more closely into information systems and management consulting literature, software technologies in general and intranets in particular are often described as means of change that not only provide access to information (i.e. documents and files) and applications (enabling certain work processes) and thereby organise work processes; they are understood to also change *how* work is done. This becomes evident in the entry on intranet software from the encyclopaedia of information systems:

> The truly effective intranet creates new opportunities for communication that overcome inefficient organizational structures and foster new forms of efficient collaboration. It serves as a model for a company centred on processes rather than departments, collaboration rather than closed doors. (Bayles Kalman, 2003: 683)

As can be seen, the quote describes the intranet as an instrument that changes communication and work processes for the better, namely as becoming more efficient. Likewise, the second part of the quote frames the intranet as being a 'model', a representation or mirror of the company that stands for a different approach towards work more generally. This becomes also obvious in the appreciation of the intranet as a technology that can be applied as a 'tool', serving as a means to an end which can be defined beforehand: "The effective intranet is a tool; it is also a model for an efficient, process-centred enterprise. It is a machine for doing business" (Bayles Kalman, 2003: 684). In fact, the notion of 'tool' emphasises the stable and finite character of a technology, thereby considering the context, i.e. the organisation, as being modifiable, for instance in the case of increasing performance or changing work processes (Orlikowski and Iacono, 2001: 123). In this manner, intranets have become part of the technology consulting industry where tech companies offer seemingly straightforward software solutions to address specific business processes or problems, as mentioned above in relation to SAP (Dörfel and Hirsch, 2012; see also Pollock et al., 2007).

Intranets carry along managerial ideas that in fact date back to the emergence of the so-called "scientific management" approach in organisation studies which is committed to the idea that work processes can be,

---

1   Quote from the Encyclopaedia of Information Systems (Bayles Kalman, 2003: 684).

firstly, predetermined and, secondly, arranged with the highest efficiency (Froschauer, 2012: 46). The central advocate of this paradigm, Frederick W. Taylor (1856–1915), emphasised the rationalisation and detailed documentation of work processes for managing businesses (Taylor, 2001; [1911]).[2] In fact, these developments worked on the premise to exercise control over managers, workers and production processes by standardising and documenting work procedures (Yates, 1989). Against this background, internal communications as a specific managerial instrument emerged, professionalising the communication with the workforce and determining work procedures in the company (ibid.: 2).

However, the somewhat one-sided perspective on managing work processes and employees was soon complemented by the so-called "corporate welfare movement", which opposed the exclusively rational and systemic understanding of workers. Instead, it emphasised the individual employee and the importance of a "more humane and cooperative atmosphere" in the factory by providing healthcare, libraries and clubhouses to workers and their families (Yates, 1989: 17). The idea that organisations are not only made of abstract work tasks and procedures, but permeated by a social fabric, found entry into the emergence of Human Relations as an additional type of management (Froschauer, 2012: 47). Evolving group norms and related dynamics as well as the motivation and satisfaction of workers became important for thinking about how work is done in the organisation (ibid.). In-house magazines or so-called shop papers served as means to establish a closer relationship with employees – they brought together a great variety of topics not only concerning the company, but also the individual worker by, for instance, discussing their professional role in the company (Yates, 1989: 17; 75–6). Obviously, workers' contributions in these papers were welcomed. However, as JoAnne Yates stresses critically, such magazines foremost assisted company management as yet another type of downward communication by prescribing ideal worker norms and workers' identification with the company (cf. Davies and Frink, 2014; Heppner, 2013).

From a historical perspective, it was the distributed construction work part of the railroad industry that made it necessary to align different stakeholders across distinct locales at the end of the 19th century. Before, correspondence happened through letters and notes carried on by messengers.

---

2   This approach was taken up by Henry Ford and further applied to industrialised mass production of which the assembly belt became a central element.

However, the commissioning of railways called for the distribution of written guidelines and especially time schedules (Yates, 1989: 4). In this context, downward communication was established as a hierarchical principle. At the same time, upward communication became likewise necessary since management became increasingly detached from the day-to-day work activities. Thus, business growth and the dissemination of work made it necessary to manage internal company communication in order to organise and control work activities. From the beginning, these developments were related to artefacts functioning as organising instruments; for instance, the press copier and carbon paper enabled the reproduction of messages and the filing cabinet was the start for more elaborated archival systems (Yates, 1989: 62; Wit et al., 2002: 56–8). Such devices systematised the storage of documents and enabled prompt access. Also, the typewriter, introduced in offices at the beginning of the 20th century, increased the production of texts. Overall, these devices and technologies reduced those time costs understood as unnecessary and inefficient and hence assisted company management in controlling employees and work processes (Yates, 1989).

Against this background, intranet technology can be understood as continuing such early communication practices of 'duplicating' and distributing internal messages across distances by making them available in the newsfeed on the starting page. Moreover, it also constitutes an archival system where certain communication procedures – news and reports about the company and its activities – are stored and ready to be accessed. However, as will become apparent, today intranets obviously move beyond these early internal communication practices as they automate work processes, for instance when it comes to ordering personal software or reporting a failure to facility management. Likewise, they make available specific applications enabling communication exchange, such as instant or text messaging. In the fashion of Web 2.0 technologies, today intranets call upon users to comment on and rate content and to make their own contributions. In fact, intranets are an early example of the so-called digitalisation of work as they aim to prestructure and control work processes as well as organise the internal communication and engage employees to contribute content and personal data (cf. Schulz-Schaeffer and Funken, 2008: 15).

In this manner, the intranet is a paradigmatic example of how a technology is understood to function and expected to deliver specific results. That is, conceived to make internal communication and work processes more efficient, the intranet is framed a managerial instrument that determines and controls work tasks. In fact, this perspective is characteristic for narratives and research on technologies in organisations where the technology is constructed as a determining force inducing predictable outcomes (Barrett et al., 2006: 7; see also Pellegrino, 2012). The primary approach within this literature is to distil relevant variables and determine so-called 'best practices' (Torres et al., 2008). Especially the implementation and adoption phase of technologies constitute a prevalent case for such research in order to define relevant factors (Heracleous and Barrett, 2001; Ruppel and Harrington, 2001).

In addition, as will be shown, resonating with ideas from the corporate welfare movement, intranets are also intended to design the company's social fabric by raising employees' identification and commitment with the company. While the topic of post-industrial management, the notion of organisational identity and related conflicts in the company I investigated will be further discussed in Chapter 3, let me outline the wider societal developments, in particular the characteristics of today's post-industrial economy, which must be considered as the broader context of my case of the intranet.

1.2   The post-industrial economy: Cognitive-cultural capitalism and "immaterial labour"

The era of industrialisation was characterised by the production of goods in large factories where the division of work, to name just one of the most important rationalising measures, ensured the efficient and effective use of labour. As mentioned above, during this time, early ideas about how to manage and stimulate workers' performance emerged with regard to how to exercise control. Specific technological advancements, such as the railroad but also the telegraph and electrical engineering more generally, constituted the necessary background for these developments (Reckwitz, 2020: 144). Overall, as Andreas Reckwitz emphasises, the industrial economy relied on the mass production *and* mass consumption of goods by the same workers that actually manufactured these mostly functional goods (ibid.: 145). In comparison to the agriculture-based economy, the industrial economy brought wealth to a relatively large number of people because of its large scale production and consumption.

The supply and demand for goods reached its high peak in the 1950s; but especially since the 1960s and 70s, the industrial economy came increasingly under pressure because of saturated and declining markets. Rising unemployment, a looming recession and the oil crisis in 1973 contributed to this development. Daniel Bell was one of the authors who described fairly early the characteristics of a so-called "post-industrial society" in which the economy consists to a large extent of services and a knowledge-based industry (Bell, 1976). Other authors, such as Scott Lash and John Urry, similarly underline the importance of knowledge and information for a globally operating economy that is based on work processes that do not simply produce specific goods, but 'manufacture' their cultural value and singularity (1994: 3; see also Slater and Barry, 2005: 1). Accordingly, the distinguishing feature of a specific product lies not anymore in its functionality, but in its 'immaterial' difference, which is obtained through a specific cultural-symbolic value.

In fact, the notion of "immaterial labour" (Lazzarato, 2006) is decisive for understanding the post-industrial economy and its work processes; as Lazzarato says, immaterial or cognitive labour encompasses the generation of knowledge and information for research and development, design, communication and marketing activities, in particular consumer research, in order to not only create the product but its context (see also Lazzarato, 2004; Arvidsson, 2005a: 241; Thrift, 2005). As Scott Lash and Celia Lury have shown, as part of these activities, brands such as Nike or Starbucks are characteristic of a global culture industry that relies on the "construction of *difference*" (2007: 5, emphasis in original) so as to address potential consumer desires. Describing this kind of work, Carolin Gerlitz underlines that

> [...] securing competitive advantage can only be obtained through immaterial differentiation, for example, by addressing niche audiences, developing design strategies or adding symbolic and sign value to material offerings.

That is, design and marketing activities are central to value production in order to generate constant demand and create new desires and affective attachments. The emergence and management of specific brands plays a major role in this development; in fact, they are described as the "immaterial capital" of today's post-industrial economy (Arvidsson, 2005a: 239). As Adam Arvidsson further outlines, the value of so-called intangible assets (such as patents and intellectual property) has increased since the 1980s, but in particular brand value has become one of the most important assets in contemporary economies (2005b: 5).[3] Altogether, because of the dependence on im-

---

3   As Gerlitz further explains, brands increasingly shape the social and cultural sphere and configure social relations since economic value production is not confined to the

material and cognitive work and the symbolic quality that defines a product, authors refer to the notion of cognitive-cultural capitalism when describing the economic characteristics of late modernity (Reckwitz, 2020: 141; see also Slater and Tonkiss, 2001; Huws, 2019).[4]

When it comes to employment relations, we witness two forms of occupation that dominate the labour market: service work of rather low-skilled workers and so-called knowledge work that engages mostly high-skilled personnel (Reckwitz, 2020: 153 et seqq.).[5] In fact, within the post-industrial economy, knowledge work ensures the necessary and ongoing innovation within society so as to develop new products, events or experiences (e.g. Stehr, 1994, 2007).[6] In contrast, service workers are employed in areas such as logistics, care, tourism and gastronomy, i.e. mostly in the low-wage sector, thereby increasingly replacing industrial work but without being protected by the governmental regulation that existed during Fordist working conditions (Reckwitz, 2020: 156–7; see also Flecker, 2017: 91 et seqq.). As Andreas Reckwitz points out, *both* types of work constitute the backdrop of the post-industrial economy; in fact, they almost complement each other since knowledge workers rely on services in order to delegate certain activities, such as childcare, cleaning and domestic work. In contrast, jobs requiring mid-level qualification, for instance in administration and in retail, have declined since the 1980s (2020: 158).

Overall, work in the post-industrial economy is understood as an individual project and symbolically valued as emotionally satisfying, thereby rather

---

factory anymore, but emerges into a variety of areas, especially through new forms of media and consumer engagements (2012: 16; see also Arvidsson, 2005b).

4   Andreas Reckwitz differentiates between industrial and late modernity; the first was shaped by rationalising and formalising efforts that became, he says, almost universal principles in society. In contrast, since the 1970s, the search for authenticity and hence "singularity" has become most prevalent – in relation to various societal domains, such as the production of goods but also as part of the formation of subjects and collectives (2017: 12).

5   Even though the telecommunication industry covers both types of work, for instance in the form of call centre agents and software developers, my research focuses on knowledge work, in particular of so-called technicians and employees working in the area of Customer Communication and Business Sales.

6   Analysing digital capitalism, Sabine Pfeiffer (2021) highlights its distributive forces put forward by online platforms, artificial intelligence, robotics, and the like. As she argues, contemporary economies rely not only on the efficient value production of goods and products, but in particular on their ongoing realisation on the market.

serving managerial interest (Alvesson and Willmott, 2002: 622; see also Reck-witz, 2017: 201–3; Flecker, 2017: 41). However, while service work is character-ized by the automation and rationalisation of activities, managerial strategies in the context of knowledge work call upon employees' subjectivity. Compar-ing literature across different decades, Luc Boltanski and Eve Chiapello (2005) show how post-industrial management depends on mobilising the individual worker, who submits to notions such as creativity, innovation, project and team work in order to comply with the 'new spirit of capitalism' that de-mands a flexible and adaptive subject.[7] In fact, people engage in economic value production by developing an "entrepreneurial self" (Bröckling, 2015) that constantly seeks to optimise his or her chances on the labour market. Thus, responsibility for one's competences and overall performance is primarily in-dividualised. These are forms of subjectification within postindustrialism that regulate people's self for the good of the company, a company that has to in-creasingly adjust to changing markets, as outlined above (e.g. Becke, 2017; Lohr, 2003).

But allow me to return to my research on the intranet; as I am going to show, not only the technology plays an important part in the case, but the internal marketing campaign that addresses employees in the context of the recent company merger is of significance, too. In fact, the branding of the merger, as I term it, is intended to gather employees around the new com-pany brand, thereby overlooking other conflicts in the company. The idea of the brand as a means for identification on the one hand, and a connecting link between employees on the other, addresses them primarily on an emo-tional level. It corresponds to the developments described above; understand-ing work as a source of identification and, moreover, as self-fulfilling indeed summarises major characteristics of contemporary knowledge work (Reck-witz, 2020: 160).[8] However, I will come back to further outline post-Fordist

---

7   As Boltanski and Chiapello explain, the new spirit of capitalism distinguishes itself from earlier versions in the sense that it has incorporated different types of critique, in particular from art and the 1968 student movement, thereby emphasising people's autonomy and authenticity (2005: 175-6).

8   As this case shows, the culturalisation of organisations does not only happen in relation to the nurturing of brands to an outside audience, but also when it comes to designing desirable corporate cultures inside the company (Reckwitz, 2017: 197 et seq.). I further discuss the notion of organisational culture in the context of research on mergers in Chapter 3.

management practices in Chapter 3, for the time being I will explain the theoretical and empirical starting points for my investigation.

1.3   Research questions and observations

Despite various functionalities and the managerial praise that defines intranets as instruments leading to more efficient work collaboration and increasing employee commitment, existing research shows that the implementation and use of intranets is more difficult than this narrative frames it (Damsgaard and Scheepers, 2000). That is, despite sophisticated design and technological advancement, intranets do not fulfil expectations in terms of usage and promised organisational change (Clarke and Preece, 2005). Often, employees' usage lies below expectations and intranets are generally disregarded in the company (Lamb, 1999; Stenmark, 2008). Furthermore, when it comes to knowledge sharing, it seems intranets do not overcome existing routines in the company so that outcomes are hard to predict (Newell et al., 2001; Ruppel and Harrington, 2001; see also Scott, 1998). In addition, despite a vast amount of research on the different aspects that intranets cover – collaboration, communication exchange, information and knowledge sharing, integration of newcomers – research on intranets is rather rare since access is especially difficult: intranets are often considered the heart of a company which must be secured from the outside (Lehmuskallio, 2006: 290–1).

Taking into account these findings, the starting point for my investigation into intranet technology has been the perceived gap between the general appreciation of intranets in the business and management field on the one hand and their rather ambiguous use in everyday work contexts on the other. At the beginning of my research, I was asking myself: What kind of expectations underpin the development and implementation of intranet technologies? And how do they play out as part of everyday work? In the course of my research, I also started to question the deterministic account of technology in general and intranets in particular. Thus, I began to ask more conceptual questions: How can we understand and frame the association of technologies, humans and work in today's increasingly mediatised office work?

Within the last decade, a variety of accounts on technology have emerged, examining different contexts of usage. Especially so-called process-approaches have pointed out the complexity of change projects and thereby described resistance as a possibly necessary stage of the change process

(Barrett et al., 2006: 8; see also Ford and Greer, 2016; Ford et al., 2008; Jones and Van de Ven, 2016). Moreover, research in the framework of neo-institutionalism has shown that new technologies may question existing understandings about work in the company and hence pointed out a "cultural inertia" when it comes to the wider dissemination of specific technologies in organisations and industries (Orlikowski and Barley, 2001: 155; see also Becker, 1995). In addition, referring to discursive analyses, research has investigated not only how different groups in the organisation may frame change projects, but also how situated projects incorporate larger narratives about technologies and their usefulness (Barrett et al., 2006: 11–2; 16). And most recently, on a theoretical layer, media studies scholars have pointed out the "mediatedness" of today's organisations, arguing for an integration of ideas from media theory into organisational theory in order to inform research on technologies in organisations (Beverungen et al., 2019).

Nevertheless, despite these insights, the dominant frame that "technology determine[s] the structure and behaviour of organizations and their members" (Barrett et al., 2006: 8) still prevails, especially when it comes to studying information and communication technologies, in particular intranets in the realm of business communication research. Leading is a rationale that investigates goals and aims and how to 'match' humans and technology (Adams et al., 1992; Ayatollahi et al., 2010; Davis, 1993). My research moves beyond such an instrumental approach that defines most existing studies by critically attending to the conceptualisation, implementation and application of intranets. The case of application is the intranet in a post-merger telecommunication business – which I call "Telecompany-X" – where the intranet technology is intended to support the post-merger integration process. My analysis unravels the involved practices and dynamics, focusing in particular on expectations towards the technology as well as how it is deployed in different work settings.

Doing so, this research contributes to understanding contemporary office work that is increasingly organised through information technologies and their applications. It asks: How is the intranet part of specific managerial and everyday work practices? Answering the question, it resorts to theories of practice and especially insights gained in Science and Technology Studies (STS) in order to analyse the subtle and intricate ways in which the intranet is part of everyday work and how these relate to the managerial idea of bringing together and connecting employees, previously from distinct companies. Thereby, I question the widespread idea that a technology such as the intranet is simply a tool serving a means to an end. Thus, instead of understanding the intranet as a 'mirror', a reflection or an abstract model of the company simply facilitating business processes, theories of practice allow to unravel how the intranet partakes in configuring the organisation, its work processes and the (increasingly) mediated communication taking place. As will become apparent, the intranet does not serve as a neutral tool – as it appears in the notion of a mirror or reflection – but adds to, interferes and entangles with management practices and employees' everyday work.

As such, my research is a paradigmatic investigation into the sociomaterial practices the intranet is part of and at the same time constitutes. It examines the expectations towards the technology, its design in the form of specific material properties as well as how they are socially appropriated when part of everyday work. I therefore explain next how theories of practice and in particular the notion of sociomateriality qualify as a research approach for an investigation into the intranet as part of today's technology-laden work settings.

1.4   Theories of practice in organisation research and Science & Technology Studies[9]

Within social theory, theories of practice have received great attention in the last twenty years as a specific form of cultural theory (Knorr Cetina et al., 2001). Focussing on the bodily and materially accomplishment of practices, they offer to rethink what has elsewhere been denoted as 'systems' or 'structures' when giving a description and analysis of the social (Reckwitz, 2003). By now, theories of practice constitute a research programme on their own, even though they rely on a variety of theoretical backgrounds, as for example Heidegger's 'being-in-the-world' understood as a practically engaged and in specific circumstances located subject, as well as Wittgenstein's theory of language-games that emphasises the implicit knowledge guiding human action (Reckwitz, 2003: 283).

Giving an overview on the different approaches in theory and research, Martha Feldman and Wanda Orlikowski (2011) distinguish between three

---

9   Parts of this section have been published in the *Graduate Journal of Social Sciences* (Schönian, 2011).

types of engagements. First, an empirical focus especially within organisational theory where the notion of practice stays rather implicit and the
empirical phenomenon is the centre of research (cf. Weick, 1995). Secondly, a
theoretical focus where the conception of practice is made explicit in order to
theoretically explain everyday activities and how they are generated, changed
and sustained in time. Here, a variety of backgrounds such as Bourdieu's
'implicit logic of practice' (Bourdieu, 1977), Giddens' 'situated practices' (Giddens, 1986), but also ethnomethodology's attention to everyday practices
(Garfinkel, 1967; Lynch, 2001), are considered as a reference. More recent
approaches, such as Actor-Network Theory (Latour, 2005) and Schatzki's site
ontology, are still understood as part of this account, even though Schatzki's
elaborate work on social practices belongs to a third, namely a philosophical
engagement with practices. Here, the practice-theoretical understanding
becomes an ontological statement where the world consists of and is only
brought about through practices (Schatzki, 1996, 2002).

Practice theorists vary in the way they present a rather sophisticated or
less elaborated concept of practices; however, they agree that a practice is defined as a 'nexus of doings and sayings' whereas the latter is seen as part of
the former (Schatzki, 1996: 89). Also, the situatedness of activities, being very
much indebted to the context and situation in which they occur, is jointly emphasised (Mol, 2002; Suchman, 2007; see also Schatzki, 2002). Furthermore,
the informal logic of all practices is highlighted, since most activities rely fundamentally on the implicit knowledge emerging through practices (Reckwitz,
2003: 291). Bodies and artefacts have been dedicated as the main bearer of this
knowledge and are therefore of great significance for the concept. In fact, this
is why the description and analysis of social practices refers to the materiality
of all behaviour which happens by virtue of bodies and artefacts (Reckwitz,
2003: 290). Thus, the knowledge underlying practices is incorporated into human bodies; moreover, it is a collective accomplishment, temporarily shared
with material objects (cf. Mol, 2002). However, when it comes to describing
the involvement of material artefacts, practice theorists offer distinct illustrations; whether objects are not just part, but in the sense of a 'symmetrical
anthropology' (Latour, 2015) also bearer of practices, is controversial (Reckwitz, 2003: 298, see also 2002a: 231–4).

Against this background, two research areas inform my conceptual take
on practice theories and hence constitute an important reference for my investigation into intranet technology.

First of all, research done in the realm of *Science and Technology Studies* (STS) and so-called 'Workplace Studies'. They have considered, since the 1980s, the material dimension of practices in the way that human and non-human actors assemble during a variety of work practices (Suchman, 2007; see also Wajcman, 2006; Knoblauch and Heath, 1999). Especially Lucy Suchman's notion of a "material-semiotic" (Suchman, 2012: 57) research approach that focuses on both, the materiality of the artefact but also the related imaginaries, has been of influence in this realm. It also includes the field of Human Computer Interaction (HCI) and Computer Supported Cooperative Work (CSCW). Instead of highlighting rules and goals as directing human behaviour, a sensibility towards the situated accomplishment of work practices and involved technologies distinguishes this research (Suchman et al., 1999, 2002; see also Hughes et al., 1991). Within this field, the computer or technology more generally is seen as actively partaking in the configuration of practices. In addition, STS has called attention to the ways in which users as well as technologies are reciprocally enacted (Oudshoorn and Pinch, 2003); neither are technologies or users simply given, nor can the effect of a specific technology be easily controlled. Both users and technology constantly come into being and are co-constructed in the accounts of software designers and developers as well as within the setting of their usage (Akrich, 1994; Wilkie and Michael, 2009; see also Woolgar, 1991).[10]

Secondly, research in the realm of *Organisation Studies*. In fact, the focus on practices has implicitly been part of a variety of research that moves beyond the idea of organisations as exclusively rational and bureaucratic institutions (Reckwitz, 2003: 285). For instance, the work of Karl E. Weick questions the term 'organisation' as it misleadingly frames a static and permanent entity. Instead, he calls attention to how activities align one another in the company, holding together the organisation as such (Weick, 1995). From this perspective, informal routines and ways of doings are foregrounded and understood as significant insights into how organising takes place (cf. Schatzki, 2006). This stands in contrast to, for instance, theories of bureaucracy or rational-choice approaches that predominantly refer to the formal structures of a company (Wilz, 2015: 256). Other approaches share a similar orientation, such as neo-institutionalism where scholars follow the idea that 'organising' happens

---

10   See Judy Wajcman's elaborate account on how STS may inform social theory, in particular when it comes to thinking about technological change beyond determinism that she describes as an often underlying principle (2002).

less by rational decision making but the *belief* in rationality, efficiency and the incorporation of these ideas into managerial instruments and technologies (Froschauer, 2012; Reckwitz, 2003: 285). In addition, the so-called strategy-as-practice research group foregrounds the activities or doings in connection with conceptions of strategy in organisations (Jarzabkowski, 2004, 2005). Also, research on organisational knowledge, understood as a situated and socially achieved accomplishment, constitutes another point of reference for this investigation (Lave and Wenger, 1991; Nicolini et al., 2003). While the initial idea of the strategy-as-practice research group was to "humanize" (Jarzabkowski et al., 2007: 6) existing research in management and organisation studies, as part of the continuing discussion of the notion of practice in social theory, a sophisticated and theoretically more elaborated engagement with the concept of practice has taken place in both realms (e.g. Seidl and Whittington, 2014; Whittington, 2006; Nicolini, 2013; Gherardi, 2012).

Research done in these fields raises awareness for the association of humans and technologies as part of work practices. In fact, the discussion about the contributing powers of artefacts, or more generally materialities, of particular relevance to my investigation into the intranet, has found its way into organisation studies under the notion of "sociomateriality". The term calls attention to the traditional neglect of the material dimension of organisational life, as Wanda Orlikowski has pointed out (Orlikowski and Scott, 2008). Prior to this discussion, organisation studies have either "ignored" this dimension, taken for granted or in its impact "minimize[d]" (2007: 1436–7, see also 2010). When artefacts are studied, it appears to be always a specific incident, as if organisations do not engage regularly and on a daily basis with materiality – in the form of offices, desks, pens as well as other technical and material devices (Orlikowski, 2007: 1437; see also Clash et al., 1994). Overall, as she emphasises, existing approaches mostly fail to notice that "materiality is not an incidental or intermittent aspect of organizational life; it is integral to it", and that technology is always part of historical and cultural processes, it does not exist in a vacuum (Orlikowski, 2007: 1436–7). Following Orlikowski's reasoning, the material is important, especially when it comes to understanding and theorising contemporary organisations that emerge through a variety of information technologies.

As can be seen, the notion of sociomateriality is a post-human account that strives to "decenter the human"; that is, it aspires to move beyond a framework that always tends to focus on the way people treat and deal with technology, questioning the "ontological separation" of humans and artefacts

(Orlikowski, 2007: 1437–8; see also Cooper and Law, 1995). In this manner, it moves beyond research on information technologies that tends to cut off effects or interactions with technology, centring either on the technology or on the human engaging with the technology, as if both humans and technologies are always comprehensible and complete entities (cf. Barley, 1986). That is, it opposes the deterministic understanding of technologies in business and management studies, as mentioned above. Instead, it describes a web or network of social and material entities, emphasising the relational capacities without ascribing a genuine substance or characteristic to either humans or non-human actors (Orlikowski, 2007, 2010). The quality of these associations must be seen as one of "constitutive entanglement", that is, a recursive, mutual engagement of artefacts and humans that brings about specific practices as well as artefacts (Orlikowski, 2007: 1437). Thus, comprehending technologies and software applications involves not only focussing on users, but on the practices that configure both technology and users. From this perspective, the intranet is not simply a tool, a mirror or representation of the company and specific processes, but partakes in constituting and configuring the organisation.

When leaving the idea of substances behind, one is able to look at the way associations in the organisation are established – not via some inherent substantial capacity in humans or artefacts, but through assembling and arranging practices (Cecez-Kecmanovic et al., 2014: 4). Practice-analyses fulfil a change of perspective in order to render intelligible social phenomena in the way they processually come about and are accomplished (Schmidt, 2012: 32). It is less a question of whether the social determines the technology or vice versa, but how both are brought about. Thus, social order is not taken for granted but investigated in situ. For instance, phenomena such as 'class' or 'gender' are not conceptually pre-defined, but considered as result and premise of, respectively for, specific practices (ibid.). Likewise, an organisation or a specific technology is not simply taken for granted, but the different practices are investigated which hold together and bring about the technology as such.

Following the focus on practices outlined above, my work understands the intranet as configured through practices – specific meanings and understandings associated with it, a know-how that enables to use the intranet in specific ways and a particular materiality that affords certain usages while preventing others. But investigating the intranet means also looking at the company's technological infrastructure, that is, other involved technologies such as phone and email communication that make work possible. Doing so, it becomes evident that a great deal of this work is the interaction through such technologies (cf. Wajcman and Rose, 2011: 950). Thus, the so-called mediatedness of contemporary work manifests itself in the integration and alignment of different devices for accomplishing everyday work.

In this sense, the practice-theoretical approach put forward in this work brings together research and analysis on the intranet in connection with the dynamics of the merger integration process. As I will show, the intranet is part of both company management's internal communication and branding practices to create a coherent, unified company after the merger as well as it is configured in employees' everyday work. Unravelling these different practices and their logics illuminates employees' ambivalent relationship to the intranet that in fact loses its identity while fanning out into a variety of applications relevant to employees' everyday work. But as my work argues, not having a definite identity in this manner turns out as both, an advantage and disadvantage; that is, from the perspective of strategic management, employees' ambiguous relation to the intranet indicates its partly failure to realise the managerial desire of company coherence. At the same time, as the second part of the study shows, the intranet is part of the company's technological infrastructure and specific applications indeed work well and are central to staff members' everyday work.

However, as a type of cultural theory, theories of practice also suggest an understanding of culture that extends existing approaches and, as I am going to show, offers an opportunity to rethink the dynamics involved in merger integrations (Reckwitz, 2002b).

1.5   A practice-theoretical understanding of mergers and organisational cultures

Examining existing studies, the dominant framework for analysing mergers and in particular the disparities in post-merger companies refers to the notion of 'culture' and 'cultural differences' (Riad, 2005; Lee et al., 2015). Doing so, groups of people are delineated by explaining their shared meaning making in relation to an all-encompassing holistic understanding of culture (Barley, 1983; see also Mol, 2002: 80). As scholars have critically remarked, the narrative of 'organisational culture' determines an explanatory agenda that is prevalent and hardly questioned, in research on mergers, but also in organisation, business and management studies and the consulting industry more generally (Schein, 2015). As Sally Riad states, it constitutes a truth whereby the notion of "'culture' has become natural to 'organization'" (2005: 1533), thus obstructing other narratives and analyses that move beyond the often conflict-laden, polarising and problematising account on mergers. Moreover, as scholars have pointed out, developments in cultural theory have not been taken up sufficiently, preventing scholars from getting new insights into the processes and dynamics involved in merger integrations, for instance when it comes to constant restructurings, the recomposing of company divisions, and employees' ongoing differentiations in the company (Angwin and Vaara, 2005: 1447; see also Patel, 2017; Rottig and Reus, 2018). Drawing on the notion of connectivity, authors have argued to look for the various ways in which associations in the post-merger company may happen, thereby moving beyond the traditional cultural perspective (Angwin and Vaara, 2005: 1448).

As this work argues, theories of practice give way to a different understanding of merger processes and address the appeal to re-think moments of connection and connectivity in the organisation. As Andreas Reckwitz outlines, existing cultural theories differ from theories of practice in the way they either centre the human mind or signs and symbols as the constitutive place of interpretation and knowledge generation (Reckwitz, 2002b: 248). He describes the first as 'mentalism' in the sense of early structuralist thinking by Claude Lévi-Strauss where culture is located in an unconscious set of rules guiding meaning making. In contrast, post-structuralist thinking, hermeneutics and constructivist systems theory are examples for cultural theories he calls 'textualism'; here, discourses, respectively communication, are the dedicated place where knowledge and symbolic structures are generated (Reckwitz, 2002b: 248–9).

Theories of practice depart from above-described cultural theories in the way they locate the social. As said earlier, theories of practice highlight the inherent knowledge tied to the accomplishment of practices, a knowledge which is not purely cognitive or just apparent in discourses and signs, but incorporated into bodies and shared with artefacts (Reckwitz, 2003: 289; see also Mol, 2002). For instance, answering emails at work or handling the variety of communication devices involves a specific bodily (as well as mental) alignment with these artefacts. In fact, these "cognitive-symbolic relations", as Andreas Reckwitz calls them, are recursively configured as part of (sociomaterial) practices and inform social action, without determining a "superstructure" in an all-encompassing manner (Reckwitz, 2002a: 213; see also Knorr

Cetina, 1999: 9–10; 247). Thus, interpretation of the world happens by virtue of socially shared practices and the involved (cognitive-symbolic) knowledge generation. As can be seen, theories of practice differ from social theory which resorts to collective norms and value in order to explain social order (Reckwitz, 2002b: 245). Likewise, they oppose rational-individualistic thinking as done in economic theory which stresses the amalgamation of individual reason and intention as the keystone when explaining the social fabric (ibid.).

Against this background, it is possible to unravel the involved practices and cognitive-symbolic relations in the post-merger company without assuming a total or closed system of cultural determination that opposes distinct cultures (understood as homogenous groups of people). That is, theories of practice assume "a hybrid combination of cultural elements stemming from different space and time" (Reckwitz, 2005: 94, own translation) and which are nevertheless brought together as part of practices. Thus, practices may consist of elements potentially from an extended time and space and which are trans-locally available (Reckwitz, 2005: 101–2; 106–7). This perspective enables one to describe the post-merger company as a hybrid formation, permeated by practices that (potentially) assemble elements and characteristics of the former two companies.

As such, the analysis adds to research on mergers within organisation and management studies by making (theoretically) apparent that, first of all, existing work practices may necessarily refer to the two companies' pre-merger differentiations, and, secondly, successful collaboration in the post-merger company must not rely on erasing the old, differentiating characteristics of the two former companies, as often proposed when two companies merge. Thus, examining the alignment of sociomaterial practices enables scholars to re-think the all-encompassing approach on culture that overlooks the composite character of functioning work practices.

1.6   Empirical Case: The intranet in Telecompany-X

The company. The fieldwork for this dissertation was undertaken in a company located in the telecommunication industry. By the time I started my investigation, Telecompany-X, as I call it, had just gone through a merger integrating landline and mobile communication in order to provide the whole array of telecommunication services to customers. Previously, in 2008 the mobile division employed 2,100 people and featured four different brand products that covered 4.6 million mobile customers and a revenue of 1.6 million euro. The landline division was the older and larger business, in 2008 it employed about 7,800 people and accounted for a revenue of 1.8 million euro while serving 2.3 million customers. Because of these differences, the merger was often described as a takeover or integration of the mobile division into the former landline business. Subsequent to the merger, Telecompany-X employed about 9,000 people, being the largest telecommunications company in the country. In 2012, the company featured 5.3 million mobile and 2.2 million landline telephony customers. The company's revenue accounted for 2.3 billion euro. A new intranet was introduced as part of an internal communications campaign intended to bring together the two formerly distinct companies.

Both companies have continuously been part of the larger business group selling telecommunication services especially in Central Eastern Europe. Despite the recent merger, the two formerly separate businesses share a common history; they both stem from the mail and telecom corporation that was founded in 1881 and which was back then owned by the state government. In 1996, the mail and telegraph corporation – which was until then administered by the Ministry of Transport – was transferred into a stock company and kept under the control of the government. Three years later, the two were separated; whereas the mail corporation stayed in full possession of the government, the telecom corporation was transferred into a stock company of which the government still holds 30,2%. In addition, the mobile part was outsourced as an overall stock company promoting its own brand and products.

The market. The businesses' separation as well as the recent merger occurred in the context of larger developments in the telecommunication market across Europe. Liberalising the telecommunication market in 1987, the European Union intended to create competition and to reduce governmental monopolies. At the beginning of this process, an increasing proliferation of numerous mobile network and service providers occurred.[11] But the emergence of the World Wide Web and of new telecommunication technologies in the 2000s increased the demand to make various telecommunication services available. Within businesses, these developments led to decreasing numbers in fixed line telephony while mobile and Internet communication numbers

---

11   Related to the liberalisation was, of course, the promise that while competition increases, charges for end users decrease. Whether the liberalisation has indeed only advantages for the consumer is obviously a contested debate, in particular when it comes to the required and in some countries still missing grid expansion (Kruse, 2004).

increased. Hence, companies faced economic pressure. The great number of mergers and acquisitions in and across Europe was a reaction to this pressure; today, the integrated provision of digital services combining mobile and landline as well as Internet and TV services has become the preferred business model for today's telecommunication companies.[12]

Staff and departments. Subsequent to the merger, Telecompany-X consisted of civil servants (called "Beamten" in German) and regular employees.[13] The company headquarter featured the main divisions such as Marketing, Sales, Human Resources, Customer Service, Internal Communications and Company Management. However, the so-called "technicians" I visited first as part of my fieldwork were located offsite in another company building. Furthermore, so-called 'field workers' maintaining the actual telecommunication network as well as 'agents' in various call centres across the country were also part of the workforce.[14] In addition, the company also employs a number of external workers which are not considered as part of the regular workforce.[15] Obviously, the merger involved a great amount of internal reorganisation, especially in terms of the integration of departments such as Accounting, Internal Communications, Human Resources, Marketing, Sales and Customer Service. Employees were to some extent integrated, but also transferred to

---

12 After the latest merger in 2014, the respective telecommunication market consists now of three companies. As market analysts say, only three to four players are able to make reasonable profits on fairly big and established telecommunication markets.

13 In this sense, the company and its workforce are paradigmatic for the merger of a formerly state-owned company and a privately owned business. However, because of civil servants not finding an adequate position in the new company, management attempted to outsource a number of employees from the former landline business into a governmentally-owned interim employment society. Obviously, this aroused a country-wide debate about the status of civil servants and involved the intervention of the company's trade union.

14 After the merger, especially call centre activities have been gradually outsourced to external agencies.

15 External workers usually support different teams in one department. One of my informants was employed as an external worker for five years by the former mobile part. Telecompany-X continued the employment. He explained to me that, so far, a permanent post had not matched his profile. He added that external workers cost more, but keep the company's headcount low. Obviously, as a partly stock driven business the company is interested in low personnel costs which have a positive impact on the stock price – while an increasing workforce produces "high overhead costs", I was told.

new positions. However, the rather technical departments related to the company's main products – mobile and landline communication, Internet and television services – remained mostly separated; also, in these departments, the 'mixing' of employees occurred rather on the middle management level.[16]

The Intranet. The implementation of "Inside-X", the official name of the intranet, occurred in summer 2011, about six months after the official merger.[17] Prior to that, a provisional intranet was set up providing in particular urgent and practical information on the company integration. For example, terminologies in the two companies differed; while the mobile division used the abbreviation 'SIM' for SIM card, the telecom part referred to 'SK' (for "SIM-Karte" in German) when referring to SIM cards. Also, the previous companies had two distinct intranets, this is why a lot of information had to be transferred to the new intranet. It included, for instance, employees' personal data stored on distinct time management applications.[18] At the time of my fieldwork, Inside-X had been online for about two months, but the data migration was still not finished; employees continued to have different applications according to their previous company when, for example, managing travel expenses or pay rolls. Thus, even though the intranet appeared in its new design, behind this 'visual coherence' old applications were still at work.

Inside-X runs in a browser and is based on Open Text, a content management system (CMS) for business enterprises, enabling companies to store

---

16   As I experienced, this reorganisation was yet not finished in 2012 when I started the second phase of my fieldwork. Asking one of my informants about her position, she was still unclear about her team's association and official name. The subsequent conversation with her colleagues in order to find out the correct name featured different terms and made obvious the extent and ongoing of reorganising activities inside the company.

17   Officially, the intranet in Telecompany-X is termed "Inside" followed by the company's brand name. However, no one referred to it using this name, the people I visited and interviewed simply said "intranet". Another, humorous description was the notion of "our internal Google". It constitutes the foundation of Chapter 5 ("Our internal Google").

18   Online data migration and software integration are enduring processes when it comes to merging two companies. As the project manager and the chief editor of the intranet told me, the new intranet in Telecompany-X featured 143 applications which had to be integrated, in addition to 40.000 pages of the former intranet of the landline division. Since my visits extended over 10 months, I was able to experience this gradual integration; while in the beginning employees according to their preceding company used distinct time management tools, in the end all were part of one system: the one previously used in the mobile corporation.

and organise large amounts of data. As the name already conveys, it is predominantly based on text, but allows the integration of different software applications such as Microsoft Sharepoint and SAP.[19] In terms of a classification, it belongs to the generation of so-called portals where applications and information can be added in a module-like fashion. As I was told, while the software was developed in the company with the help of an external agency, the content was mainly assembled and implemented by the chief editor of the intranet. The image below shows the starting page of one of my informants:

Figure 1: Intranet starting page: "Inside-X"

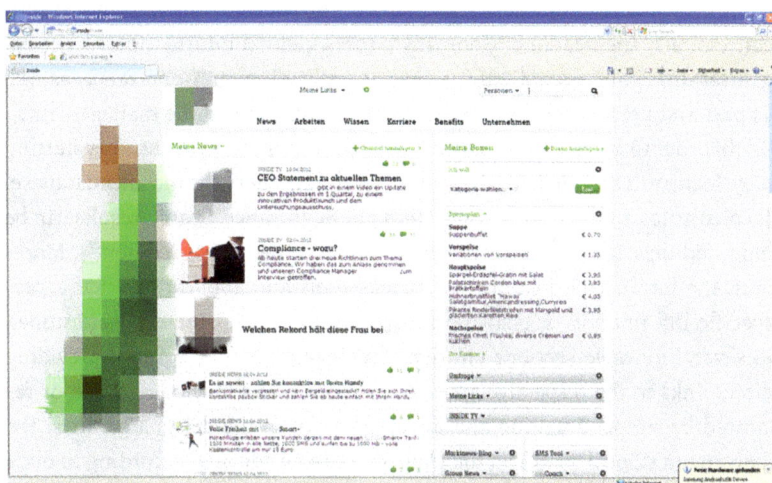

As can be seen, on its starting page, the intranet displays the company news section – called "My News" – prominently located at the centre. It features specific news on the employee's work division, but different 'channels', as they are called, can be added. Each post can be liked or commented on. Apart from the news section, the intranet assembles a variety of company information as well as applications for specific work processes. First of all, the pull-down menu at the top covers the sections "News", "Work" ("Arbeiten"), "Knowledge" ("Wissen"), "Career" ("Karriere"), "Benefits" and "Company" ("Unternehmen"). Each of these headlines stores specific information; the section

---

19 Microsoft Sharepoint is a web application system that manages corporate data content. It may be used as an intranet, as data and file base or as a search tool.

"News" comprises by default general news on the company. It also provides a download button for the company's in-house magazine. The other sections store information on company procedures and guidelines. For instance, the section "Work" features a subdivision "Everyday Work" that compiles information on employment law and the application of the company's Facility Management. The headline "Knowledge" covers the subsection "Health and Safety" where information on the company's medical service, its opening times and contact details are stored. The headline "Career" contains the internal job market as well as information on the company's performance management and the employee promotion scheme; as one of my informants framed it, it assembles the "company's expectations" towards employees. The section "Benefits" lists all companies where staff members of Telecompany-X receive special concessions. The headline "Company" stores general information on the organisation, i.e. an organigram, a central application on the intranet, as well as past and present business reports and information on the management.

In order to access stored data directly, the top right of the intranet starting page features a search field where employees may query the intranet database. It constitutes an important application on the intranet. Search results can be modified through pre-set categories ("general", "people" or "content"). Moreover, the intranet also comprises various tools and applications that access specific information or enable certain work processes. These are subsumed in several movable sections entitled "My Boxes" ("Meine Boxen"), providing direct links to the respective application. Such boxes may be removed or relocated by simply dragging and dropping them in the designated area. The daily menu ("Speiseplan") on the right side can be adjusted according to one's company location and the respective canteen. It is followed by a sequence of more applications; one addresses a survey ("Umfrage") evaluating the new company brand, "My links" assembles individually defined links and the intranet's video channel, "INSIDE TV". Four more applications are displayed, referring to specific news about the company's market ("Marketnews Blog") and the larger corporation it belongs to ("Group News"). The starting page also features two more important applications: the "SMS Tool" that sends short messages to mobile phones in and outside the company and the "X-Coach" which stores information on the company's products and services as well as customer data, predominantly used in Customer Service.

As can be seen, the starting page is the central gateway for entering information and applications on the intranet. Most of the content is stored 'behind' the starting page and involves employees to look or search for it by navigating through the website or by referring to the search function. In addition to such stored content, it features various applications which employees use frequently during the day. These applications involve different degrees of formalisation in how they predetermine users to specific procedures. On a regular working day, I was told, employees start their PC and automatically access the intranet when logging in to the company network. Most of them consult the daily menu first and perhaps quickly glance over the newsfeed.

However, as I learned during my investigation, especially the search function and the corporate directory in connection with the organigram constitute two central applications for my informants. As will become apparent, the ways in which these applications are integrated into existing work routines tell us about both successful and failed moments of technology implementation. Overall, the study also shows that my informants' initially expressed disregard of the intranet does not only relate to its setup – which makes it indeed a rather ambiguous device –, but must also be seen in the context of these work practices where the intranet slips into such practices and becomes rather indistinguishable to my informants.

1.7   More than a machine for doing business

The intranet described above serves very well the idea of an internal communication platform enabling access to various company information and communication tools for everyday work. By way of making available information as well as applications that assist the communication exchange among employees, such as the SMS-tool or Microsoft Sharepoint, it corresponds to the expectations of (efficient) collaboration already inherent to early office devices intended to distribute internal communication and determine work processes. In fact, the intranet defines to some extent such work processes: specific applications standardise certain work procedures, for instance in the case of reporting a failure to the company's Facility Management or ordering personal software packages. In this manner, the intranet in Telecompany-X is less involved in the specific work of the different departments as this happens predominantly in relation to other software technologies dedicated to the specificity of the respective work division. Instead, the intranet constitutes and is part of the company's technological infrastructure, bringing together content and different applications, thereby making, for instance, certain communicative practices and other work processes possible.

But, as my analysis shows, in addition to the work-related layer, the intranet also carries managerial practices of normative control intended to increase employees' commitment to the new company (cf. Kunda, 2006; Barley and Kunda, 1992). Within business and management studies, communication approaches are understood to support a company's post-merger integration processes by, for instance, fostering a new company identity (Balle, 2008). This resonates with the Internal Communication's branding campaign in Telecompany-X that promotes the new company brand on the intranet starting page while aiming to erase 'old' traces of the two businesses. As such, company management expects the intranet to encourage coherence and togetherness across the company. Thus, the intranet is designated a "change agent"; the term usually describes executives on the middle management level, understood as a vital link between management and employees in the way they translate managerial strategies to the workforce, thereby affiliating employees into the new company (Buick et al., 2018, see also Ford et al., 2008). However, in the current case, the intranet is designated a change agent as it carries practices of (post-industrial) culture management, in particular corporate and internal branding. In this way, the intranet is intended to set an example of the new company and to promote the new identity and brand to employees.

As my analysis demonstrates, such practices only partly resonate with employees. That is, examining the intranet from the perspective of the work practices it is part of, it is not surprising that the various layers of the intranet – company information, communication tools for exchange and collaboration as well as the corporate branding campaign – are a conglomerate that makes the intranet a central, but also an ambiguous device, serving contradictory logics. As will be shown, assembling both the Internal Communication's campaign on its starting page as well as applications assisting employees' everyday work, in particular their communication among each other, employees devaluate the managerial campaign of coherence. That is, employees prefer applications related to their work and, in comparison, designate Internal Communication's branding campaign as playful and superfluous. In fact, the two types of content on the intranet contradict each other and support employees' ambivalent relation to the intranet. These findings underline the specific difficulties of the intranet's starting page that combines a variety of logics. Furthermore, the materiality of the intranet newsfeed storing its content contributes to this disregard since it enables employees to constantly postpone the reading. Overall, the managerial idea of using the intranet to increase company coherency and of normatively determining employee's commitment to the company after the merger appear as very much detached from the everyday work and contradict how employees make sense of their work and the post-merger company more generally.

The second part of the study zooms in on the intranet-in-use and the ways in which it proves to be a (un)successful working tool. Investigating the two main applications on the intranet, the search function and the corporate directory in connection with the organigram, I show how using the intranet as part of everyday work is a complex undertaking that is informed by existing work routines, other technologies, specific software applications, and employees' immediate interests.

In particular, looking at the search function provides insight into how a technology (dis-)integrates into existing work routines. That is, studying how employees actually work around the search function, it becomes evident how technologies are made workable tools in a particular work setting, despite their seemingly functional deficiency. Thus, saving links in the browser, communicating with employees as well as exchanging emails with colleagues shows how the intranet is integrated into older, existing routines. It makes evident that different elements in this setting, such as the immediate feedback from colleagues which is encouraged by the open place office, contribute to working around the search function. Thus, the analysis illustrates that the 'matching' of humans and technologies is rather a matter of alignment with the existing working infrastructure at hand, the physical setting of the office and, nevertheless, also the working culture of the specific work setting or department. This has consequences for the design and development of software since it highlights the complex relationship between the technology, its setting of usage and the people using it.

In contrast to the search function, the corporate directory and the organigram on the intranet turned out as well-used applications, informing employees' email and phone communication. Especially, they enable to understand incoming emails by identifying the often unknown sender. As I learned, knowing the departmental affiliation as well as the hierarchical status of the sender allows an employee to understand the request and to write the appropriate answer. In this manner, the intranet upholds formal organisational structures and established hierarchies in the company. As becomes apparent, the communication in Telecompany-X engages various technologies, such as the intranet and the specific application of the directory and organigram, but also landline and mobile phone. It underlines the infrastructural quality of the intranet and respective applications. Indeed, a great amount of everyday interaction is relying on this infrastructure and the interplay of the involved devices.

Through all the chapters runs the question to what extent the intranet is indeed involved in bringing together, that is connecting employees on the level of everyday work collaboration, but also of providing a sense of togetherness, after the merger. As elaborated above, it is the promise of intranets to first of all enable work collaboration in efficient ways. But investigating the intranet and specific applications in Telecompany-X, it becomes apparent that the intranet is an ambiguous device, both hindering and supporting connection and work collaboration among employees. Thus, asking to what extent the intranet indeed brings together employees after the merger, I show that such aims are not easily achieved and that it goes beyond simply adjusting the intranet to employees' needs.

For instance, examining how employees orient themselves in the post-merger company, the study shows that referring to the previously two distinct companies is a significant form of making sense of the integration process and the emergence of the 'new' post-merger company. This observation stands in contrast to Internal Communication's branding campaign that aims to erase 'old' signs of the former two companies by installing a new company culture and by promoting the new company brand and identity to employees. That is, erasing all signs of the previously distinct businesses stands in contrast to employees' insisting on the two corporate identities which, I argue, must not only be understood as a form of resistance, but as a form of ongoing identity work and of making sense in relation to everyday organisational processes in the post-merger company.

One of the central debates in the context of the merger concentrated on the different corporate cultures of the two distinct companies where the mobile part distinguished itself from the landline business because of employees' hands-on work attitude and flat hierarchies in the company. However, looking at the ways in which the directory and the organigram are a constitutive part of employees' communication via email, it becomes apparent that despite this debate and the presumed differences, the formal hierarchical and departmental structure is an important 'knowledge device' in the everyday work of employees from both former companies that helps making sense of the new company. By 'knowledge device' I refer to the importance of knowing other employees' departmental affiliation and their hierarchical status when interacting in the company, for instance when interpreting email messages. As will become apparent, in contrast to the managerial idea of a shared, hands-on post-merger corporate culture, the intranet rather sustains pre-existing organisational, especially hierarchical, structures in the company.

Overall, the case of the intranet makes apparent that today's so-called knowledge work of which the telecommunication sector is a paradigmatic example, is obviously emerging through a variety of technologies, that is, 'old' communication devices as well as more sophisticated software applications. Thus, the study shows that knowledge work does not only involve expert knowledge, as often pointed out in relation to dealing with "epistemic objects" (Knorr Cetina, 1999), but knowledge that emerges in relation to how various technologies entwine with one another (cf. Beverungen et al., 2019: 623–4). This type of 'mundane' knowledge work, as I call it, pervades relations and work processes in the company. As a result, today's knowledge (or rather: communication/interaction) worker has to invest efforts into making the different technologies work and to contextualise, that is, interpret and make sense of the data or information he or she receives through these technologies (Schulz-Schaeffer and Funken, 2008: 19; see also Wajcman and Rose, 2011).

The study makes also evident how the intranet combines understandings of work and technologies paradigmatic for contemporary discourses about the so-called 'digitalisation of work'. These ideas include the steering and determination of work processes, and the exercise of control – in the current case especially in relation to employees' emotional commitment to the post-merger company. Of course, ideas about control and determination of work are not new, as discussed in the beginning of this text. Nevertheless, the intranet and the case of the company merger reveals them in certain ways: showing how the intranet undermines managerial expectations calls into question the widespread appraisal of technologies, especially the ways in which they are often celebrated as straightforward solutions to a variety of problems societies face today.

1.8   Chapter outline

The study's setup concentrates on the intranet as a window into, first of all, the expectations towards this technology and, furthermore, the specific work practices linked to the most prominent applications it makes available. Hence, the study juxtaposes managerial expectations of company coherence with employees' everyday uses of the company's intranet, in particular of the starting page, the search function and the corporate directory and organigram. Against this backdrop, the study also sheds light on how these expectations and work practices relate to (dis-)connecting employees following the merger.

Subsequent to the introduction, Chapter 2 reflects the study's methodological approach, in particular how I gained and maintained access into Telecompany-X and how the 'object' of my research and related questions emerged as part of the research process. The sequence of analytical chapters begins with a discussion of the post-merger setting of the company: Chapter 3 examines the context in which the intranet is located; namely, the framing of problems in the post-merger company. As will become apparent, the company is permeated by ongoing identity work and regulation of both employees and management. That is, we learn that management has apparently undertaken regulating efforts to erase old signs of the previous company identities in order to install the new company brand and identity. Employees make sense of these efforts by resorting to mainly two strategies: First of all, they narrate and thereby uphold and manifest the two companies' differences and, secondly, normatively describe and request the unity of the company by overlooking former differences, respectively by downplaying them as a natural fact. In this manner, both strategies almost echo the managerial desire of coherence, as a form of resistance to or as adopting the wish of a unified, coherent company.

Overall, the reported narratives correspond to research and literature on merger integration processes that describe the fragmentation of the post-merger company as problematic and especially the first strategy as a form of employee resistance. Furthermore, the chapter also makes evident that previous managerial identity regulation now serves as an obstacle since it obstructs the implementation of the new company identity. But from the perspective of my informants and the work happening in the company, employees' "cultivating difference", i.e. their insisting on differences, constitutes a shared reference point and an important way of making sense of the new, post-merger organisation and of understanding post-merger conflicts and the formerly distinct products and services. In addition, findings also suggest that the extent to which employees have been involved in previous identity work and whether or not they have been affected by restructurings also impacts how employees deal with the integration process.

Chapters 4 to 6 examine the three most relevant applications on the intranet – the starting page, the search function and the corporate directory in connection with the organigram – and unravel how they participate in configuring specific work practices. But Chapter 4 also constitutes the counterpart to Chapter 3 in the way it presents the management's solution to the problem of (the perceived) company fragmentation: the intranet as the central business portal is understood to set an example of the new company in the way it promotes the new brand and company to employees. It is part of the Internal Communication's branding campaign intended to increase employees' commitment with the new company and to install a hands-on, proactive work culture among employees after the merger. But, as the analysis shows, assembling disparate logics, the starting page appears to employees as divided. That is, employees devaluate the campaign and related applications because they consider them to be a waste of time and hence superfluous. This stands in contrast to work-related applications and content of the starting page, which are regarded as necessary and more important. Thus, while the campaign is intended to connect employees through logics of commitment and identification, employees seem instead unified in how they neglect this type of content.

Chapters 5 and 6 focus more closely on the intranet-in-use and investigate what I call 'mundane' knowledge work. The notion emphasises that today's knowledge work is not exclusively comprised of so-called expert knowledge, but of one that is predominantly communicative and that emerges in relation to different technologies and applications, such as mobile and telephone calling, but also email writing.

Following this agenda, Chapter 5 investigates the practices around the corporate directory in connection with the organigram and how they inform employees' technology-mediated interaction at work. That is, not only is the colleague's image on the directory relevant, also the organigram is important for locating people in the company in terms of their departmental affiliation and their hierarchical status. Only with reference to these characteristics are employees able to understand requests they receive as email messages and as part of the internal company network. Furthermore, such insights also inform how to approach one another in the company, not only via email and phone, but also when it comes to face-to-face interaction. Overall, illuminating the involved rules and techniques employees make use of when referring to the corporate directory and organigram, it becomes apparent that these applications contribute to upholding a specific interaction order among employees that preserves the hierarchical as well as departmental division of the company. This, in fact, stands in contrast to the ideal worker norm of the "Einfach Macher" put forward in the Internal Communication campaign. Nevertheless, as I argue, because the applications assign departmental belongings and hierarchies, they also provide employees a sense of the new company after the merger.

Chapter 6 examines the practices around the search function, especially how employees work around it and thereby sustain existing work routines. While at first glance the problem appeared entirely technical, since employees' search queries apparently do not correspond to the database's classification system, the chapter shows that the software's 'matching' with 'user's needs' and the overall acceptance of a technology are intricate matters that necessitate taking into consideration the context in which the technology is put – that is, the characteristics of the respective work setting. While the concept of workaround in software development refers to the shortcomings of an existing technology, the chapter illustrates how it may serve as a window into understanding how technologies successfully align with one another. These insights are relevant for the development and design of intranets in the way they question concepts such as technology acceptance and usability that focus either on the user or the technology.

The conclusion summarises the insights gained from the study and outlines the implications that go beyond this specific case. First of all, the merger appears to be still ongoing in Telecompany-X which becomes obvious in staff members' continuous and ongoing references to it. It is actually part of the current identity of the new company which is not only apparent in the ongoing identity work, but also in 'old' work routines that associate with the two companies' former software applications and technologies and, overall, with the different products and services that are now provided under 'the same roof', that is, in the merged company. Therefore, the study questions the widespread understanding within research and literature on mergers that, in order for the two companies to come together as one, it is indeed necessary to erase all signs and traces of the former companies. Rather, such signs and traces are indeed relevant for handling the everyday work in the post-merger company and, potentially, serve as a starting point for discussing how work is and should be done in the new company.

Secondly, the case of the branding campaign on the intranet and employees' devaluation of this content shows that the configuration of different, in fact contradictory logics on the intranet may lead to an ambiguous relation among employees to the technology. But in the case of the intranet in Telecompany-X, I show that the intranet's specific quality is its rather 'loose' script which enables employees to leave content considered as irrelevant aside and instead to focus on those applications that are relevant to their work. Therefore, another implication concerns the idea within business communication and management studies to determine and control work processes with the help of technologies such as the intranet; it may be similarly important to think about their sense of open- or 'looseness' so as to engage the 'many' users. Furthermore, the ways in which the intranet partakes in work practices casts doubt on isolating the intranet from the work setting in which it is put, as concepts such as technology acceptance and adoption and also the notion of usability suggest. In fact, a workable intranet is not only a question of specific functionalities and personalisation features, but of taking into account existing work routines, including the spatial setting of the office, and the existing technological infrastructure of which the intranet is part.

Altogether, answering the question to what extent the intranet indeed brings together employees of the former two companies, the analysis shows a fragmented and multi-layered picture. In fact, designating the intranet an integration agent, it has indeed difficulties living up to these expectations – at least when it comes to promoting the new company identity and brand to employees. Nevertheless, the insights gained in relation to the search function and the corporate directory and organigram point at shared work routines among employees; they agree on a specific interaction order that orients towards departmental and hierarchical structures in the company. This contradicts most widely the Internal Communication's branding campaign which aims to install a hands-on, proactive work culture among employees that moves beyond hierarchies. Surprisingly, the organigram seems to be a central device for providing an overview and making apparent how different departments hang together and hence assists employees in getting a sense of the whole of the company. From this point of view, the intranet indeed supports the company's coherency.

These insights have obvious consequences for thinking about organisational development that is in contemporary businesses often connected to information technologies; first of all, the practice-theoretical research approach sensitises one to examine the work settings into which the technology is put. It lays bare the rather hidden work practices and routines which resort to a variety of technologies and specific applications on the intranet and hence brings to the forefront what usually stays implicit and covert. Indeed, existing routines and employees' well-developed competences, the spatial setting of the office as well as the material properties of the technology are relevant and provide insight into understanding the workings of the intranet and specific applications. In this manner, the study confirms that the formalisation of work processes through technologies relies in fact a great deal on informal work routines that somewhat associate as part of work practices.

The focus on practices also makes apparent that key to effective work practices is the overall alignment of different technologies and applications which I describe as the primary characteristic of 'mundane' knowledge work. Thus, the successful integration of a new software or technology is less a question of matching users and technologies or a single application, as often framed in software development and design, than of understanding the respective workplace and of making sure it integrates into the existing work setting. As this work further argues, it is the variety of applications and functionalities the intranet as a specific type of technology assembles, but also the involvement of additional managerial politics that makes it especially hard to determine beforehand how the intranet is in fact used. This is very apparent in the current case; while the corporate culture management efforts aim to install a unifying hands-on work culture that moves beyond the hierarchical as well as the departmental structuring of the company, the use of the directory and organigram as part of everyday communication practices reinforces those organisational principles.

Therefore, this research suggests to conceptualise technologies not as individual agents that install, for instance, another work culture or more efficient work processes. Rather, it suggests to, first of all, take into account the different logics and layers of a technology in connection with other applications as part of the respective work setting so as to understand how they align into workable configurations.

2 Researching the Intranet in Telecompany-X: Methodological Considerations

> "Just as the project was redefined as a range of practices [...], my site was likewise the outcome of my research practices and various methodological devices for seeing, linking together and tracing out a space corresponding to particular analytical purposes."
>
> *(Henriksen, 2002: 36)*

In the quote above, Dixi Henriksen emphasises that the 'object' of her research did not pre-exist her study, but was configured in the process of the research itself, hence only emerged in relation to her fieldwork, the activities it encompassed and the methodological approach she developed. In this chapter, I similarly aim to not just state, but also unravel the methods involved and the circumstances of my research which led to a very specific account on intranet technology. As I experienced, undertaking empirical research is very much informed by the development of the process itself, that is, the situational opportunities and chances emerging along the way that shape data generation and analysis. For this reason, literature on qualitative research methods suggests making transparent and reflecting on how meaning is generated and insights are gained as part of the research process.

In what follows, I elaborate first of all the methodological rationale informing my research. It considers the intranet as a disseminated object, not just across the company I investigated, but also across the different sites of my fieldwork. Subsequently, the chapter presents and discusses my fieldwork by tackling the following questions:

How did I access 'the field' and the organisation I investigated?
What kind of methods did I make use of?
How did my role as a researcher affect the data generation?
How did I proceed analysing my data and 'writing up' the research?

Similar to the literature on methodology, I differentiate between the process of data generation and analysis, even though the two very much go together, even inform each other. Obviously, there was a stage in my research where I mostly looked at my data as part of the analysis; but understanding and interpreting, Dvora Yanow emphasises, already happens during the fieldwork as well as before entering the field (Yanow, 1996: 35). This also applies to my theoretical considerations and specific research interests I had prior to and while entering 'the field'. But in order to enable a comprehensive overview and to align my research to the academic standard, I stick to this differentiation and report separately on how I generated and analysed my data.

2.1 Methodological rationale

My research on intranets was grounded in an initial interest in technologies and organisations, but, as will become apparent in this chapter, it was further configured in the course of my fieldwork. My initial research puzzle, the increasing implementation of intranets and people's reported disregard, directed my perspective in two directions: to examine the concepts and understandings underpinning the development and design of intranets and to study how intranets take part in everyday organisational life. Moreover, as already stated in the introduction, my theoretical interest in theories of practices obviously configured my empirical research, too. Especially, the discussion in social theory in general and in organisations studies in particular about a conceptualisation of the material dimension of organisational life was influential for my investigation (cf. Orlikowski, 2007).

Against this backdrop, my study relies on ethnographic methodologies, but, as will become evident below, I distinguish my approach from an ethnography as such since my research did not rely predominantly on participant observation, as usual in ethnographic research (van der Waal, 2009). Instead, my study follows the intranet across different sites in Telecompany-X combining methods such as interviews, document analyses and an exploration of the technology *in situ*. This exploration happened as part of undertaking visits at staff members' workplaces where I asked for a 'guided tour' through the intranet. In fact, while doing so, my research moves close to what has been termed a "multi-sited ethnography" (Marcus, 1995), a reformulation and more recent utilisation of ethnographic methodologies. It departs from assuming the territorial boundedness of a culture understood as a closed entity manifesting itself in rules and routines and instead proposes a geographically distributed understanding of social phenomena (Marcus, 1995: 98).

Elaborating the idea of multi-sited ethnography as a research imaginary particularly well fitted for research in Science and Technology Studies (STS), Christine Hine highlights that it first of all serves as an orientation for the researcher in thinking about his or her object of study (Hine, 2007: 656). As she explains, the multi-sited imaginary lays emphasis on the fact that the researcher actively constructs, as she says "crafts", the research object while conducting fieldwork. Following this understanding, my research does not assume a reality out there, ready to be investigated, but conceives of realities, of research 'objects', as actively configured while part of the research process. Hence, understanding how intranet technology is conceptualised and part of everyday organisational work must not be investigated in one place, but can be found – in accordance with the conduction of fieldwork – in different sites and settings (e.g. Mol, 2002: 160; Scheffer, 2002: 372; see also Hirschauer, 2001; Law, 2004; Law and Urry, 2004).[1]

As becomes evident, the multi-sited rationale corresponds well to the understanding about technologies and organisations outlined in the introduction, an understanding that questions the straightforward existence of discrete objects and concepts (Suchman, 2005; see also Hine, 2007: 664). Instead, it acknowledges the multiple ways in which intranet technologies come into being, as part of programming and design considerations, but also while constituent of everyday work practices (Mol, 2002; Bruni, 2005). Likewise, Lucy Suchman describes the notion of "configuration" as a methodological programme; doing so, she underlines the importance of tracing how humans

---

1   Following this understanding, my text refrains from using the notion "collecting" data, predominantly referred to when describing the methods involved in a research study. Misleadingly, the term purports a reality out there, waiting for the researcher to be 'collected', i.e. studied and investigated. Instead, I use the term "generating" data so as to emphasise the circumstances of the research setting and the active involvement of the researcher in constructing and configuring the research – prior to the actual fieldwork and already happening while undertaking observations and interviews (cf. Yanow, 1996: 34–5).

and machines are 'con-figured', that is, how they align with one another in specific ways (2012). From a methodological point of view, this requires in particular "thinking about the discursive and the material together" (2012: 50) that assemble as part of technological projects and the respective practices (cf. Reckwitz, 2008: 190).

In addition, the idea of configuration is also a reminder that one's research must not necessarily evaluate the technology from one angle, but recognise the variety of "actors, relationships, labours and contradictions" (Suchman, 2012: 53) and the technology's possible "indefiniteness" (ibid.: 55) so as to reveal who is included and perhaps what is overlooked or disregarded in this process. As can be seen, the perspective encourages one to investigate the manifold and possibly contradictory logics involved in the implementation and appropriation of the intranet.

Following these considerations, I started my research by interviewing people working in the area of software programming and development and the wider field of knowledge management. However, the main body of research is a study on how one intranet is configured as part of a merger integration process in a telecommunications company. This close investigation into the work practices of which the intranet was part added specific topics and insights. Altogether, the different parts of my study built upon each other in the sense that the first part of interviews and the insights I gained there concerning the development, conceptualisation and implementation of intranet technologies were later important for understanding and analysing my fieldwork in Telecompany-X.

2.2   Entering field sites: Initial interviews

Looking back on how my empirical research proceeded, it is not surprising that in relation to the distinct sites of my fieldwork I adopted different research strategies. The initial, explorative part was a fairly obvious first step and a rather straightforward endeavour; it involved conducting semi-structured formal interviews with software developers, so-called 'knowledge' and 'intranet managers' and people working in software consultant agencies. In contrast, gaining access to a company was a much more challenging task and required me to constantly adjust my research strategy. But, as I am going to show, this was an important step since it made me refine my investigation and generated specific research questions in association with my initial research puzzle and focus.

The initial interviews I undertook were a way of getting in contact with 'the field' I was aiming to research. In particular, with the help of a fellow student I got in touch with a network of software programmers organised in a so-called 'office community'.[2] As I learned, most of these developers had university degrees, but not necessarily in informatics; their programming expertise was often gained through 'learning-by-doing', a strategy very common in software development. However, the fact that they had studied at university made them open to me as an academic.

The initial research period socialised me into this community of software developers and programmers which involved, for instance, attending an office party which happened regularly once a year. This rather informal event provided an opportunity for me to get in contact with potential informants for my study.[3] Thus, while getting in touch with knowledge and intranet managers working in different offices and organisations, I soon moved beyond this one office community. The last stage of this research phase comprised two interviews in a social media/internet consulting agency that conceptualises and implements intranets, but also other software applications and systems.

The table below provides an overview of my interviewees, their job positions and the organisation:

---

2   An office community (called "Bürogemeinschaft" in German) is a loose affiliation of freelancers sharing a flat as a working space. Some of the people working there were also registered as a company, consisting of two to three people. The office I visited included not only software developers, but also graphic designers and one person maintaining an online web platform for cultural events.

3   Also, during my research, I was looking for a part time job and hence applied for a job in this Bürogemeinschaft. My position mainly involved the content management of an online platform. This job post lasted for about a year.

Table 1: Interviews with software developers, knowledge/intranet managers and IT consultants

No.	Date	Name	Job title	Organisation
1.	09/2010	Harald	Software Developer	Self-employed, own business for IT services
2.	05/2011	David	Knowledge Manager	Non-profit organisation, health care sector
3.	04/2011	Alexan-dra	Knowledge and Intranet Manager	Research organisation, formerly Intranet Manager in a globally operating business consultancy
4.	07/2012	Paul	Knowledge Manager	Governmental organisation
5.	06/2012	Georg	Software Consultant, CEO	Social media/internet consulting agency
6.	07/2012	Maria	Software Consultant, expert in 'usability'	Social media/internet consulting agency
7.	09/2013	Max	Software Developer	Self-employed (own business for IT services); also, working part-time for Telecompany-X

All interviews were conducted at my informants' work places, except two of them (no. 1 and no. 5), which took place in a café. During most of these interviews, the atmosphere was rather informal since I had previously met the informant at the party or in the office. Two of my contacts were also established via an online social network platform for professionals; my initial informant introduced me through this platform to people he considered relevant for my project.[4] I undertook with both of them an interview and one became a mentor-like colleague with whom I met a few times in order to discuss the insights I had gained.

The interviews with software developers familiarised me with concepts and understandings in the realm of software programming and development.

---

4   As part of my research on intranets, I became a member of two social network platforms for professionals, Xing and LinkedIn. As a member of these sites, I joined groups focussing on intranet technologies. However, getting in contact through this platform with people I did not know was not very successful in terms of getting responses to my requests. Nevertheless, my profile served as a way of making myself and my research officially visible to those I was in contact with as part of my research.

Moreover, the interviews with knowledge managers and software consultants focused on the implementation and integration of technologies into specific work settings and discussed how to conceive of the relation between organisations and technologies. Both parts helped form my understanding about software technologies more generally and intranets more specifically. In this way, they also served as an inspiration for my subsequent empirical study on the intranet.

The interviews were rather open in the beginning, but as I developed an understanding for what I was studying, I adjusted my research perspective and my interview guideline. For instance, initially I had asked my interviewees somewhat broadly about the experiences they had while conceptualising and implementing intranets; usually this served as a good starting point for their illustrations. But once I had read about the concepts and topics some of my informants referred to, I started to ask more specific questions, for instance about design principles or the development process.

Obviously, in the beginning, the specific vocabulary especially in software development constituted a challenge since the field was completely new to me; for instance, I had to become acquainted with the so-called "waterfall model" (cf. Daum, 2021: 31), a rather old-fashioned way of delineating sequences in the development of software that puts emphasis on a strict and hierarchical division of work responsibilities. In contrast, a more recent concept is the notion of "agile methods" which describes a rather flexible approach towards the design and development of software. As my informants told me, it is a specific form of project management that enables one to adjust the development process to the individual circumstances of a software project. The literature classifies agile management as belonging to a third paradigm in the history of software design and development, that is, a move away from defining standards, as done before, to an incremental approach, thereby recognising the sometimes unpredictable dynamics in the development process (Pflüger, 2004: 275; 295 et seqq.). By now, the approach has developed into a management paradigm, emphasising the need of contemporary organisations to be adaptable to increasingly changing environments (Madsen, 2020). As Timo Daum stresses, the concept was initiated by IT experts and people working in software development and programming in order to encourage a more team oriented and flexible work culture. But the "spirit of agility" (Daum, 2021: 36, own translation) developed into a management paradigm – in fact 'dispositive', he says – that puts pressure on the individual who increasingly has to adjust to the concept's requirements, in particular the digital tracking of specific work tasks and responsibilities (ibid.: 34 et seqq.; see also Sauer, 2021). As can be seen, my understanding of the field grew gradually in relation to the people and the research literature I investigated. These insights assisted me in understanding and later also analysing my informants' responses.

But not just the concepts my informants referred to, also the role I was attributed was informative and constituted a way of understanding the settings I investigated. For instance, I increasingly felt discomfort when my informants working in a media/internet agency asked me to report on "best practices" I might have heard or known about. This discomfort concerned, first of all, my self-understanding as a researcher; in fact, I did not want to and felt incapable of instructing my informants since I was still in the process of getting insights, thereby still refining my understanding about software technologies in general and intranets in particular. But, as I realised, the search for 'best practices' and universal solutions puts forward an understanding of technologies that also occurs in the business communication literature on software technologies (cf. Amcoff Nyström, 2006). That is, working with concepts that explain and define the relation between software and organisations (as, for instance, the terms 'usability' and 'organisational culture' do) often serves as a guiding principle. In fact, these concepts illustrate very well the ways in which software tools are approached and understood to work; "best practices" are widely accepted and a valuable information source within software development and the business communication literature.

In contrast to this general approval of software technologies, the interviewees I met in the context of the local network of office communities did not emphasise the existence of best practices. Instead, they tended to devalue the universality of software products and services they worked on. This relates, I figured, to their common background sharing a rather critical attitude towards the tech industry. In fact, adopting this attitude appeared as a common agreement, a bonding point, among them.

From the beginning, I was aiming to also investigate one intranet *in situ* in order to illuminate how and to what extent the intranet indeed participates in an organisation's everyday work. As will become apparent, finding an organisation and entering Telecompany-X refined my study and generated more specific research questions.

2.3 Extending sites, aligning focus: Telecompany-X

Each time I visited Telecompany-X, I received a visitor card that enabled me to enter the different locations of the company. However, the process of getting and maintaining access was a more difficult, less straightforward endeavour. As I am going to illuminate next, it involved constantly reconsidering my access strategy and adjusting my research interests along the way.

But let me first give an impression of the physical barriers when entering the organisation that in fact corresponds to how I experienced the company while trying to gain and maintain access. The headquarters, which was a fairly new building, featured a large counter where I registered and received the visitor card that let me through electronic barriers. In contrast, one of the smaller buildings I visited had a front door and another automatic double door system that secured the entrance:

Figure 2: Building entrance (view from inside)

Entering the building in this manner, I was somewhat intimidated and had to rethink whether I met the somewhat suddenly apparent security standards and whether I was indeed eligible to enter the building. However, let me reflect on the developments and discuss my research approach in greater detail.

2.3.1   Gaining access

Literature on ethnographic research in organisations describes the process of gaining access as a central, but also very demanding and difficult stage of the research. One of the reasons put forth is the importance of a company's public reputation which might be at risk when someone from the outside enters the company (van der Waal, 2009: 27; see also Feldman et al., 2004). Furthermore, in my case, the intranet as the stated primary research object appeared to reinforce the difficulties; intranets are described as 'under-researched' because of the difficulty of accessing a company's internal network which is usually secured from the outside (Lehmuskallio, 2006: 291). Following these observations, it is not surprising that finding a company and gaining access took a while and included several attempts; nevertheless, in my case, the issue of maintaining access turned out to be most difficult. One reason was my entry 'from bottom up' which meant I had to constantly negotiate my position with employees in the company. Secondly, as I further learned, the organisation was not prepared to provide access for a longer period of time to someone not regularly working in the company. Allow me to explain the insights I gained one by one.

Initially, I had several "selection criteria" for a suitable company. For instance, one criterion was the dissemination of work processes; I wanted to find a company that operates across different locations and where the intranet is involved in 'bridging' these locales. But, first of all, I had to find a company that was indeed willing to provide access. Relying on my personal and professional network, I got in contact with three companies showing an initial interest in my research. But before negotiating the details of my visit, all three rejected my enquiry "because of organisational reorganisation" or "resource problems".

Subsequent to these rejections, I asked one of my former interviewees for advice and how to perhaps adjust my enquiry. She suggested shortening my cover letter and condensing my request since, as she said, "these days, employees hardly would have time to read a detailed explanation". Moreover, she recommended stating upfront the possible benefits of my study for the company so as to increase my chances. Subsequently, the letter, instead of featuring a text with paragraphs, consisted of an introductory passage and a few bullet points summarising the "practical realisation" of my research and the "possible utilisation of results". Hence, in attempting to gain access, I tried to make myself valuable to the organisation and thereby adjusted to the realities of the businesses I was in contact with and that were pointed out to me. Or, in other words, in the process of gaining access I adopted some of the logics of the field I was aiming to research.

Of course, such an adaptation is not uncommon in the field of qualitative research; in fact, as part of my fieldwork in Telecompany-X, I even further adjusted my research approach. It is important to say that in the end neither version of my cover letters were successful; once more, it was my personal network, another fellow student, through which I established contact and finally gained access to Telecompany-X. My initial contact person, Walter, was a former classmate of my fellow student and at the time of my visit he was a "team leader", working at the middle management level in Telecompany-X. Yet again, he had studied and saw his involvement as an opportunity "to support a PhD research", as he said.[5] He in fact promoted the implementation of the fairly new intranet to me as an interesting case for my study. By then I was relieved having – apparently – found an open and supportive environment for my study.

2.3.2 Maintaining access

However, from the beginning, my initial contact Walter, my "gatekeeper" or "key informant" (van der Waal, 2009: 29), made clear he could only assure access as far as his department, Operations Support Systems (OSS). After I had introduced my project, he promised that he would inform his team of eight people (who he was the manager of) and ask them to participate. In addition, he also put me in contact with the chief editor and the project manager of the intranet and both agreed to being interviewed. These two were my first contacts located in the headquarters of the company; following this interview – which helped me to develop an understanding for the intranet and in particular the expectations towards it – I already felt as if I had made my way forward into the company.

---

5   This personal relationship made it less necessary to point out the value of my research. Nevertheless, at a later stage, I was confronted with this logic again when attempting to negotiate a longer period of observation in Telecompany-X.

Within Telecompany-X, my project was described as a PhD research student being interested in the intranet. In accordance with Walter, I decided for a start it would be best to 'visit' people at their workplace and investigate *in situ* what they do and how they make use of the intranet.[6] In fact, I was aiming to negotiate a period of participant observation, but since I sensed a rather hesitant attitude towards this request, I decided to first of all enter the organisation and revive my request at a later stage. In fact, visiting people at their workplace in this fashion made sense to the setting and people I was intending to research. Finally, three members of staff agreed to be visited. As one of my informants told me, Walter had promoted my project saying those participating would also "learn something about the intranet"; apparently, this was the experience he had had during my visit and the incentive he provided to his colleagues.

In fact, such an incentive was indeed necessary since many employees underlined that they hardly make use of the intranet, thereby highlighting their lack of value for my study. While there are several reasons for such a reaction – amongst others, employees' wish to not be kept away from work, or possible feelings of intimidation because of the research situation – I learned at a later stage that this also relates to the somewhat invisible, but also ambiguous character of the intranet. Specifically, as my study shows, the intranet and applications are part of work practices, but while slipping into these practices, the intranet becomes rather unnoticeable and is often not recognised as such. Furthermore, some parts of the intranet are also disregarded and considered as irrelevant by employees. As my work argues, not having a definite identity in this manner turned out to be both an advantage and disadvantage; that is, from the perspective of strategic management, the ambiguous identity indicates its partial failure to realise the managerial desire of company coherence. At the same time, as the second part of the study shows, the intranet aligns with other technologies so that specific applications indeed work well and are central to staff members' everyday work.

However, coming back to my informant's comment encouraging his colleagues to participate in my project, I was glad when I heard it since, obviously, my visits kept employees from work. Of course, the comment confirmed

---

6   Since Walter was located on middle management level, he informed the Head of Department about my project and request. She approved and I was able to interview and visit those employees willing to participate. Astonishingly, I did not have to sign a non-disclosure agreement, or the like.

again the logic of being valuable to the company I pointed out earlier as part of the process of adjusting my research to the field. In fact, this logic made me again aware of the still precarious state of my research.

Nevertheless, the impression of having already made my way into the company was supported by the fact that not only my initial contact, but also the chief editor and the project manager of the intranet appeared to be very open to me as a researcher. When I expressed my surprise at this, I was told that employees in Telecompany-X are used to journalists or researchers visiting for one or two days. In addition, most of the people I got in contact with were around my age and had studied in the past or were still studying alongside their work. Hence, the rather familiar and informal atmosphere I had experienced during my interviews with software developers et al. seemed to continue in this new environment.

But as my research went on, this impression changed and I felt I had to actively position my interests as a researcher. Precisely, it turned out that the access I was asking for – to observe and participate in a department for a few weeks – departed from the acknowledged paths in the company. Unfortunately, the chief editor of the intranet left the company shortly after our interview.[7] At first, the new editor showed interest in my project and supported my request to contact departments so that I would be able to observe staff members. But after several email and phone conversations she made clear that her efforts had failed and that all departments she had asked were suspicious of letting someone enter even for only a day or two; in addition, she underlined again the lack of benefits of my study for employees as another reason for the rejection. Apparently, one Head of Department only approved handing out questionnaires to selected employees.

However, even though some of the reasons might have been an excuse, survey research as the only available approach was not the path I wanted to take, so I adjusted my strategy in order to maintain access. In fact, at that moment, I was already under pressure since in the meantime half a year had passed and so far, I had only conducted four visits in one department plus the interviews with the project manager and the former chief editor of the intranet.

---

7   Just to note; the job of the chief editor of the intranet is a 20hrs per week part-time position. This was somewhat surprising to me as I assumed the intranet to be a central technology of the company that involves a lot of content maintenance and resources.

In the given situation, I decided to contact one of my informants in the headquarters who had previously shown interest in my project; in conceptual terms, I made her another "key informant" for my investigation. Initially, I had been in contact with her because the project manager of the intranet pointed her out to me; she supervised another central software application, the so-called X-Coach. The application is predominantly used in Customer Service; it features information about the company's clients and products and guides call centre agents through customer calls. In the course of the interview, my informant suggested to visit one of the company's call centres which I gratefully took on. But after a day in the call centre, I decided to stick to my initial interest in the intranet. This decision related to two considerations; first of all, at the time of my research, call centres had been researched extensively and, secondly, to me it seemed at this point that the intranet was in various ways entangled with the overall situation of the recent company merger and was therefore of more interest to me.

When I told her the difficulties I was experiencing, she put me in touch with six colleagues possibly willing to be part of my project. Three of these agreed to being visited; from there I continued my way through the company; as previously, I asked my informants to point out other colleagues in the company. In doing so, I moved further across different departments in Telecompany-X. As can be seen, I did not just have one "gatekeeper" or "key informant" with whom I was negotiating my presence in the company, but at least three people that were relevant for how my fieldwork proceeded.

The table below gives an overview of the interviews and visits I undertook in Telecompany-X:

Table 2: Interviews and visits in Telecompany-X

No.	Date	Type	Name	Job title	Department[8]
1.	07/2011 09/2011	2 visits (incl. initial contact visit)	Walter	Head of Inventory & Provisioning	Operations Support Systems (OSS), so-called ' technicians'
2.	09/2011	Interview	Silvia	Chief Editor Intranet	Internal Communications
3.	09/2011	Interview	Martin	Project Manager Intranet	Internal Communications

4.	09/2011	Visit	Frederik	Software Developer	Operations Support Systems (OSS), so-called ' technicians'
5.	09/2011	Visit	Thomas	Software Developer	Delivery Management, Operations Support Systems (OSS), so-called 'technicians'
6.	11/2011	Interview	Mrs. Ross	Head of Service Teams	Service Process Design, Customer Service (responsible for "X-coach")
7.	11/2011	Visit	Birgit	Call Centre Agent	Service Line, Customer Service
8.	04/2012	Visit	Katrin	Service Team Manager	Customer Service ("Stabsstelle")
9.	04/2012	Visit	Stephanie	Service Quality Manager	Service Design, Customer Service
10.	04/2012	Visit	Gloria	Promotion Manager	Team Sales Channel Development; Residential & Small Business Sales
11.	04/2012	Visit	Viktoria	Information Manager	Customer Service, Team Information Management
12.	05/2012	Visit	Manuel	Accountant, Business Sales	Performance & Financial Management
13.	09/2013	Interview	Max	Software developer, Customer Experience	Works part time for Telecompany-X and his own company (IT services and software development) *

* My very last informant belonged to the network of independent software developers, but he was also employed part time in Telecompany-X. I used this interview – which was in fact a longer conversation in a café – as a way of getting feedback on some of my interpretations and insights.

As the table shows, my interviews and visits in Telecompany-X extended over 10 months and were divided into two phases: the first phase comprised the initial contact visit, the interview with the project manager and the chief editor of the intranet and four visits in the Operations Support Systems (OSS) department, team "Inventory and Provisioning". In addition, I interviewed the person responsible for the "X-coach", the company's information tool used in Customer Service, and spent half a day in one of the company's call centres accompanying a call centre agent. The second phase of my fieldwork started about three months later, and this time my visits extended across different departments. While the early interview with the chief editor and the project manager of the new intranet explored the expectations towards the software, I was able to contrast these with observations I made regarding how the intranet was part of the everyday work in distinct settings in Telecompany-X.

Each of my visits lasted between 45 minutes and 1.5 hours comprising a 'guided tour' through the intranet. At the start of these visits, I always assured my informants that I would completely anonymise their personal data. Most of my informants were located in open space offices or in offices they shared with one or two colleagues so that often their colleagues were included in the conversation; hence, the atmosphere was mostly informal and rather chatty. All the workplaces I studied featured a variety of technological devices; each informant had his or her own work desk with a personal computer and one or two screens (sometimes also a camera), a landline phone, a mobile device and a headset. One of my informants, located in the middle management, was working at his laptop only. A few had an additional laptop on or besides their desks. The software technicians in the OSS department also had an "emergency computer" below their desks – in case the regular one broke down, I was told.

2.3.3   Two groups of employees

As part of my study, I got in contact with two types of employees circling around my two key informants: software developers, called 'technicians', and staff members with a background in Customer Service.[9] While the first

---

9   All my informants were employed permanently; only one was a so-called 'external', who was working for the company for about five years, intermittently changing teams and departments. So far, the company did not have a permanent post for him, he told me. This is often the case when it comes to "stock-driven companies", he further ex-

group was a team in the Operations Support Systems (OSS) department, those related to Customer Service were spread across different departments and groups such as Information Management, Business Sales & Financial Management and Residential & Small Business Sales.[10] Since my visits in the OSS department took place first, the data generated there, and the insights gained from them, served as a basis from which to contrast my observations in other settings. The following paragraphs provide some notes on the two groups and the work they pursue.

First of all, the employees I visited were located at different sites of the company; the technicians were in a building complex rather remotely outside the city which, before the merger, were part of the landline business. As I learned from Walter, my key informant and team leader in the OSS department, the technicians were taken over from one of the company's suppliers about half a year before the business integration. Nevertheless, as I found out, they associated themselves with the former landline business and also used some of the previous software applications. All other staff members were either situated in the headquarters or in one of the smaller branches of the company. Most of the employees with a background in Customer Service used to belong to the former mobile division.

Furthermore, as I learned, the technicians in the OSS department worked in the area of "Inventory and Provisioning" which, broadly speaking, maintains the telecommunication network. It does so by managing the inventory (cables, switches, nodes, routers, etc.) and ensuring the relevant connections and the configuration of different systems along the network. It also processes faults and new customer requests. The work centres on the so-called "Cramer application", a standard software application for monitoring and mapping telecommunication networks: while assembling the data from different systems, it maps these in relation to distinct work tasks that have to be per-

---

plained, "they rather keep the headcount low and possibly pay more for external employees in order to keep a good stock price".

10   The minimum unit in the company is a team. Each team has a team leader who functions as the direct supervisor. The next higher unit is the "group" who consists of about three to seven teams. These groups again belong to a department, such as Customer Service, Operations Support Systems or Business Sales, which is the next higher, hierarchical unit. Above the departments are the managing directors, one responsible for finances, one for sales and another for technology. As I got to know, the size of a team varies depending on the group and department; sometimes a team has only four or five members, but occasionally teams in the company have up to 20 members.

formed. For instance, a new order often requires the engineers 'in the field' to unplug and reconnect certain parts, as my informants described it, meaning parts somewhere along the physical telecommunication line have to be recoupled. Such a task was visualised in the system so that an overview of the whole work process becomes possible.

In the course of my visits, I found out that one of the primary tasks of the technicians was the configuration, that is, the adjustment and coordination, of different systems that were part of the telecommunication network. This involved the development of software which was nevertheless different from the software development I had learned about before. That is, the technicians in the OSS department did not start from scratch, so to speak, but the Cramer application they worked with regularly required a limited customisation at specific interfaces, i.e. software development, because different data sources along the network are not always compatible. Only the adjustment ensured the communication between the different parts and hence enabled the overall functioning of the network.

As can be seen from these descriptions, the intranet appears to not belong to the core of what my informants do as everyday work; however, my study shows that the intranet is nevertheless part of and constituent for their work. This was not obvious in the beginning since most employees, especially the technicians, always emphasised their disregard of the intranet. But finding out about the rather intricate ways in which the intranet was indeed part of their work was important also in the sense that it informed my subsequent investigation in other departments and hence gave me the possibility of comparing the data from the OSS department with the insights I gained in the other settings of the company.

The second part of my fieldwork in Telecompany-X extended across a greater variety of departments; as mentioned earlier, the staff members I got in contact with had almost all (except one) a background in Customer Service, mostly working as call centre agents. To give an impression of the variety of work they were doing: One of my informants, still part of Customer Service, was now responsible for the maintenance of the software used in the call centre ("X-Coach"). Her work included the update of data in the so-called 'back end' of the software. Another informant, Stephanie, had also worked as a call centre agent but was now part of the team "Service Design" where she coordinated and conducted the training of agents at the hotline.

Another employee I visited, Gloria, labelled "Promotion Manager", worked in the department called "Residential & Small Business Sales". Her position was split; she spent half of her time on maintaining contact with small businesses that sell the company's products, the other half she invested in collecting and processing promotional data which was later also published on the intranet. Another informant, Manuel, worked in the Business Sales department – more precisely, as part of the group "Performance & Financial Management" – where he examined and evaluated the customer accounts of larger corporations, serving as the point of intersection between Controlling and Accounting.

Overall, studying the two groups of staff members around my two key informants was not only a pragmatic decision, but made specific analytical contrasts apparent. That is, the technicians turned out to be far more hesitant towards the corporate branding campaign and the managerial efforts of culture management implemented after the merger in contrast to staff members with a background in Customer Service. They appeared as more open and accustomed to these measures. As the work argues, the differences shed light on the distinct local workplace culture that also shapes how staff members engage with the specific content on the intranet. These observations touch upon questions of group coherence and the manifestation of identity and cohesion among staff members beyond the merger differentiation. In this manner, the development of my fieldwork sensitised me to processes of identity formation that exist besides the dominant topic of the merger.

Altogether, at the time of my fieldwork, internal company dynamics were otherwise very much determined by processes happening in relation to the merger. I had the impression that people were very busy with themselves and with the reorganisation of the company – departments changed, new titles were announced, people were integrated, some changed jobs, others remained in their position. In addition, the company was also very present in the media since the previous management had been involved in a corruption scandal. It included the former CEO and other members of the board as well as politicians and lobbyists. As the investigation committee found out, during the 2000s, the company management had financed a network of people involved in the illegal funding of political parties, money laundering and the manipulation of company stock prices. Media interest was high at this time and new reports and revelations occurred almost daily. I did not make any reference to the reports myself; sometimes my informants made comments as well as fun of the management and the current media interest. I understand these as my informants' efforts to distance themselves from these events and the former company management.

But the time of my fieldwork turned out to be an insightful research setting since the company was in a state of transition, still adjusting to the merger and new organisational processes. Moreover, the two phases of my fieldwork were beneficial for my research, not only when it comes to extending the sites I visited and, as said above, my informants' different affiliations, but also in regard to the investigation and the analysis. That is, extending my visits over a longer period of time was related to the constant negotiation about my position, but, fortunately, the two phases made it possible for me to follow up on the changes on the intranet and the related processes in the company. In addition, it also enabled me to distance myself from the field site and to already examine the data I generated and revise my questions and interests. For instance, while in the beginning I was totally focused on studying how the intranet is part of the ongoing of different work practices, I soon realised the centrality of the merger for understanding the intranet in this context.

In fact, the process of constant negotiation made me aware of the organisational structures that turned out as to some extent "resistant" towards my study (Scheffer, 2002: 372). That is, my request to observe different staff members at their workplace for a day or two went apparently outside the acknowledged pathways; neither was I a visiting journalist for a day, nor a trainee. The reactions towards this request – "I mean, what do you want to see?" – and the advice to instead interview people by phone and to hand out a survey illustrate not only my informants' understanding about social sciences and empirical research, but also made me understand the setting I was researching. It first of all made apparent what is institutionally acknowledged as means of research in Telecompany-X. Furthermore, it made me revise my first impression of a very open and flexible company and instead to recognise Telecompany-X as permeated by formally closed and also hierarchical structures. But, as I am going to discuss in the following, since my overall entry into the company had not followed these structures, I kept relying on the personal network I had established so far which enabled me to move beyond official pathways.

2.4   Generating field data: Opportunities and limitations

Making my way through the company in the described manner had, obviously, effects on the data I generated. As already said, my entry into the company was not, as is usually the case when researching organisations, a top-down entry. Instead, I was in contact with people from the middle management level and the regular personnel. Thus, I did not interview one of the CEOs or the Head of Internal Communications. This would have been a possible last stage of my research, but after I had made this way through the company, I hesitated since once the company management became aware of my research it might demand to double-check my data.[11] However, while reviewing my data, I realised that the insights I had gained through the project manager and the former chief editor of the intranet, both part of Internal Communications, can very well be seen as outlining a managerial perspective on the intranet. Actually, within Telecompany-X, the Internal Communications department is directly subordinated to the CEO. Thus, balancing pros and cons of a possible contact with company management, I decided against this option and worked with the data I had generated.

Secondly, following a person's network pays attention to the voices that are apparent and heard while possibly overlooking the so-called "silent" voices that are nevertheless relevant for the phenomenon one investigates (Yanow and Schwartz-Shea, 2009: 68; Yanow, 2009). Silent voices are, for example, the people that stay invisible in the company, such as temporary staff or cleaning personnel. In relation to my research on the intranet, I recognised that, for instance, engineers working 'in the field', i.e. along the physical telecommunication network, or agents in the call centre were those that stayed rather invisible in my research. In fact, whereas employees in Telecompany-X are officially asked to spend time on the intranet, employees working as call centre agents in Customer Service were advised not to lose time while reading or browsing the intranet. Hence, the intranet was apparently intended only for some employees while others were excluded. Nevertheless, subsequent to my visit in the call centre, I deliberately chose to not follow up this line of research, but include this insight in my reflections and to bear it in mind during the analysis.

2.4.1   Company visits and 'guided tours' through the intranet

My fieldwork in Telecompany-X comprised the above-described visits I undertook at staff members' workplaces as well as semi-structured formal and

---

11   In fact, in the course of gaining access, I was in touch with one company that asked me to do my research under the company's supervision.

informal interviews. The visits were the centre of my investigation; for the most part, they focused on employees' handling of the intranet. Usually, I started by asking for a 'tour' through the intranet along the content and applications my informants use most often. In fact, these 'guided tours' through the intranet resemble what is called "Think-Aloud Method" in usability testing (cf. Clemmensen et al., 2009). But thinking aloud focuses on the individual, in particular participants' decision-making and related cognitive processes, often initiated by prescribing specific tasks beforehand. My 'guided tours' had another focus, namely "observing materiality in actions" (Royer, 2020: 15) which captures the material artefact within the net of the practices it is part of. I consider the guided tours as rather belonging to the realm of Media Studies where scholars as part of so-called "search experiments" observe and accompany how people browse websites (Mager, 2010: 12–3).

Doing so, I was able to trace how the intranet is part of staff members' everyday work, and furthermore, how they navigate through and explore the intranet. As a methodological approach, I consider my visits and especially the tours as more informative than formal interviews because they happened at people's workplaces and included the everyday office scenery; hence, they gave an impression of and made me experience the field site. Obviously, I was interrupting employees' everyday work so it was not at all a 'natural' situation. But, as said in the beginning, my methodological approach refrains from assuming a 'natural' or 'objective' reality that awaits to be investigated. Instead, it is based on the assumption that crafting one's research involves enacting the different realities that bring about the situations that are of interest (cf. Law and Urry, 2004).

In this manner, the guided tours made apparent the intranet's particular materiality, manifesting itself in my informant's (implicit) know-how about certain features on the intranet. Thus, accompanying my informants and 'touring' the intranet, I soon became aware of the applications they use more often and those they rather explored and tested in relation to my presence. Of course, these were of interest to me, too, since they showed me how my informants navigate and explore the intranet in situ. In fact, this first-hand experience happened more often; especially within staff members' open-plan offices, my visits proved themselves valuable also as a social opportunity to observe, for instance, how the technicians in the OSS department interact with one another in relation to using the intranet.

In fact, as Hirschauer and colleagues point out, within the social situation of the interview, and, I want to add, the visit, participants not only tell about their private life, they may also enact specific ways of dealing with each other, e.g. they perform their relationship (Hirschauer et al., 2015: 3). In a similar manner, but in relation to researching processes of identity formation in an organisation, Langley and colleagues underline that their interviews not only provided insight into staff members' explanations, but were likewise "sites of identity work" (Langley et al., 2012: 143) where identity was enacted and negotiated. Following this understanding, the interview situation becomes an "empirical situation" (ibid.) in which researchers may *experience* – either staged or in situ – how couples interact with one another or how staff members negotiate their belonging, as I did in Telecompany-X.

As can be seen, such an approach refrains from a 'naïve' understanding of interviews that considers them as merely obtaining information. Actually, during my visits, the transition between the situation of an interview and moments of observation were indeed fluent. For instance, as I experienced in the technicians' office, my visits provided the opportunity to observe how the technicians work around the search function of the intranet through immediate exchange among one another. In this manner, they enabled me to observe the relationship between my informants and the intranet. Likewise, I witnessed how the technicians distanced themselves from managerial control by making fun of corporate culture management efforts. At the same time, the visits had also moments in which I interrogated staff members about the development of the merger or the internal communication in the company.

As part of my visits, I recorded conversations and took notes on the work setting and how my informants navigated through the intranet. Also, I asked some of my informants to make screenshots of the intranet starting page and some applications they made use of. Furthermore, I collected various internal and external documents such as the company's internal employee magazine and a business magazine intended for stakeholders and the industry. In addition, I also examined company presentations on the Internet and read newspaper articles, in particular in relation to the recent merger the company had gone through.

Some of my visits also continued as informal talk, for example at the street corner close to the headquarters since my informant was about to go home. In such a setting I did not have my recording device at hand, but took notes afterwards. For instance, I learned about the company division running between people sitting in the headquarters and the technicians located remotely, outside the city centre. As the employee told me, "they [the technicians] do their own thing, the departments here [in the headquarters] are the important ones; Sales, Marketing, and so on, they make the money!" I remember this quote well since I was surprised; to me it seemed that the people I had visited, the so-called 'technicians', upheld the core of the company, the telecommunication network in relation to the services the company makes available. However, such a conversation was important for me in order to develop an understanding about internal company logics.

2.4.2   In there, but outside: Shifting research positions

Telecompany-X as a new research setting challenged me, not only in terms of getting access and of understanding how the intranet is part of the everyday work of my informants, but also in the sense that I became part of a large organisation where I wanted my work to be taken seriously. Of course, my lack of knowledge about almost everything felt fairly big and demoralising in the beginning. Also, my initial informants in the OSS department were all male, so I worried they would notice this lack of knowledge and dismiss me as just a student girl coming along asking a few questions. However, in dealing with this situation, I came up with a strategy allowing me to transform my uncertainties and lack of knowledge into a resource and thereby adapt to the research setting: at the start of each visit, I assured my informants that I knew less about their work than they did and that I would treat them as 'experts' on their work. Moreover, I also underlined that I would rather ask questions and double-check my understanding instead of making too many unspoken assumptions. Proceeding like this was helpful in the sense that the situation lost its tense quality not only for me, but also in case my informants appeared to be intimidated by my presence. In these situations, I also emphasised my organisationally 'independent' or external position as a researcher, meaning I was not appointed by company management, which also contributed to a less tense and relaxed atmosphere.

This in fact external position was at some point deliberately chosen. In the course of negotiating my access, I had also considered following established organisational structures by applying as a trainee to Telecompany-X. But I was told that this involves a strict and fixed application process which would have deferred my research once more. And more importantly, I realised that in becoming institutionally part of the organisation, I would lose my position as a researcher in favour of going 'native'. In fact, emphasising my interests as a PhD and social science researcher – this is how I labelled myself – was a way of separating to some extent my position from internal structures and understandings in the company. For instance, this label made clear that I was not evaluating my informants' performance, the ways in which they use the intranet, and reporting to the management, a connection I obviously did not want my research to make. Even though this position as an outsider made my presence in the company constantly precarious and felt in the beginning like a weakness, I later realised that this was an advantage; it brought me closer to my informants and allowed me to follow my interests as a researcher and to refrain from becoming institutionally utilised (cf. Suchman, 1995: 59; 63).

Continuing my way within the company gradually changed not only how I experienced the organisation, but also my position as a researcher. Personally, this was also a path towards becoming a 'social science researcher' by learning to make my research interest explicit in this setting. In connection with a closer explanation of my research approach, emphasising my interests also served as a justification device, warranting my hesitation towards interviewing employees by phone only and instead insisting upon arranging further research visits.

Initially, I expected my German background to be of more importance than it finally turned out, or at least this is the impression I got. Neither was I familiar with the local dialect nor with the rather difficult relationship that appears to exist between Austrian and German people. The only explicit mentioning of my background occurred while discussing contemporary work conditions that demand people to be increasingly flexible – as my informant said: "You had to be flexible, too, right?" in reference to me moving to Austria and in order to highlight an important characteristic of today's working world. Another informant asked me whether or not I live in the same city, "because of your accent", as she said. In this particular case, I felt she wanted to present the company to me as a flagship company, for instance by emphasising the newly decorated open spaces for staff to hang out. But this modus of presentation decreased once we sat at her desktop and she started browsing the intranet. Overall, I got the impression that even though once I had said a word, my informants immediately recognised where I come from, associating myself as a researcher with the institute I was part of (which is well known) was helpful in making this issue fade from the spotlight.

To sum up, conducting my empirical fieldwork, I had to take into account the challenges and opportunities at hand. That is, prior to my fieldwork, I was of course making assumptions about the company and my approach, which methods to use and the like. But upon gaining access into the company, I realised I had to continually revise my strategy and thereby adjust pragmatically to the situation at hand (Scheffer, 2002: 353). This is in fact what Stefan Laube has called "ethnographic opportunism" in analogy to insights gained in Science Studies on the embeddedness of scientific facts (2013: 61–4). It describes the researcher's ability to be attentive to the situatedness of ethnographic research, in fact of empirical fieldwork more generally, that emerges in specific contexts and which enable, but also restrict the investigation. In my case, this was indeed a time-intensive undertaking, but following this path, I developed a position consistent with my research interests.

2.5   Analysing field data: Crafting the research narrative

Extant literature describes the analysis of qualitative data as having an open beginning, making sure it emerges in close proximity to the people and settings the researcher is studying (Glaser and Strauss, 2009). In contrast to this rather theoretical description, my analysis of data was a less isolated process and took place while still generating field data. As already explained in relation to the circumstances of my fieldwork, the different time periods of my investigation gave me the possibility to examine some of my material before entering the field again. Thus, my analysis involved an exchange between moments of analysis and further data generation which enabled me to adjust my questions and interests based on the already gained data (Laube, 2013: 42). In addition, the analysis was also informed by theoretical considerations I had prior to the actual investigation as well as insights emerging along the way. This interplay has in the end enabled and restrained, simply *configured* my study (Yanow, 2009; see also Yanow and Schwartz-Shea, 2009).

But theoretical interests and propositions do not grant the research narrative and relevant themes. So far, I have reported on the circumstances of my fieldwork and explained the contexts in which I generated my field data. In the following, I discuss how I examined my data and thus bear witness on how I selected the themes and topics of my analysis.

First of all, my field data comprises audio recordings of formal interviews with software developers, intranet and knowledge managers, and of formal interviews and visits in Telecompany-X. As already mentioned, the field data encompasses also screenshots of the intranet and relevant applications and notes on company settings and employees' workplaces as well as various company documents such as the internal employee magazine, a business magazine intended for industry and relevant stakeholders and company presentations on the Internet.[12] In the beginning, I looked at these data sources as broadly providing information on the company, but this perspective was further configured in the course of my study. For example, at first, I simply read through the different articles in the internal employee magazine, but once I had become aware of the internal campaign promoting a specific work attitude among employees, I noticed especially the ads for this campaign in the magazine. As such, the magazine was a "visual aid" (Scheffer, 2002: 365), an additional way of making sense of the organisation while emphasising the campaign as a specific insight for recognising and linking analytical themes.

In line with the periodical pattern of my fieldwork, I did not transcribe all interviews and visits at once, but in different stages. Indeed, the transcription of interviews was a first step in the analysis since I got an overview of themes occurring in the data. In a next step, I read more thoroughly through the interviews and generated codes for specific topics. Whereas in the beginning I developed codes for all possible topics ("open coding"), at a later stage I coded selectively, that is, I concentrated on the analytical themes I had already found and looked to see whether or not they appear in my data ("focused coding") (Emerson et al., 1995: 150–67). For example, in the beginning all kinds of topics emerged such as the gender-bias towards male dominance in software development. Or, as already reported earlier, I had a code that referred to the ways in which the intranet excludes certain employees, for instance call centre agents. However, in the course of my analysis, I decided to set some of these topics aside while focusing on the ones from which I finally crafted my research narrative.

In relation to recognising how the intranet was part of everyday work practices, the audio recordings of my visits turned out to be especially important. As I realised, they did not only record verbal expressions, but also the clicking of employees' cursors while touring the intranet. I made a note on these sounds in the transcript since in connection with the verbal expressions and fieldnotes from the respective visit, the sound was an additional reference point for understanding how long my informants had to look for information and how long they scrolled through a page, respectively how fast they clicked away to another page. Thus, the sound provided another insight

---

12   In total, my data encompasses 292 pages of interview transcriptions (single spaced) plus 6 screenshots. I also transferred my fieldnotes describing the work settings, atmospheres and other observations from a note pad into 21 pages typed data.

into how familiar staff members were with a particular page or application on the intranet.

Altogether, asking questions about my data material was helpful when aiming to find analytical topics; as Emerson and colleagues point out, in order to reconstruct members' meanings, one has to interrogate the situation at hand by asking: "Who does what, how and when?" Doing so, the researcher is able to reconstruct expectations or specific problems and the solutions people develop under given circumstances and the means and tools they refer to (Emerson et al., 1995: 146; 152; Laube, 2013: 67). Furthermore, as part of the seminar on "Situational Analysis" with Adele Clark at the Institute of Advanced Studies (IHS), I developed different kinds of maps that served in the beginning as a way to reflect on my project more generally. At a later stage, in relation to the empirical data, this approach helped to analyse the relations between different elements of my research; for instance, between the intranet in Telecompany-X and the internal branding campaign. Similarly to Emerson, guiding questions of the analysis are: 'What makes a difference/what matters in the situation?', 'to whom?' and also 'in relation to which element or device?' (cf. Clarke, 2005). Thus, the approach takes into account that a situation of enquiry encompasses heterogenous elements, including non-human entities. In the process of interrogating my data, specific topics and themes emerged; obviously, my theoretical interests in practices, the relevant literature and my role as a researcher have also been constitutive in this process.

2.5.1   Selecting analytical themes from interviews with software developers and others

The interviews with software developers, intranet and knowledge managers and media consultants occurred at the very beginning of my study, hence the data touched upon a great variety of topics such as the modelling of the development process and current trends in software design, for example the increasing personalisation of software. But it also covered a more specific discussion about intranets, that is, their history and emergence, expectations towards intranets as well as several stories about failed intranet implementations. Some of these topics and terms occurred repeatedly and, as will become apparent, turned out to be significant for the analysis and overall structure of my dissertation.

For instance, while explaining their experiences with technologies in general, I noticed my interviewees frequently opposed humans and technologies, treating them as fundamentally separated entities that nevertheless affect and work on each other in often mysterious ways. This understanding, I realised, conceives of software technologies as straightforwardly solving work tasks, such as the exchange and distribution of information and knowledge across the organisation. It resembles the literature in management and business studies that praises software 'tools' as means of organising work processes more efficiently, as explained in the introduction. However, in connection with my research in Telecompany-X and my theoretical interests in practices, I started to critically examine these assumptions and, instead, to look at the workplace setting as a critical resource for understanding how (software) technologies are part of everyday work.

Another key term my informants invoked frequently was the notion of "usability". It refers to the degree to which the software is considered as 'user-friendly', as easily applicable. In the discourse, it is a criterion of quality – the greater the usability, the better the expected appropriation by the prospective user. Within this conception, tracing back users' 'needs' and 'wants' is an important step so as to create a potentially successful technology. Thus, the user becomes the central point of reference while other factors, such as the workplace or a specific work setting, are rather disregarded. In the context of my research, this concept was important for finding out how users on the one hand and the software on the other is imagined and envisioned – in my informants' accounts, but also more generally in software design and development. These ideas were also central for thinking about and analysing my research in Telecompany-X; in fact, they inspired Chapter 5, which discusses the intranet's search function in relation to notions of usability, technology acceptance and adoption.

Another concept mentioned repeatedly by software developers, but also knowledge and intranet managers was the notion of 'organisational culture'. It played a significant role in my informants' narratives, especially when explaining failed software implementations. In short, this concept considers organisations as groups of people that share norms and values manifested in routines and ways of doing. It has become a catchphrase, especially in the consulting industry. According to my informants, organisational cultures are often inert, sometimes even resistant and may prevent the successful implementation of a technology. These statements echo a great amount of business literature that describes corporate cultures as the decisive factor when it comes to technology implementations. At the same time, the literature also frames organisational cultures as potentially manipulable. In fact, these understandings are two sides of the same coin, so to say, meaning that either the technology or the human part is described as the obstacle, thereby highlighting again the fundamental separation and confrontation of humans and technologies, as mentioned above.

However, when it comes to my informants' statements on this topic, I noticed especially among the software developers and knowledge managers a widespread devaluation of technologies. As I realised, this devaluation expressed my informants' resistance towards an industry that marketises technologies and software applications as the solution to a variety of organisational problems. As said, I made sense of this insight as a form of agreement by my informants which they share as a very loose community of independent software developers and knowledge managers.

As can be seen, the interviews with people working in the area of software development and the wider field of technology implementation, including knowledge and intranet managers, unfolded a set of analytical topics – the fundamental separation of humans and technologies, the more specific relationship between potential users and software, the configuration of potential users as groups of people sharing norms and values and of having specific needs and wants, the missing account on the workplace – which sensitised and stimulated the analysis of my data. But when coding my interviews and visits in Telecompany-X, the list of analytical themes got even longer, so that I had to make further selections.

2.5.2   Identifying analytical topics from company visits and 'guided tours' through the intranet

Following the multi-sited rationale, I started to look in particular for those topics that connect and inform the different sites of my study. For example, the classification of organisations as featuring a specific 'culture' occurred not only among the interviews, but also in relation to my visits in Telecompany-X. In fact, the notion of culture, mostly in connection with 'difference', became a central theme for understanding the internal discourses after the merger. Moreover, it also made apparent what was conceived as the organisational problem: the cultural separation of the company.

As I learned, the intranet was expected to tackle this problem – but to my astonishment it did so not by simply distributing internal information, but by being part of an internal corporate branding campaign that promotes the new company and its brand to employees. In fact, at the time of the first phase of my fieldwork, Inside-X had been launched for about half a year. As the chief editor told me, a small online survey was conducted after the first two weeks, in which about 1,000 employees participated. Apparently, 66% stated that they like the intranet "very much", whereas only 7% did not like it "at all". As the project manager of the intranet underlined, "[...] at the end of the day, it [the intranet] was well received, for an intranet, the reasons, well [...] perhaps euphoria about the new brand [...]". Despite the fact that he seemed to downplay his expectations towards the intranet ("well received, for an intranet"), I was quite surprised by the link between the intranet and the new company brand, but his framing already points at the specific expectations towards the new intranet in this context. As I found out, company management considered the intranet to set an example of the new business and to gather employees around the new company brand with the aim of installing a coherent company identity.

In addition to providing insight into the central role of the intranet as a 'change agent', I was surprised by the rather limited interest in employees' actual handling of the intranet. In fact, not only the project manager, but also the chief editor appeared satisfied with how the intranet apparently found approval among staff members. Apart from the initial survey, the intranet was regularly evaluated once a year. As I was told, 95% of participating members apparently "used" the intranet, but without further explaining what this usage actually implied. This finding is especially interesting in light of the fact that employees automatically log on to the intranet when accessing the web browser on their personal computer. Nevertheless, both the chief editor and the project manager were satisfied with the numbers, since in total, 80% confirmed they "have a look" at least once a day which both underlined is "not that bad" and in fact shows that it is used "intensely". However, I understand the limited investigation into how employees indeed use the intranet as less an expression of disregard than an example of how a certain agenda is being implemented without in fact further pursuing its realisation. It obviously encouraged my research interest, in particular the investigation of what 'usage' in this context actually means.

Altogether, the concept of organisational culture, the internal corporate branding campaign as well as the managerial desire for a coherent company identity turned out to be central analytical themes for understanding the intranet in Telecompany-X. These topics served as the basis for Chapters 3 and 4 which discuss the company's conflictual situation after the merger and the configuration of the intranet as a change agent that carries managerial practices of internal and corporate branding intended to solve perceived struggles.

In my descriptions above, I deliberately chose the terms 'astonishment' and 'surprise' in order to emphasise also my own sensemaking that was significant regarding the topics I later turned to in my analysis. In fact, the literature on ethnographic research describes reflecting on one's own understanding as a source of knowledge that emerges while "'living' in two worlds", as Dvora Yanow says (1996: 45). That is, making sense of one's own world and likewise of the world one is researching creates a space to reflect on assumptions that are confirmed, but also expectations that might be disappointed. As Yanow further emphasises, this is where puzzles and tensions – possibly in connection with additional questioning – may lead to a purposeful route into understanding the research setting (see also Laube, 2013: 58).

This twofold sensemaking became very evident in relation to another experience I had while getting in contact with new people in the company. In the beginning, I addressed my initial contact Walter by using the colloquial German "Du". I was introduced to him through a friend and he was about my age so this appeared fairly natural. However, making my way through the company I somehow became increasingly insecure about how to approach my informants; they sometimes addressed me using the formal "Sie", but this varied in relation to my informants' age and position; unfortunately, I did not recognise any pattern I could follow. This is why I started to use the formal "Sie" which nevertheless sometimes felt inadequate and made the situation more official. Sometime later in another conversation, one of my informants told me about the differences between the two formerly separated companies; one concerned how people address one another – as my informant said, those stemming from the former mobile part were used to the colloquial "Du", while employees from the landline division usually relied upon the formal "Sie". As I further learned, subsequent to the merger, these different ways of approaching one another were a conflict issue on which a lot of discussion focused. While experiencing it first-hand (of course, differently from my informants), my own entanglement made me aware of the issue and underlined to consider how relevant it seemed to my analysis. Indeed, as will become apparent, I encountered the question of how to address one another again in relation to analysing my visits and the touring of the intranet and related applications.

Allow me to return to how I proceeded analysing the data. In fact, while the analysis of interviews proceeded rather straightforwardly, when assessing the transcription of my visits and 'guided tours' through the intranet, I referred again to the idea of situational analysis and the approach of map-drawing. Even though situational maps are intended to locate the research project in a broader sense, I used the idea of the situation as an analytical category for taking into account the 'micro' situation of the intranet and the involved practices. For instance, being part of and hence constitutive to specific practices, the starting page, but also the search function and the corporate directory in connection with the organigram proved themselves as central applications to specific situations. Other applications such as the messenger tool on the intranet were used extensively, too, but turned out not to be as central and instead subordinated to the larger practice of everyday communication and interaction. However, visualising the different practices as part of situational maps was helpful for analysing how the involved elements relate to each other and how they constitute the situation of enquiry (cf. Clarke, 2005: 86 et seqq.).

In addition, translating relevant passages for the text at a later stage was another opportunity to reflect on the words my informants made use of, and their meaning. Thus, the translation served as another chance to distance myself from the data I generated. In relation to these translations, I obviously paid attention to my informants' colloquial expressions and double-checked all of my translation (also those of the intranet screenshots and other material) with a native English speaker who has been teaching German for years. However, some of the terms, such as the notion of the "Einfach Macher", I explained and kept using the German term.

2.5.3   Organising analytical themes and topics

Following the central and constitutive practices the intranet was part of, I was able to organise the different analytical topics. First of all, the specific situation of the merger and, in connection with it, the implementation of the intranet turned out to be central topics and served as starting points for my analysis. Therefore, Chapter 3 ("Cultivating differences") is the 'prologue' to the dissertation as it analyses the dynamics of the merger, in particular the perceived conflicts around the two former companies and their identities. Chapter 4 ("The divided intranet") serves as a counterpart as it illuminates how the intranet is expected to tackle these conflicts by promoting the new company and brand to employees. In particular, through analysing how employees make use of the starting page, the different logics – one attending to everyday work and the other to the corporate branding and culture management efforts – became apparent. The two categories "everyday work" and "playing around" refer to the contrasting logics and constituted the core of the analysis.

Chapter 5 and 6 zoom in on the practices around the corporate directory and organigram and the search function. From there, I develop a set of arguments for understanding the utilisation of intranet technologies and for attending to the workplace as a significant category. In particular, Chapter 5 ("This has to be coordinated") engages with the everyday mediated communication as a central characteristic of what I call 'mundane' knowledge work. That is, examining the practices around the corporate directory and organigram on the intranet makes apparent that everyday interaction in Telecompany-X is a very much coordinated activity sustained by an array of everyday technologies. Thus, while knowledge work has been often described as involving expertise in relation to very specific technologies, my analysis points out the alignment of different devices and applications and the emergent knowledge as central characteristic of this work. In addition, the issue of how employees address one another plays a part in this context, too; as the chapter shows, the hierarchical ordering across the company – a somewhat contested issue during the merger – also manifests itself in these 'mundane' communication practices.

Foundational for Chapter 6 ("Searching our internal Google") were my informants' reports on the non-functioning of the search function which encouraged my investigative interest into how employees indeed work around it. I had learned about the notion of the workaround during the interviews with software developers and programmers; it describes how users circumvent a certain technical failure of a software or technology. Referring to the concept, I examine how employees (dis-)use the search function and hence redefine the workaround as a valuable source for getting closer to understanding the characteristics that make a workable technology. Thereby, I critically revise concepts such as usability and technology acceptance and adoption.

As can be seen, the different chapters address distinct research communities and scientific debates; that is, Chapter 3 and 4 analyse the merger process as well as the entanglement of the intranet with measures of corporate culture management, thereby taking into account discourses about corporate branding, organisational identity work and normative control. Thus, this first part of empirical chapters critically interrogates bringing together intranet technologies with measures of culture management. Moreover, as mentioned above, while Chapter 5 refers to research in organisational studies and organisational sociology on knowledge work and the partaking of technologies, Chapter 6 tackles debates in software/technology development. Both chapters argue for a close examination of how technologies are used and, in accordance with the perspective on practices, show that less the individual technology, but more the interrelatedness of different technologies – which I describe as 'mundane' knowledge work – is characteristic to contemporary work and critical when thinking about workable technologies.

3 Cultivating differences: Orientation and sensemaking in the post-merger company

As outlined in the previous chapters, when I started my fieldwork in Telecompany-X, the company had just gone through a merger integrating landline and mobile services. Previously, the telecom business ("Phone-Y") was primarily concerned with fixed network operations and increasingly also internet services. Founded in 1996, the mobile division ("Mobile-X") was the first available mobile phone network operator. Both companies had, obviously, different corporate identities, i.e. an individual logo in connection with the associated company brand. The mobile part's company logo consisted of black colour with a silver signature and the main company brand was likewise black with a yellowish-golden pattern. The landline company logo was based on green and red squares and a black font on white background, it did not have a separate brand logo. Despite the mix, green was understood to be the foundation of the landline's colour scheme whereas the mobile company was associated with the black colour. The different corporate logos and their colours defined both companies' promotional and advertising material and their activities in public.

I encountered the differentiation between "black world" and "green world" for the first time during my visit in the call centre of Telecompany-X. The agent used these terms in order to refer to the different responsibilities at the hotline; belonging to the "black world" described agents that usually stemmed from the mobile division and that dealt with mobile phone services. Being part of the "green world" designated agents who had a background in the landline business and hence were associated with topics around landline services. As I was told, prior to the merger, agents were educated as so-called "all-around agents" responsible for all kind of topics. Subsequent to the merger, they were assigned to specific subjects such as "technology", "accounting", or "products". Thus, call centre agents had to learn about the procedures of the respective other, the mobile or landline part, in one of the specific areas.

Based on these logos and specifically the colours, people in the company associated green with the landline business and black with the former mobile company. The differentiation was also mentioned in employees' accounts; for instance, talking about the merger with Gloria from Residential and Business Sales who was formerly part of Mobile-X, she also referred to these terms by pointing out:

> I mean, still one year after the merger, it is being asked: 'Were you black or green world?' and 'back then it was like this', and [...] 'at ours, it was like this' and 'at yours, it's like that'; it is still 'at ours' and 'at yours', yes, it is still like that, also because we still have extremely many systems that run parallel and where you have to enter with different user [names], because it hasn't been managed yet to bring all down to a common denominator.

As I learned throughout my investigation, the notion of black versus green world was still widely used among employees in Telecompany-X in order to allocate people and coordinate work in the post-merger company. Apparently, traces in the form of different routines and work procedures of the former two organisations still existed; as Gloria underlined, especially the integration and alignment of the corporate network had apparently not happened yet so that people still used their 'old' user name and application, for instance for the company's time management system. In fact, it seems that employees made sense of the merger and related processes by referring to the two former companies and by pointing out the differences. Thus, in doing so, employees identified one another and conveyed their former belonging. As I am going to show in this chapter, such differentiation and identification were central modes of orientation in the company.

However, Gloria's statement above appears to also lament the fact that these differences still exist and are talked about, even though a year had passed. This resembles a comment by the project manager of the intranet who likewise pointed out that after the merger, the company was still permeated by an internal division: "[...] well, in some areas, we still have two worlds, unfortunately, but one can see it is very encompassing and complicated the whole thing, such a change." The interview took place about a year after the merger and, similar to Gloria cited above, he complained about the division in the company that still endures; apparently, the desired transformation into a company consisting of just one world had not succeeded yet. Also, instead of naming the merger, he used the term 'change' which in the literature occurs often in connection with 'management', describing the strategic restructuring and reorganisation of business companies, especially in the case of merger integrations (Lauer, 2014).

Indeed, my informants' statements correspond to other employees who described the fragmentation of the company as a problem that has to be eliminated or at least tackled. Such an opinion resonates with the existing literature on mergers and acquisitions within the wider field of organisation and management studies; post-merger companies are often described as suffering from internal conflicts across various organisational levels as a result of merger processes (Vaara, 2002; see also Kansal and Chandani, 2014). Within this framework, different management styles, constant restructuring and employee resistance in the form of orienting to past organisational identities are understood to interrupt the smooth running of work processes. They are considered to hinder the successful accomplishment of mergers and acquisitions, that is, the realisation of anticipated and estimated objectives such as increasing business production and company efficiency (Haleblian et al., 2009).

Against this backdrop, the chapter first illustrates the existing framework for understanding merger processes in research and literature. Subsequently, it attends to how employees in different departments make sense of the merger and the managerial desire for coherence. The concept of sensemaking describes organisational members' attempt to (retrospectively) grasp the ongoing of activities happening in the organisation (Weick, 1993: 635; see also Weick and Roberts, 1993). As Weick and colleagues outline, sensemaking is a collective process that happens when taking part in interrelated and coordinated activities.[1]

As will become apparent, the ways in which employees make sense of the merger can be described as forms of organisational "identity work" (cf. Alvesson and Willmott, 2002: 622); identity work describes employees' ongoing discussion and related activities of who they are as part of the organisation they work for and identify with. As research has shown, identity work occurs

---

[1]   Referring to organisational sensemaking, Weick and colleagues oppose organisational theorists that foreground decision making as central and most important activity for analysing organisations. Instead, he suggests to look how meaning is accomplished as part of the ongoing of routines and activities taking place in the organisation (Weick et al., 2005: 412).

increasingly in cases of managerial "identity regulation" (Alvesson and Will-mott, 2002: 625), that is, in the context of efforts to implement and prescribe a new company identity to staff members. Thus, employees' continuous iden-tity work points to managerial practices that aim to establish a new company identity in Telecompany-X. While Chapter 4 further outlines the campaign in the context of the setup of the intranet, this chapter analyses, first of all, how employees deal with the merger and the managerial desire for coherence by illustrating the narratives and (post-)merger controversies in the company.

In fact, my analysis shows that despite the managerial call for a new and coherent organisational culture and identity, the formerly distinct companies and their historically grown identities are still an important point of refer-ence. First of all, referring to the previous companies often is a pragmatic way of making sense of the merger since the company is permeated by var-ious traces of the two former businesses. Secondly, both identities are also utilised as part of employees' ongoing identity work and the narratives they refer to: The first upholds and nostalgically manifests as well as laments over the companies' differences; in fact, it is a central and dominant narrative. The second approach almost contrasts this idea in the way it downplays the merger by naturalising and overlooking the distinctiveness of the former two companies. While the first narrative can be understood as a form of employee resistance, the second approach corresponds to the managerial prescription of wholeness as it follows the normative request to emphasise the unity of the new company. In doing so, employees apply a form of self-correcting strategy that deliberately overlooks the differences of the former two companies.

In this manner, the different narratives and related strategies also provide insight into how different departments and work settings – mainly Customer Service/Communication and the software technicians in the Operations Sup-port Systems (OSS) department – are affected by the merger and hence relate differently to the integration processes.[2] They make evident the various other divisions in the company that run across the dominant, merger dominated differentiation between "black world" and "green world"; as I show in this chapter, the company is permeated by numerous forms of "culture contact"

---

2   I refer to a practice-theoretic informed notion of strategy; it underlines that communi-cation, in particular the narratives people employ in organisations, are a specific type of doing and that storytelling contributes to making sense of the situation at hand (Fenton and Langley, 2011; see also Seidl and Whittington, 2014).

(Bateson, 2000: 61), in the form of departments, but also work settings and local work cultures.

3.1 Merger processes in research and literature: Corporate cultures and organisational control

Mergers and acquisitions are a well-researched area within management and organisation studies; however, the leading framework emphasises the potential for conflict in mergers. This idea has found its response in the proliferation of merger case studies in strategic management research aiming to identify determining variables in pre- and post-merger companies (Cartwright and Schoenberg, 2006). Giving an overview on mergers and acquisitions within organisational studies, Angwin and Vaara distinguish three perspectives that populate existing approaches; the first constitutes the strategic management focus that predominantly examines whether managerial strategies concerning, for instance, knowledge and skill sharing, deliver expected outcome (2005: 1446). The second perspective highlights the so-called 'social impacts' of mergers on employees, for example increasing uncertainty and employee resistance. The third perspective centres on 'cultural differences'; here, the distinctiveness of two merging corporations are understood as the main obstacle generating various conflicts in post-merger organisations (Angwin and Vaara, 2005: 1446). As the authors state, while the first two pick up specific problems within organisations, the perspective on 'cultural differences' offers an explanatory framework for a variety of issues, for instance country-specific problems in globally operating companies, but also conflicts around organisational identities (e.g. Langley et al., 2012; Tanure et al., 2009).

Studying the literature on 'cultural difference' more closely, one can see that this perspective is accompanied by dramatic notions such as 'collision' or 'culture clash', highlighting the difficulties of merger integration processes (e.g. Buono and Bowditch, 2003; Lee et al., 2015). In fact, explaining how organisations deal with distinct cultures, this perspective offers three possible scenarios; either cultures stay separated, one dominates the other or the two coalesce (Schein, 2003: 23). Nevertheless, the concept of culture delivers also the solution: knowing the different cultures enables one to adjust them, or to install the necessary means in order to do so (Schein, 2003: 163). Thus, by referring to 'consistent' or 'coherent' cultures, management and organisation studies' scholars reveal a somewhat steering understanding of corporate cultures as distinct characteristics of organisations (Barley, 1983).

In fact, this understanding rests on two assumptions; at first, strong and coherent cultures are necessary for successful company performance and secondly, they can be "designed" and "manipulated" through strategic management and human resources (Barley and Kunda, 1992: 383; see also Maldonado et al., 2018). As Barley and Kunda point out, the notion of culture addresses employees not just as rational, but as emotional beings that may increasingly show commitment and identify with the organisation they work for (1992: 382–3). In this manner, the concept relies on a normative rhetoric that subordinates the individual employee to the whole of the company. Consequently, efforts in the realm of culture management, as these activities are called, direct attention to employees' subjective experiences so as to increase work quality and efficiency (e.g. Morrill, 2008: 24; see also Müller, 2017; Willmott, 1993).

A similarly prevalent idea discussed in the context of merger integrations is the conflictual potential of distinct organisational identities. First of all, the concept of organisational identity describes "[...] members' collective, shared sense of who they are as an organization" (Corley and Gioia, 2004: 175), thus emphasising the internal perspective of employees and their understanding of who they are and what differentiates them as a company (Clark et al., 2010: 397). Like the concept of organisational culture, it rests on the assumption that identities are manipulable. Likewise, it aims to change people's selves in favour of a strong identification with the company so as to ensure the company's successful post-merger performance (cf. Olie, 1994). In fact, the increasing discussion in recent years around notions of service and quality management, but also human resource management more generally shed light on the prevalent understanding of employees as advocates of a specific corporate culture which share a sense of self that is bound to the organisation's identity (Willmott, 1993: 522; see also Kunda, 2006; Tuckman, 1994).

3.2 Post-industrial management practices: Organisational identity work and regulation

As can be seen, similarly to the concept of culture, the notion of organisational identity follows the idea that identities may successfully be implemented by aligning employees through strategic and communicative measures (Pratt et

al., 2016: 444). As already outlined in the introduction, such managerial approaches belong to the post-industrial economy that distinguishes itself from
industrialisation and bureaucratic and hierarchical structures with flexible
and changing forms of work and working conditions (Macdonald, 1991; see
also Vallas, 1999). Thus, while the era of industrial work aimed to control and
determine work processes and involved specialised tasks, the management
of so-called information and knowledge work demands new organisational
structures and managerial practices that bind employees and unleash their
skills for the good of the company (Vallas, 1999: 73).

But how do these managerial practices engage employees? As authors have
shown, such practices address the "production of subjectivity" (Alvesson and
Willmott, 2002: 624), that is, the creation of a flexible employee who identifies
with his or her work and who is able to adapt to constantly changing work
conditions and job responsibilities (cf. Bröckling, 2015). Thus, post-Fordist
management counts on notions of value and respective emotions, worked
into internal training programs and company events as well as promotion
schemes that shape employees' identity construction. In fact, while being the
objective of such measures, employees are positioned as "identity worker[s]"
(Alvesson and Willmott, 2002: 622) that have to orient to and internalise these
managerial messages.[3]

However, authors agree that organisational identities may change when
put under pressure from the outside, for example through market adapta-
tions, or internally, through reorganisation and restructuring (Clark et al.,
2010: 398). A specific case of organisational identity change is obviously mergers and acquisitions where established concepts about a company identity
are called into question. Indeed, conflicts around distinct group identities
and related work practices frequently permeate post-merger companies, often resulting from managerial "pressures for sameness" (Langley et al., 2012:

---

3 Following Giddens, Alvesson and Willmott describe the concept of self-identity as a
reflexive process that the individual is part of when engaging in his or her social-cul-
tural life. It is a likewise unconscious but also conscious interplay of identity work and
identity regulation (2002: 625–6). In fact, according to Giddens, the modern individual is more prone to engaging in identity work as identities have become more fluid
and less stable. This, the authors state, makes the modern individual more open to
associate themselves with corporate identities but, at the same time, it may also serve
to 'emancipate' the individual as it allows for various alternative and altering identity
conceptions (Alvesson and Willmott, 2002: 624; 636–7).

137), that is, the managerial effort to install a consistent organisational identity in the company after the merger. As mentioned above, such managerial
measures are described as "identity regulation" so as to underline the exercise
of control that is related to the induction of, for instance, corporate values,
compliance guidelines or ideal worker norms (Alvesson and Willmott, 2002:
625). In fact, by determining the existing and regulating narratives, company
management may exercise control as it normatively defines employees' self-
images, their sense of purpose together with their feelings towards and identification with the company.

Because of the coercive character of these measures, identity regulations
often operate in specific "frameworks of power" (Brown, 2019: 14); that is,
power relations define who is the addressor – often company management –
and who the addressed and whether or not employees feel obliged to take up
such messages. Nevertheless, Alvesson and Willmott state that identity regulation "[...] encompasses the more or less intentional effects of social practices
upon processes of identity construction and reconstruction" (2002: 625) which
may be either "[s]trategically employed or produced by actors in their everyday interactions [...]" (2002: 635). Thus, identity regulation is *not* restricted to
managerial interventions exclusively and employees must not be understood
as submissive to such efforts. Rather, Alvesson and Willmott assume a proces-
sual and interactive formation of identities which rests on employees' identity
work, including their (dis-)engagement from managerially defined conceptions (2002: 621; see also Langley et al., 2012: 140). As can be seen, employees'
self-constructions happen in the context of managerial regulation and ongoing, everyday identity work that all contribute to negotiating employees'
belonging to the company. In this manner, managerial discourses and practices are involved in the construction of corporate identities, but the existing,
possibly work-specific and local cultures may have an impact, too.

However, when it comes to research on organisational identity, authors
have underlined that concentrating on people's self-understanding and descriptions risks leaning towards uniform and stable conceptions, thereby possibly disregarding disparities and differences (cf. Alvesson et al., 2008: 14).
Likewise, the excessive use of and orientation towards the concept of corporate culture has been criticised; in particular, the lack of and vague definition of what the term culture actually means has been the centre of criticism
(Angwin and Vaara, 2005: 1447). Furthermore, as Sally Riad says, it is the preferred rationale for understanding mergers and acquisitions, almost constituting a "regime of truth" (2005: 1533) that is not questioned anymore, thereby

preventing other ways of making sense of what is happening when organisations merge. In fact, following the (sometimes blurring) notion of culture, often a holistic understanding prevails that fundamentally separates employees from one another by configuring them as homogenously distinct groups of people.

Thus, both concepts, that of corporate culture and of organisational identity, have to be treated with caution; as said above, they put forward a steering understanding that conceives of corporate cultures and identities as possibly being manufactured and manipulable. Such a framing easily overlooks how strong cultures and the identification therewith may create a very tight system of legitimate behaviour that hinders organisational development and creativity (cf. Alvesson and Willmott, 2002: 636; see also Kärreman and Alvesson, 2004). Also, various local cultures in the sense of communities-of-practice are necessary for the development of specific knowledge in the company (Brown and Duguid, 2001; Lave and Wenger, 1991).

Following these insights, I share a hesitant attitude towards the concepts of corporate culture and identity; instead of simply assuming the existence of a fixed identity defining culturally different groups of people, I follow the understanding put forward by theories of practice and ask how difference first of all comes into being. Thus, I understand the different narratives as ways of *doing*, as *narrating* difference. In this manner, they constitute a type of resistance towards, while also echoing the managerial desire for coherence. At the same time and as already said above, the constant reference to the two previous companies can also be seen as a form of orientation in the merging company which assists employees in making sense of the integration process. Therefore, I suggest to consider the reference to the former green and black world as a *shared* reference that enables employees to categorise and explain distinct work routines and procedures which apparently still exist in the post-merger company.

Obviously, such a perspective differs from management studies literature and also the management in Telecompany-X that treats any reference to the two former companies as a problem only. As the next chapter illustrates, company management has set up an internal communications campaign that resorts to measures of culture management, in particular corporate and internal branding, in order to wipe out the 'old' company brands and identities. In contrast, this chapter underlines the importance of the existing and historically grown identities of both former companies for the merging company. Moreover, it points to a possible downside of past managerial identity work and regulation: it obstructs the development of a new corporate identity, in particular through current measures of culture management.

In fact, when it comes to identity change, Corley and Gioia highlight the permanent, continuing character of organisational identities, but also underline the importance of a state of "ambiguity" the identity has to pass through in order to change (Corley and Gioia, 2004: 200–1). This finding stands in opposition to the immediate implementation of a new company brand and identity through communicative, especially branding, methods, as done in Telecompany-X.

Altogether, by highlighting the importance of both previous company identities for everyday work, my analysis departs from the dominant understanding in management and organisational studies. That is, it questions the managerial idea of simply erasing the former, historically grown company identities through methods of culture management, in particular internal and corporate branding, and points at the limits the design of corporate cultures and identities may face. Instead, it emphasises the integration potential of orienting to the former two companies as shared points of reference. Moreover, by providing insight into how different departments – Customer Service/Communication and the software technicians in the OSS department – are affected by the merger and relate differently to integration processes, it shows that cultural difference – that is, difference in how work is done and understood – runs across the company, possibly undermining the merger differentiation.

3.3   Caught in difference: Orientation in the merging company

The two previously distinct companies share a common history, but, according to employees, have developed as relatively distinct businesses. For employees, the merger obviously created a great deal of uncertainty in terms of job security and position. As the chief editor of the intranet explained to me, at the time of the merger, many people in the company did not know whether they would keep their jobs or move to another position or whether they would leave the company altogether. In addition to being in an uncertain state about their general future in the company, employees were also part of processes of restructuring and reorganisation. The main departments such as Accounting, Sales, Marketing, Internal Communications and Customer Service were put together so that some employees changed their job position. Only the technology-laden departments and respective teams were kept largely unchanged since operations for mobile and landline businesses work separately. Thus, subsequent to the merger, most employees dealt with members from the other company on an everyday basis, sometimes working together in close connection.

As already mentioned, shortly after the merger, Internal Communications launched a campaign – of which the intranet was part – and which highlighted the new company brand and identity as the new shared point of reference. It is not surprising that employees responded in various ways to the pressures associated with the merger in general and the campaign in particular. As I learned from Gloria who I quoted in the beginning, during the integration period, advertising material from the two former companies was used among employees from the former landline division in order to express discontent with the merger:

> [...] actually, we had employees who for some time wore in defiance Phone-Y-branded clothes and were walking around like this in the company. Or merchandising products, old branded stuff, was hung up on the wall; I still have a pen, too [*she reaches across her desk, shows me the pen*].

According to Gloria, this was done in opposition to the merger and the dictate to become one company, conceived at the expense of losing one's organisational belonging. Obviously, such activities were forms of resistance; this becomes even more evident in relation to the efforts undertaken by company management in order to remove all material related to the formerly separated companies:

> Yes, well, people went through the company examining old stuff, but in the end, one cannot take away employees' things [...] well, it was called upon and asked that all things which still feature the old brand [...] to deliver them somewhere so that they can be destroyed, but many were sentimental and kept things and this was eventually ok because one cannot force people to burn their books – in that kind of way.

As we learn, at the time of the merger, employees were asked to eliminate old advertising and merchandising products such as calendars, pens, T-shirts, notebooks and the like. Moreover, workplaces were examined in order to check whether employees resisted this appeal. I asked Gloria who these people were; she did not remember but guessed they belonged to Internal Communications. The explicit statement that people should not be forced to burn their books is, of course, a heavily loaded notion referring to Nazi Germany when books were burned and destroyed. In light of this description, the merger appears as indeed powerfully enforced and imposed on employees, very much directed 'from above'. It also exposes the managerial directive to prevent the continuation of the formerly separated companies embodied in the old materials. Obviously, keeping and celebrating nostalgically the 'old' material in this context – as was done in relation to hanging up posters and wearing T-shirts – is a way of showing and performing resistance towards these managerial concerns.

As can be seen, orienting to the previously distinct businesses and their corporate identities appears to be a widespread activity in the merging company and happened on several layers; company management did so with reference to collecting old advertising material, while employees did the opposite by deliberately wearing and exhibiting such materials. In fact, during my research, especially employees from the former mobile company still underlined their former belonging to Mobile-X by emphasising the comparison between a bureaucratic and an innovative start-up company culture so as to differentiate between the landline and the mobile business. In German-speaking countries, complaining about bureaucratic work procedures is a well-known discourse, especially when it comes to governmental institutions. Likewise, the understanding that so-called start-ups are particularly innovative, assembling motivated, hands-on people, complements this understanding and is also a very common description in the ordinary management discourse; thereby, Phone-Y is labelled as the 'other', lacking such positive characteristics.

In fact, these narratives correspond to Alvesson and Willmott's description of how organisational discourses have to connect to the ways in which employees define themselves as part of the company. As they underline, the mere existence of such discourses is not decisive, they have to appeal to employees' self-constructions in order to exert control (2002: 628).

Against this backdrop, my informants from the mobile division described colleagues as either belonging to 'them' or 'us'; as will become apparent in the next section, other features such as the companies' distinct market positions, their different ownership statuses and the conflict around how employees address one another were used to re-enact such differences. Within this framing, another state of mind was insinuated to belong to 'other' staff members, thereby sustaining one's own former identity construction and company belonging (cf. Alvesson and Willmott, 2002: 631–2).[4] However, at the time of my fieldwork, I also experienced other ways of dealing with the post-merger company. Employees' identity work did not always emphasise the separation of the company, but appeared to deliberately overlook former differences, even downplaying them as a natural fact. In doing so, employees normatively described the unity of the company and attempted to bring the ongoing discussion about difference to an end. Altogether, I understand these different strategies as echoing the managerial desire for coherency – as a form of resistance, or as adopting the wish of a unified, coherent company.

3.4   Making sense of the post-merger company: The discursive construction of (in-)distinctiveness

The narratives which I discuss in the following provide insight into how employees made sense of the merger, namely by involving themselves in different forms of identity work. Doing so, it becomes evident that employees are not only objects of managerial identity regulation; they actively take part in framing their own belonging and their own, as well as the other company's identity. Thus, circling around the two former companies and their brands, the narratives shed light on the previous identities and the ways in which employees have taken up ideas which they associate with the black or the green world. When it comes to company management's identity regulation, this turns out to be an obstacle as the previous identities seem to hinder the acceptance of the new company brand and identity. Within this framework, employees relating to the former company identities are considered as problematic as they reinforce a company divide.

3.4.1   Upholding difference: "These were totally different worlds clashing"

As outlined in the methodology chapter, the two previously distinct businesses share a common history; that is, only in 1996 were they separated:

---

4   This type of 'othering' is a common way of constructing social identities, in particular with reference to power relations. Among others, Zygmunt Bauman has written on the production of dichotomies in modern society (1993; see also Rohleder, 2014).

Mobile-X was outsourced keeping its own brand while Phone-Y – in association with the postal service company – was kept in (partial) ownership by the government. As former employees of the mobile division explained, this put each of the companies in a very different position on the telecommunication market; while Mobile-X competed with various other mobile service providers, Phone-Y had a relatively stable position advocating its "monopoly". As Gloria, who formerly worked in Mobile-X said, this situation made the landline business "untouchable". She further explained:

> [...] these were totally different cultures because Mobile-X had the competition; it was very stressful on the market, very dynamic, we always had to react within five minutes, we had very short response times, within a day everything was turned around 360 degrees, all proceeded rather informally, everyone was arranging things backhandedly [...].

The statement invokes the image of a lively business one associates with many so-called 'start-ups' from the 1990s. Referring to Mobile-X's market position, she explains how the competitive environment stimulated a particular working atmosphere, denoted as 'culture', in Mobile-X. As she emphasises, a constantly changing market required handling things very fast, without following pre-set structures or formal arrangements. Following this understanding, the specific market environment apparently had an impact on how work was effectively done in the company. This, obviously, stands in contrast to Phone-Y, which was, according to Gloria,

> [...] not flexible, they did not have any competition, they were market leader, effectively they had a monopoly position, that is, they did not have any stress, they did not face any threat from outside. Certainly, fixed network sales dropped and they lost turnover, but they did not have anyone attempting to take them over, or to frighten them in any other way.

In this quote Gloria frames Phone-Y as the opposite of the dynamic and changing work setting in Mobile-X. While everyday work in Mobile-X is described as dynamic and fast, within Phone-Y it appears as laid-back and less stressful, according to Gloria, because of the company being owned by the government. It seems that the different ownership status spared employees in the former landline division from having any pressure and worry in relation to their work. Furthermore, the notion of 'threat' and the mention of a possible takeover emphasises again the market situation of Mobile-X and underlines its distinct work culture. Both quotes serve as a way of creating a specific view on Mobile-X: By contrasting the former mobile part with the landline division, she configures a specific identity of Mobile-X that highlights seemingly positive attributes about the company and its employees such as being flexible, very hands-on and oriented towards their work.

As can be seen, the reference to both companies' market positions enables Gloria to differentiate the two, unravelling from there the two companies' distinct cultures. Furthermore, the statement also highlights the symbolic importance of the corporate identity. In doing so, Gloria develops the image of Mobile-X as an adaptable company in constant movement. Not explicitly mentioned, but underpinning her quotes is the image of Phone-Y as, in contrast, a strictly organised company, based on formalities and bureaucratic procedures. In fact, this perceived difference between Mobile-X and Phone-Y gave rise to various other associations among employees, all understood to confirm such an opinion; for instance, as I was told, in the former mobile part of the company, an "open door policy" was upheld, signalising seemingly positive features such as transparency and team work, whereas in the landline part, office doors were rather closed.

However, due to the distinct ownership statuses – Phone-Y was owned by the government and Mobile-X was an entirely private business – the landline business employed civil servants who enjoyed a particular pension scheme. These "Beamten", as they are called in German, are non-terminable. In the public discourse, Beamten are related to bureaucratic and very formal work procedures. An important feature is the implementation of hierarchical structures upon which everyday work is based. This is performed through the utilisation of file memoranda, called "Aktennotiz" in German. These memoranda are protocols detailing individual activities in relation to specific work procedures. Usually, they are approved and authorised by the direct manager and then move around the organisation, involving relevant people according to the hierarchical order. Hence, work procedures may take time since following the hierarchical pathway usually involves different people and possibly departments across the company.

Obviously, yet another, less critical account of the use of file memoranda is possible, too. While former members of Mobile-X understood the use of documents as representing a bureaucratic and hierarchical order, one may also emphasise it as a means of making internal work procedures and decisions (partly) transparent. That is, file memoranda document and also justify in a sense how certain decisions are made and, for instance, how company money is spent. Filed in a ring binder or these days rather stored on an internal server, they constitute a lasting memory detailing important work procedures and events within the company. Nevertheless, as part of the discussion about the two companies' differences, employees formerly part of Mobile-X used the reference to the above-described "Aktennotiz" to position the former landline business as a bureaucratic organisation that operates through the implementation of hierarchies.

Of course, the use of file memoranda stands in contrast to how work was reportedly done in Mobile-X. First of all, since it was a stock company, it had only regular employees and did not employ any civil servants; as my informants emphasised, Mobile-X employed largely young people and featured flat hierarchies across the company. Thus, it was considered a 'young business' which was growing very fast at the beginning. Again, Gloria, the promotion manager in Residential and Small Business Sales I quoted earlier, described Phone-Y simply as "bureaucracy, highly structured" and explained the different work procedures:

> [...] when we were integrated, it was an extreme change because here [at Phone-Y] everything works through documents and you won't get anything, everything that's leaving the official path, it was impossible, nobody reacts or gets in touch, totally different work attitudes, well, at ours it was somehow 'not possible is impossible', over there it was 'it's not possible, it has always been like this and we do it like this', these were totally different worlds clashing [...].

According to her statement, the documentation of work procedures was the fundamental way in which Phone-Y was organised. Furthermore, her framing ("when we were integrated") suggests that from her perspective, the mobile part was integrated into the former landline division, conveying the impression that the mobile part was indeed merged in the landline business. In fact, this is an understanding I encountered also in other employees' accounts; mostly, they referred to the telecom part as being the older and larger business, therefore the 'smaller' and 'younger' mobile division was being integrated.

However, it seems that subsequent to the merger, Gloria and her colleagues from the former mobile company wrote emails (the preferred way of communicating in Mobile-X, I learned) and wondered why they did not get a reply, let alone any feedback from employees previously stemming from the landline division. This called into question how collaboration was done and, apparently, also challenged so far established work routines. This difference makes her conclude that employees in the other part must have had "different work attitudes", hence a different mindset about how working together has to be organised. Obviously, such an attitude stands in contrast to 'her' company where things were handled without considering official pathways, by simply making things possible.

The understanding that employees have different work attitudes also becomes apparent in a statement by Walter, the group leader in the OSS department. While he considered employees formerly part of Mobile-X as flexible and open to changing job positions, he assumed people working in Phone-Y would share the expectation of working in one company until their pension. And he finished by saying: "I think this is a big difference – whether you rather like one option or the other, and hence people do things differently." Again, the different attitudes and assumed motives are considered to manifest themselves in the everyday work and to be recognisable as part of this work.

In fact, the described narratives resemble those Alvesson and Willmott have pointed out in relation to research on how identity work and regulation are enacted. For instance, within their overview, they point out that "[p]roviding a specific vocabulary of motives" (2002: 629) is often invoked in order to determine how employees should relate to their work. Furthermore, defining and categorising one group in contrast to the other – in the form of 'us' vs. 'them' – is obviously another common way of enacting difference which was indeed invoked numerous times by my informants (cf. Alvesson and Willmott, 2002: 630). Altogether, these narratives correspond to the understandings of work I have outlined in relation to the post-industrial economy; employees from the former mobile part appear to show features of a flexible, hands-on work attitude which is labelled more adequate, even superior to the one employees from the former landline seem to exhibit.

In fact, such a framing plays also a part in the next narrative to which I dedicate a separate subsection as it is one of the central topics I encountered in Telecompany-X. As described in the methodology chapter, it also involved me as a researcher when I was confused how to address people in the company. The topic also returns in Chapter 6 in the context of the corporate directory and organigram on the intranet. As will become apparent, while in this chapter the implementation of hierarchies and a formal way of approaching one another is ascribed to the previous landline business only, Chapter 6 unravels how the intranet in the form of the corporate directory and organigram configures everyday work interaction, thereby suggesting a rather widespread application of formal and hierarchical logics in the company.

Approaching one another: 'Du' vs. 'Sie'

The German language offers two ways of addressing other people; the colloquial 'Du' and the formal 'Sie'. While the first is used when addressing family, friends and people one is close to, the latter is the standard way of approaching adults one is not familiar with. Of course, how this topic is handled differs locally, but some broad directives exist. For instance, the older person is supposed to offer the informal 'Du' to the younger counterpart, otherwise people rather use 'Sie'. Whether or not one may reject such an offer and whether this rejection has to be justified is already a contested issue. The situation becomes even more complicated in case other features such as hierarchy enter the setting. Clearly, as those speaking German probably know, a person's hierarchical position matters when it comes to addressing one another, and especially within organisational settings people from the higher management are usually addressed formally ('Sie').

Against this background, it is perhaps not surprising that the central narrative illuminating the differences between the two former companies centred on the distinct ways of employees approaching each other in the company. As I was told, at the beginning, these different routines created confusion among employees of both companies. When I asked Viktoria, formerly part of Mobile-X and now working in the sales department, what it actually means that two companies are different, she told me the following story:

> Well, an example, probably the clearest way to explain it, within Mobile-X we were all on a first name basis, everyone, this was a company philosophy, it doesn't matter **who** [emphasis in original] stands in front of you, even B. [surname of the former company CEO], even if it was him, it just didn't matter. [...] this has not really been properly solved, there was the merger and within Phone-Y it was not, well, they had 'Sie' or 'Du', and then, hm, you often rub somebody the wrong way [...]. Well, that's something, [...] there has to be a conversation somewhere, it's got to be decided from the top down, how it's going to be now, because it's a cultural thing.

According to her statement, *everyone* within Mobile-X approached each other in the same way, namely by referring to each other's first name and by using the German colloquial 'Du'. The emphasis that this arrangement even included the CEO makes everyone within the company seemingly equal. But the notion of "company philosophy" suggests that this arrangement was rather imposed on everyone in the company, hence it makes evident that within Mobile-Y superior personnel prescribed how to address one another, too. Apparently, the seemingly equal way of addressing each other had in particular an internal function supporting the company's identity formation among colleagues. Obviously, Viktoria overlooks such a perspective; she rather emphasises the contrast to Phone-Y where the formal German 'Sie' and the last name was apparently the standard way of addressing each other and where employees used the first name only for colleagues they knew personally.

Viktoria's statement suggests that she has indeed taken over the company philosophy of the former mobile division. This is somewhat remarkable since in the quote she calls upon management to give a clear directive or to initiate a conversation – even though she has just devaluated organisational hierarchies and emphasised positively the seemingly equal treatment of management and employees in the previous mobile division. In fact, as I learned, the issue of addressing one another was discussed in team meetings and online on the provisional intranet, but without a final, definite instruction from the management. As my informants told me, it was left rather indistinct for a while so that in the end employees were asked to use the formal 'Sie' as a standard and only address people informally ('Du') if they knew each other well.

But, as will become obvious next, not even spoken language was necessary for employees to recognise someone from the 'other' company; as again Gloria from the former mobile company explained, how people were dressed already made it possible to differentiate employees:

> [...] one could see this immediately, I mean you can recognise this by simply looking at the style of clothing [...] by now it is not that bad anymore, but at the beginning you immediately knew which world they belong to, also as concerns the age average, we are much younger, over there is the average between 40 and 45 and at ours it is about 30, 35.

Her quote describes very well the implicit know-how that employees referred to when determining who belongs to which former part of the company. Apparently, no official or formal distinctive feature was necessary in order to categorise colleagues. The style of clothing was enough of a sign exposing the difference. Since the interview occurred about 10 months after the official merger, she describes the present situation as "not that bad anymore", a very normative phrase suggesting that these differences are not desired and have in the meantime somehow decreased. It must clearly be seen as resonating with the managerial prescription of company unity mentioned before. I also refer to this quote since this is one of the rare times where the age difference between the former two companies was spelled out; the two companies have been described in terms of 'young versus old' but, astonishingly, the actual difference appears as rather small.

In contrast to emphasising difference, another form of identity work underlined the (desired) coherence of the 'new' company. But let me explain this way of making sense of the merger in greater detail in the following section.

3.4.2   Overlooking and downplaying difference, nurturing coherence: "That doesn't exist anymore, the division"

So far, I have shown that especially employees formerly part of the mobile company tended to discuss and underline their distinctiveness and, while doing so, often also devaluated the 'other', the landline business. In contrast, the technicians I visited did not engage very much with the merger and the differences of the former mobile part, they rather overlooked them and thereby tended to nurture the company's coherence. As already described in the methodology chapter, when I asked Frederik which division he initially came from, he said that everyone from his team apart from the team leader stemmed from the Phone-Y business. Furthermore, in his department, the mixing of employees apparently happened largely on the middle and higher management level:

> KS: And you are mainly from, I'd say, the old Phone-Y? Or how, I mean before it was –
> Frederik: Well, this team, yes. Walter [name of team leader] has swapped, well swapped, you almost can't say this, but before he was Mobile-X.
> KS: Alright. This happened only just now?
> Frederik: This is a while ago – last year in autumn. [Addressing his colleague] The merger, the real one? Early mid-year last year it must have been.
> KS: Did any other changes happen back then, I mean, the teams are now mixed?
> Frederik: I think, a great mix did not happen, well, I'd say, this is always stupid to say 'mobile part', 'Phone-Y-stock', well, here, at this site, this was a pure Phone-Y location and in this way, it is very Phone-Y-heavy, well, I have the feeling what happened, on the management-level it has been mixed a lot,

yes. Using the example of Walter [his team leader], he was Mobile-X before. Well, a lot more happened there, concerning the mix.
KS: Ok. But not on –
Frederik: On working level less so, one has to say.

According to Frederik's description, his team remained largely unchanged. But in contrast to his statement that suggests his team has been part of the landline division, his team leader, Walter, told me that everyone from his team was brought over from one of the company's suppliers shortly before the merger. However, he apparently associates himself with the former landline business; as I learned, employees in his team still used the previous time management tool formerly part of Phone-Y. In comparison to the accounts discussed in the section before, it seems that for him, it is not necessary to point to the two companies and their different identities. In fact, not even the word 'swapped' ('gewechselt' in German) for describing the team leader's previous belonging to Mobile-X seems to be appropriate for denoting the company change. He also does not enter the debate about differences and distinct ways of working and instead, deliberately overlooks them by correcting himself saying that to refer to the former distinct businesses is somehow not good ("stupid to say"). Moreover, he asks his colleague when the "real" merger happened; it appears that for him, the integration process proceeded in different steps or involved different events so that the exact date is not memorable anymore. Overall, the short conversation suggests that the technicians' department, and Frederik's team in particular, has not been affected very much by the merger and processes of reorganisation, hence his rather calm attitude and little reference towards the merger.

In a similar manner, Manuel, working as an accountant in Business Sales, also did not enter the discussion about the two companies and their differences but instead emphasised the working together of both groups of employees, assuring me that now the company is "fully mixed, yes, fully mixed, that doesn't exist anymore, the division. Yes, very deliberately, it has been jumbled up." Thus, Manuel underlines the managerial approach of intentionally mixing employees from the two former companies. It seems to me that both Frederik correcting his own comment as well as Manuel describing the company as now being mixed, is informed by an unspoken rule, a normative guideline that highlights the new, coherent company and deliberately overlooks and forbids the stressing of the division (possibly) still running through it. In fact, while employees from the mobile division complained about the notion of black and green world still existing in the company, both my informants here seem to either ignore or have taken up the managerial dictate of coherence, that is, they do not engage with the differentiation, but present to me a unified company, as desired by the management.

Another narrative I encountered described the companies' differences as a natural fact and emphasised that two companies *must be* different. I call this a form of "downplaying by naturalising" as it refuses to consider the former two companies' distinctiveness as a problem, an idea that underpins the managerial directive to become one. It differs from the informants quoted above but nevertheless also nurtures the coherence of the company by downplaying the problematic view on company difference. I also consider this narrative as an attempt to disengage from participating in the ongoing identity work and to bring the discussion of differences and associated conflicts to an end.

The informant I refer to is Viktoria, who I already mentioned and who was formerly part of Mobile-X, working in the area of Customer Communication. Before, I reported on how she identified herself with the mobile division's corporate identity of being a non-hierarchical company expressed in the widespread use of 'Du'. However, in this case she insisted on the different ways of information provision in the previously distinct companies and underlined that

> [w]henever a business has gone through a merger, for some time, this is a fact, that's neither positive nor negative, that's a fact, a route has to be found, because both companies must have handled things differently, and presumably this information provision constitutes the middle ground in relation to how it has been before [...]. Anyway, it must have been like this, because, I believe, there aren't two companies that have the same information flow, this is simply the case, this is why I see it very neutrally.

According to her statement, the truth about mergers is the merging companies' *being different*. And because of their distinct work procedures, the post-merger company has to develop a new way of handling work processes. In fact, the new appears to consist of the two old ways somehow 'meeting' in the middle. The repetitive declaration "that's a fact" implies the existence of a universal, that is, an unquestionable truth about merging companies. Moreover, she appears to downplay the potential conflict of the merger by saying that this must be considered as neither negative nor positive. In fact, insisting on this opinion, she emphasised:

> […] the Phone-Y business exists already longer than Mobile-X, well, and be-
> cause of this there is already a cultural difference, logically, this is, well, I
> don't know, if you put together Apple and Philips, perhaps, since Apple must
> be considered as the youngster.

Again, the quote lays bare an apparent knowledge about mergers where history, that is the temporal existence of an organisation, is a variable generating
culturally different organisations. Her reference to two well-known companies is again an attempt to downplay the possible disputed circumstances of
the merger (in the sense of 'no emotion, simply coping'). Moreover, the term
"logically" makes it appear as a somewhat natural consequence, hence her
framing of the two companies as culturally different is taken as a natural, unquestioned and accepted reality. And she goes on saying that the merger has
not been too much of a problem:

> Well, I think this is normal, […] I think there are companies where it has been
> much more dramatic, certainly, where in parts you've heard that real battles
> for dominance ["Rangkämpfe" in German] took place, I didn't witness that,
> perhaps on higher levels, I don't know, but not on the level where we are.
> Well, there was rather the interest for the other team on the other side.

Again, she describes the merger as less stressful and highlights that no fight-
ing about positions took place, in comparison to other companies. Instead,
she delegates such confrontation to higher management levels (similar to
Frederik above) and underlines her team's openness towards the respective
other team in Phone-Y. Underlying her account is a somewhat positive description of the merger, less conflictual and especially open minded for her
part. Apparently, as she also explained, before the merger, teams and departments had been in contact in the form of visits in which employees from
the respective other company examined their counterpart's work procedures.
Hence, the two companies were not completely unfamiliar and, as her statements suggest, the merger was less conflictual than in the previous accounts
described above. Even though subsequent to the merger her department, Customer Communication, was comprised of employees from both companies:

> Yes, indeed, the aim is that everyone does it from everywhere, yes, and it
> works quite well over here, […] even though originally, I stem from the mo-
> bile part, I do also landline topics, the only difference, I have to ask more
> when it comes to landline topics, the logic in the background, the technical
> procedure is different, it makes a difference if an order is entered into the

> system via landline or via mobile phone [...]. But these are things, everyone had to learn it in the original business, these are in some cases long-term processes, [...] well, we have the advantage that we got the information here, the contact person we may ask [...].

According to Viktoria, following the merger, her team deals with both landline and mobile services. Thus, Viktoria had to become familiar with new work procedures in relation to landline products that are obviously processed differently. But instead of complaining, her account distinguishes itself because of the positive emphasis on the post-merger situation. In fact, pointing out the benefit of the situation, that is, the necessary knowledge being already present in the company, she highlights a positive aspect of the merger and underlines that such processes naturally take time. Thus, while previous accounts emphasised the conflicts around the merger, she seems to downplay possible conflicts and the differences of the former two companies and naturalises them as inevitably given.

3.5   Integrating post-merger identity work

The idea that two companies are different, in fact *must* be different, and that this is a problem that has to be tackled, is a prevalent understanding I encountered not only in the management and organisation studies literature, but also among staff members and management in Telecompany-X. As I have shown, concepts such as corporate culture and organisational identity are leading ideas explaining difficulties in post-merger companies; most often, they frame these conflicts as the clashing of two homogenously distinct groups of people that are fundamentally divided by different work routines, specific understandings or management styles. It is not surprising that management and employees in Telecompany-X have also picked up these ideas in the context of the company's recent merger. Nevertheless, as scholars in organisation studies have suggested, such concepts and framings may also prevent making sense of merger processes beyond these understandings.

Against this backdrop, the concept of identity work and regulation enabled me to examine more closely processes of identity formation and attribution among employees and to analyse the interplay of identity work and regulation. In fact, the orientation towards both former company brands – as done in relation to the notion of black and green world – underlined not only their importance for both former companies, but also shed light on the historically grown corporate identities as well as previous identity work and regulation in the former two companies. As it has become apparent, employees seem to retain their old identities in the process of losing it; that is, the managerial prescription to disengage from the previous identity and associate around the new company brand motivated some to even further hold on to the old identity.

Together with the Internal Communication's branding campaign I outline in the next chapter, it appears that, in the context of the merger, company management is trying to tackle a problem of its (partly) own making. That is, the emphasis on generating a strong organisational culture and identity through methods of corporate culture management seems to stand now in the way of bringing together the two former companies. Of course, processes of identity formation take place without managerial identity work and regulation, but the previous development of a strong corporate identity seems to make employees insist on retaining their former identity. Still one year after the merger, especially employees from the former mobile part followed the idea of the clashing of cultures by highlighting their distinctiveness as an adaptive, innovative company, thereby devaluating the 'other' part, the previously governmentally owned Phone-Y business. In fact, the comparison between the two former companies in this way is remarkable because the narratives employees of the former mobile division refer to correspond to the understandings of work I have outlined in the introduction. They have taken up and hence self-evidently defend the normative prescription of a committed and flexible employee that dedicates herself to the company.

However, reproducing the difference of the two companies in this manner can indeed be seen as a way of exposing discontent with the merger – especially, since the mobile part was understood as being integrated into the landline division, despite being the younger and, at the time of the merger, more profitable organisation. But, reportedly, also the landline division presented traces of former identity work and regulation. Both levels of engagement, the nostalgic praise of old material but also of *narrating difference*, that is the talking about these incidents and reported differences, must be understood as displaying discontentment with the merger and the managerial prescription to become one 'coherent' company. But I want to highlight that, apparently, the wearing and praise of old material took place at the time of the merger while the discussion of differences occurred about a year after the merger when I visited the company. Thus, varieties exist as to *when* these forms of discontent happened as well as *how long* they persisted.

This brings me to the other narrative I reported on, dealing with the merger and the managerial prescription of wholeness by overlooking or downplaying the distinctiveness of the two former companies. As stated, some of my informants explicitly corrected the mentioning of the former two businesses or underlined the mixing of employees in the post-merger company. This strategy also included the downplaying of difference by describing the existence of differences as a natural fact and self-evident truth. Altogether, despite variations, I consider both approaches as following the managerial desire for coherence – by adopting or de-emphasising the need to become one. In fact, both approaches are underlining the unity of the company and can be understood as an attempt to put the discussion about differences to an end. Even though these insights do not tell whether or not a possible division still impacts work collaboration in the company, they nevertheless point out some of the discussions that happened at the time of my research. In particular, the latter case suggests that among some of the employees I visited, the managerial campaign had had the desired effect since employees appear to have taken up the normative idea of company unity – at least when presenting the organisation to the outside.

However, I want to stress that the mentioning of the two former worlds at the time of my research (one year after the merger) must *not only* be understood as performing resistance. In fact, as I learned, from my informants' point of view, the reference to the two former companies was in some cases a very pragmatic way of making sense of the merger as part of everyday work: the notion of green and black world also served employees to deal with, that is, to categorise and understand, (un-)familiar work routines and procedures now part of the post-merger company or to handle the different software systems running parallel. As I reported above, old software tools as well as distinct ways of answering and sending out emails apparently still existed and most employees worked now on both, landline and mobile services, thus collaborating across former divisions. In this manner, the differentiation between green and black world can be seen as a shared reference that allows employees to make sense of work processes in the new, now 'mixed' company; that is, to attribute and understand reported incidents and hence make sure work can proceed.

Against this backdrop, the managerial attempt to erase the previous identities is surprising as it neglects the constitutive aspect of the previous identities. As said earlier, research on identity change has shown that corporate identities may have to pass through a state of ambiguity in order to change (Corley and Gioia, 2004: 201). As the authors underline, identity ambiguity differs from identity conflict; whereas conflict describes the competing existence of two or more identity concepts, as in the case of Telecompany-X, ambiguity refers to the state in which the interpretation and meaning of a specific identity is unclear (cf. Corley and Gioia, 2004: 199). Likewise, the notion of "transitional identity" (Clark et al., 2010) describes a provisional identity that emerges from discussion and debates about the desired company. Even though the cited study is based on data from top management employees, the notion of transitional identity highlights the contribution of a third, temporal identity that is loose enough – in the sense of a boundary object – to associate employees around envisioning the prospective company (Clark et al., 2010: 429; see also Bechky, 2003: 326; Star and Griesemer, 1989).

Such observations obviously differ from what I experienced in Telecompany-X. As said above, the managerial attempt to erase previous identities encouraged some employees to hold on even more strongly to them; in this manner, a transitional identity may have contributed to circumventing such a confrontation. Even though authors in organisation and management studies state that it is difficult to determine how organisational identities change, they agree on the fact that such processes *have to be managed* so that employees engage with a new one. In fact, one of the important steps in processes of identity change is described as "identity destabilization" (Clark et al., 2010: 413) which happens foremost in relation to contextualising the merger in a specific sense, for instance by designating it as both a threat to the existing status of both former companies and also as a positive way to cope with market pressures. Such a reframing opens the path to thinking about a shared future in the form of the envisioned company and encourages the leaving behind of previous identities. In addition, as authors underline, a provisional identity may also serve as a stabilising factor in the otherwise rather uncertain conditions of merger integrations (Clark et al., 2010: 428).

However, as can be seen in the case of Telecompany-X, identity regulation and identity work influence one another; that is, the interplay between the two might lead to contrary or unexpected results. As Ann Langley and colleagues found out, managerial regulation may be challenged not only with reference to employees' identity work, but also in relation to a more general necessity to uphold departmental and local distinctiveness so as to preserve existing knowledge and work cultures and hence accommodate employees to position themselves in the new company (Langley et al., 2012: 163). In fact, such a perspective makes evident that post-merger companies are permeated by differences and cultural boundaries that move beyond the former two (or more) companies and that are worth striving for. This, in fact, becomes also apparent in relation to the technicians group and employees with a background in Customer Service; as I am going to show in the upcoming chapters, they indeed show differences in how they handle the intranet and specific applications which is very much tied to their local work culture.

In addition, the technicians in the OSS department were obviously differently affected by the merger than employees in the headquarters, in particular the Customer Communication/Service departments; as we learned, only their team leader changed while they kept on working as the same group. It is therefore reasonable to assume that the merger did not play too much of a role in their everyday work. It appears that also their location – away from the headquarters, a little outside the city – contributed to them being relatively less engaged in the ongoing identity work that underlined the two former companies' differences. In fact, as becomes apparent in the following chapters, I observed a specific sense of togetherness among the technicians which related to how they interacted with one another. For now, I want to stress that their spatial distance to the headquarters, but also in the sense of not being very much involved in post-merger difficulties in their own team, made them appear more open to take up and internalise the managerial message of company coherency and of being altogether more at ease when it comes to describing themselves as part of the post-merger company.

In fact, these findings resonate well with results from Ann Langley and colleagues' study on how employees negotiate their group identity in the context of merger integration processes. As they underline, spatial circumstances and everyday work practices are important and contribute to how identity regulation and identity work take place (cf. Langley et al., 2012: 161–2). As they found out, it makes a difference whether or not employees are in contact with one another on a daily basis so that everyday work provides opportunities for identity work and related conflicts in the form of, for instance, maintaining different work routines. In fact, this was the case described by one of my informants who reported on the distinct ways of answering emails. As said, while the main departments were mostly integrated, the technical departments were largely kept the same. Thus, being affected by the merger in the form of working with employees from the 'other' company was not equally

distributed in the company. As a result, different departments or work settings may need distinct interventions when it comes to managing the merger.

In this chapter, I have illuminated how employees oriented towards their
respective former company and how they made sense of processes in the post-
merger company. In doing so, I have provided insight into conflicts and related discussions that took place during and after the merger. Despite the
conflictual potential of ongoing identity work, I have argued that both black
and green world can also be seen as *shared points of reference* that may serve as
a starting point for discussing working conditions and how work should be
done in the new company. Potentially, this shared reference point may also assist in figuring out the advantages and disadvantages of certain work routines
and forms of collaboration. In doing so, I want to call into question the common lamentation about the still existing division in post-merger companies
that is based on the widespread understanding that a post-merger company is
only successful when both former identities are entirely removed or previous
cultures fully coalesce. In fact, creating an overall homogenous company is a
risky endeavour as this possibly means losing local cultures and their knowledge that are actually constitutive for specific departments or groups in the
company.

However, as I am going to show in the next chapter, management in
Telecompany-X foremost counted on measures of culture management, in
particular corporate and internal branding, in order to bring together the former two businesses and ensure the company's performance after the merger.

4 A "medium of Internal Communications" and an "employee-portal": The divided Intranet

The previous chapter has described and analysed the dynamics and reported conflicts in the company during and after the merger. As has become evident, employees followed distinct strategies while making sense of the merger; most dominant was the understanding that the two companies *are* different and that difference is somewhat problematic. Other strategies tended to overlook and downplay the two companies' differences and explicitly called for the companies' unity. As I have shown, despite their differences, these approaches echo the managerial prescription of company coherence; while the first strategy can be seen as a form of employee resistance, the other approaches tend to ignore or to distance themselves from the appeal. Altogether, the different strategies correspond to existing research and literature on merger processes and can be subsumed under the notion of organisational identity work; it describes how employees negotiate their sense of belonging and identification with the company they work in. In particular, the intensity of identity work during and also after the merger has shed light on previous identity work and managerial regulation in the two former companies, apparently now preventing employees from gathering around the new brand.

Departing from the dominant understanding of mergers that considers company difference as a problem only, I have tried to illuminate the integrative abilities of the reported narratives and conflicts. That is, after the merger, from my informants' point of view, the reference to the two former companies was often very reasonable and also contributed to making sense of the new organisation. In fact, the company turned out to be permeated by various traces of the two previous businesses in the form of distinct know-how and forms of collaboration, different software applications and related work processes. Thus, the ongoing references can also be seen as enabling employees to understand and recognise these processes. Such an approach takes into account that research on mergers and acquisitions suggests nurturing ambiguity and developing a transitional identity in merging businesses.

However, this idea stands in contrast to how company management in Telecompany-X has put efforts into developing a new, shared corporate identity. In fact, as becomes apparent in this chapter, the central understanding – the two companies are different and that this is a major problem after the merger – was the background against which the new intranet as part of a company-wide Internal Communications campaign was implemented. Explaining and analysing the campaign, the chapter unravels the managerial expectations towards the intranet in contrast to employees' handling of the intranet, in particular the starting page. In doing so, it illuminates the different logics that underpin the current setup of the intranet. In fact, as will be shown, this setup contributes to employees' overall ambivalent relationship to the intranet. From the perspective of strategic management, this may appear as a failure since it does not realise the managerial desire of company coherence. However, from the perspective of my informants, this setup nevertheless works well as it allows leaving content they consider as irrelevant aside and instead focus on those applications they need as part of their work. As I argue, in this manner, the intranet engages the 'many' users which I describe as one of the central qualities of the intranet and its starting page.

4.1   The intranet's starting page and newsfeed

To begin with, allow me to present again the intranet starting page. Based on my experiences and research, I expected the intranet in Telecompany-X to be recognisable as a platform distributing and sharing internal content and information. As stated in the introduction, intranets usually create and sustain the 'inside' of a company by making available internal news, documents and applications aiming to organise the internal communication of a company. Therefore, I was somewhat astonished when I first saw "Inside-X", as the intranet is officially called. The intranet is by default the starting page of the web browser, that is, when logging in to the company network, employees automatically access and open the intranet. To recall, this is a screenshot of one of my informant's intranet starting page:

Figure 3: Intranet starting page: "Which record does this woman hold in Telecompany-X?"

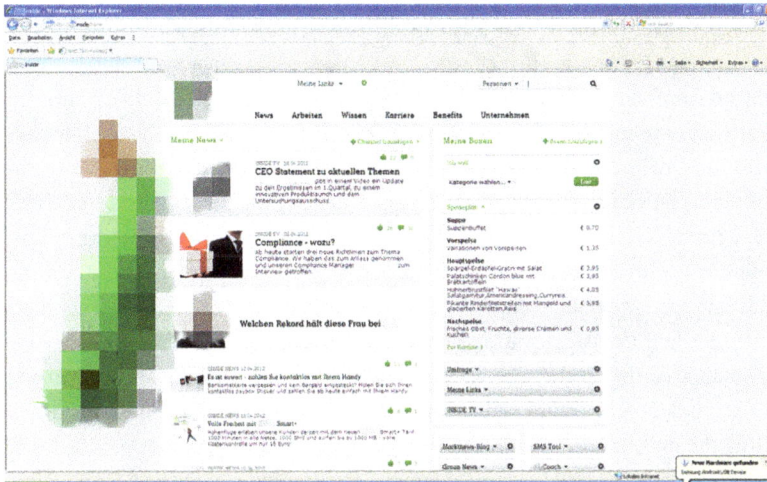

As already described in the introduction, the pull-down menu at the top covers sections labelled as "Work", "Career", "Knowledge", "Benefits" and "Company", thus assembling various information on the company's procedures and guidelines and employment law. For instance, the headline "Knowledge" includes the subsection "Health and Safety" where information on the company's medical service is stored. Likewise, the headline "Career" contains the internal job market as well as information on the company's performance management. The section "Benefits" lists all companies where staff members of Telecompany-X receive special concessions. General information on the company, that is, an organigram, business reports, information on the management, etc. is stored under the headline "Company" ("Unternehmen"). The top right of the page features a search field where people may search the intranet database; results can be further modified through pre-set categories (i.e. "people", "content", "application" or "general"). However, the prominent section in the middle is called "Meine News" which is by default comprised of general news on the company and more specific news on the person's work division.

On this day, the newsfeed at the centre displays a video statement by the CEO addressing the first quarter business results and the current investigation committee.[1] Below, the caption refers to a video about new compliance guidelines. Both videos appear under the headline "Inside-TV", the company's internal video channel. The less central news entry further down reports on the company's new mobile charges and a new cellular payment option. Borrowed from social media, every news entry features a so-called "like button" as well as the possibility to leave a comment. In fact, as such, the starting page appeared to me at first rather as the company's external webpage than the intranet. Obviously, I was aware of the official company logo and its brand, so I immediately recognised the design of the intranet based on the same colours – green and white.[2] But the newsfeed at the centre of the website did not appear to me as showing topics oriented towards company members only. Rather, the themes it presents – for instance, the picture of the blond woman accompanied by the headline "Which record does this woman hold in Telecompany-X?" – conveyed the impression of a news page on the Internet. Only the daily menu, located at the right side, disturbed this impression and hence made apparent that this is indeed the company's intranet.

While further looking at the starting page and reading over the articles, the impression prevails that despite making information on company procedures available, the starting page presents the company and its activities in a very positive way, mostly highlighting the progressive or 'innovative' character of the company's activities or the new brand. This includes also the presentation of staff members in the form of the blond woman featured in the news section. Clicking on the story, it tells that she is the youngest shop manager in the company, a dedicated employee, "full of commitment". The narrative continues saying that she is enjoying her responsibilities while motivating and managing colleagues; in fact, this is "exciting and demanding", she is cited as saying.

Not just this story – which is obviously framed as a story of employee success –, but generally the ways in which the company and its activities are

---

1   As said in the methodology chapter, at the time of my fieldwork, Telecompany-X's management was confronted with allegations of corruption involving collusive behaviour of lobbyists and politicians, thus the CEO's video statement on the first quarter business results and the investigation committee.

2   For reasons of anonymity, I have removed the company logo and the employee's name which is usually displayed at the left side, respectively on top of the page.

presented on the intranet make the starting page appear as an advertisement: it advertises the company to its own employees. The news entry on new payment methods, for instance, carries the headline "It's time – pay by phone, contactless" which sounds indeed similar to an external advertisement. Also, the message about new mobile rates features the caption "Full freedom with new mobile charges", this time indeed the same slogan as in the public advertisement. This character also continues in other headlines and content on the intranet when, for instance, employees are addressed in the context of contests and prize games, covering largely topics in the telecommunication business.

Having encountered the intranet in such a way, I was asking myself: How can this form of advertising the company to employees be explained? What kind of managerial practices, especially understandings about the organisation, accompany this strategy and what are the – possibly unintended – implications of it, in particular concerning the implementation of the new intranet? In fact, my first impressions already hint at the intranet being a carrier of practices of culture management that do not only address employees' behaviour inside the company, but likewise their relationship to the outside. In particular, the intranet assembles management strategies of employee-identification described in the literature as corporate and internal branding (Kärreman and Rylander, 2008; Müller, 2017; see also Punjaisri and Wilson, 2007). As I am going to show in the following, they are part of an Internal Communication campaign that aims to install a coherent company culture and identity after the merger.

4.2   Branding the merger: Corporate and internal brand management in Telecompany-X

The company merger and the new product brand were officially celebrated and presented to employees in a company-wide induction event. In fact, this event was mentioned by all my informants, some showing enthusiasm, some rather making fun of this well-staged performance. As I was told, different versions of the new brand logo were presented, for instance one featuring a graffiti-style and which was designed on stage by a break-dancer. Another one, a rather formal black and red logo, was uncovered in relation to a piano player. As the project manager of the intranet underlined, the overall "brand introduction campaign" was conceptualised as being very extensive and covering multiple steps and the involvement of staff members. It coincided with the public advertisement campaign of the new brand.

Subsequent to this introduction, an application on the intranet was implemented allowing employees to design their own brand logo, which featured afterwards on the person's intranet starting page. As one of my informants involved in the redesign of the company shops highlighted, the different versions referred to the idea of a flexible, adjustable brand logo of the new company. The officially designed logos were afterwards used for public advertising, depending on the event or season; for example, one made of fir needles was used during Christmas, or the piano player was utilised as part of the company's art and culture sponsoring.

The new logo design was internally well considered; the above-mentioned informant further told me that the new company name was deliberately chosen referring to the name and product of the former mobile division. For this reason, the new company and brand logo had to feature one of the colours of the former landline division. The design team decided in favour of green so that the company's 'old' green was combined with a "refreshing" white in order to convey, she said, a "new and young brand". The development of the new brand was considered internally as very important and classified as secret. In fact, employees involved in the redesign were asked to sign a non-disclosure agreement confirming they would keep the information within the team, also because the logo was likewise intended for the general public and part of the upcoming advertisement campaign.

As can be seen, the narrative on the design of the new logo describes the merger as a seemingly balanced, well-considered undertaking, as if conflicts can be settled by means of designing the right company logo. It fades out disagreements and frictions occurring in the context of the merger and the possible power imbalances between the two companies and also between the management and employees. However, on basis of these considerations, it is not surprising that my informants mostly referred to the merger by using expressions such as "brand re-launch", "brand implementation" or "brand changeover". Thus, the outlined activities around the new company brand and the internal introduction campaign shed light on managerial strategies that intend to promote a strong identification among employees with the new company brand. In fact, it resonates well with the measures of corporate culture management I have described in the previous chapter and that attempt to normatively control and manipulate employees' behaviour, attitude and emotions towards the company (cf. Alvesson and Willmott, 2002; Kunda, 2006).

As a managerial concept and practice, corporate branding developed in the 1990s in association with external product marketing. Increasingly applied to employees inside business companies, it aims to create commitment to and identification with a company through its brand (e.g. Mosley, 2007; Papasolomou and Vrontis, 2006). Whereas in the beginning this management practice occurred predominantly in the service-oriented industry, it has become a common way of addressing employees in business companies (Kärreman and Rylander, 2008). By now, corporate and internal brand management are a research area within marketing that investigates how employees' individual behaviour changes in relation to increasing alignment with a company brand, thereby fostering performance and motivation (Burmann and Zeplin, 2005).

Corporate and internal branding intend to shape the symbolic meaning of the brand and the company. Therefore, authors in critical management studies underline that corporate branding can be understood as the "management of meaning" (Kärreman and Rylander, 2008: 107) that engages in communicative processes of generating value so as to positively attribute it to the brand. Furthermore, when it comes to the founding of organisational identities and related processes of identification, branding is understood to increase the affective connection among company members (cf. Kärreman and Rylander, 2008: 105). Thus, both corporate and internal branding aim at encouraging employees to take up brand values and identify with them.

However, internal branding goes even further; it does not only impose the brand on employees, but makes employees "act as 'living brands'" (Müller, 2018: 44) so that they adjust their behaviour and hence carry and promote the brand message to the outside. Scholars have termed this notion "brand-centred control" (Müller, 2017: 12), underlining the extension of the mechanisms of normative control when employees internalise brand messages (usually addressing the public). It encourages employees to reflect their behaviour not just in the context of the company, but also with reference to external audiences.

As can be seen, corporate and internal branding practices align with ideas about post-Fordist management I have outlined in the previous chapter. Departing from bureaucratic and hierarchical forms of work, such management strategies count on shaping the individual so as to secure commitment and identification with the company. In fact, as scholars underline, while methods of culture management are still grounded on a lasting engagement of the organisation with its employees, especially internal branding has emerged in relation to precarious employment conditions and the rise of the brand as a monetising asset (cf. Müller, 2018: 46; see also Kornberger, 2010). Thus, by making employees all-encompassing 'brand ambassadors', internal branding practices address the short-term and flexible character of contemporary work conditions and provide means to nevertheless control employees' activities and their commitment to the company.

While proponents of internal branding often invoke notions of employee empowerment, research has shown that internal branding increasingly undermines the work-life boundary as employees become representatives of the brand – not just as part of their work, but also their private life (Müller, 2017: 16). Furthermore, critical management scholars indicate that branding risks the creation of "branded robots" (Müller, 2018: 45) at the expense of losing employees' creativity and their innovative engagement in the company. In addition, internal and corporate brand management focus on employees' individual behaviour and the internalisation of brand messages, hence addresses employees' mind-sets and attitudes. It does not engage with the work context employees are part of and the emerging understandings and conditions of work that, it can be assumed, contribute to how employees relate to the company, too.

Against this background, the chapter first illuminates the intranet as a "medium of Internal Communications"; that is, as part of the internal and corporate branding campaign introduced in the context of the merger. In doing so, I outline the expectations towards the intranet that I learned about from the project manager and the chief editor. Among other media, the intranet was awarded a prominent role so as to advertise the company and the new brand to employees, thereby inducing identification with the new business. In the second part of the chapter, I contrast these efforts with insights gained from employees' handling of the intranet.

As will become apparent, corporate and internal branding on the intranet creates a 'divided intranet' and a tension in employees' appreciation of it. That is, the intranet assembles different logics, namely one that describes the intranet as an "employee-portal" that provides access to content and applications relevant to employees' work and one that defines it as "the management's speaking tube" that predominantly distributes messages from Internal Communication and company management. Accordingly, employees consider the intranet both a "playground of Internal Communications" as well as a "tool of purpose" that supports and enables certain work processes. In this manner, employees prioritise work-related applications in contrast to tools and content that follow the managerial idea of internal branding and organisational identification. In fact, such efforts on the intranet are considered a waste of time and altogether devalued.

However, examining the intranet-in-use also makes apparent time constraints employees experience which lead to a constant deferral of reading the news section, despite the newsfeed's archival function. Nevertheless, employees' handling of the intranet also points out a slight difference between my informants from different departments and their willingness to engage with the intranet; while employees with a background in Customer Service turn out to have a sympathy towards some of the efforts of corporate and internal branding, the technicians show a greater disregard towards these efforts.

Overall, the analysis suggests that the branding campaign on the intranet does not fulfil expected results as it divides the intranet into a work-relevant part and one that is devalued and considered a redundant distraction. In fact, this constant comparison prevents employees from engaging with the corporate and internal branding measures on the intranet. In the vocabulary of Science and Technology Studies, my investigation shows how the entanglement of intranet technology with efforts of culture management (corporate and internal branding) configures a user that does not correspond to employees and their understanding about work and the overall working conditions in Telecompany-X (e.g. Oudshoorn and Pinch, 2003; Woolgar, 1991). As I argue, such contradictory logics encourage an ambivalent relation among employees to the intranet.

4.3   The intranet as a "medium of Internal Communications"

The two previously separated companies, Phone-Y and Mobile-X, each had their own intranet, the one from the landline business being rather decentralised, the chief editor told me, meaning each department had its own application and mostly also its own interface. In contrast, the intranet of the mobile part was more inclusive and rather centralised, with one person being responsible for the content. Ahead of the merger, a provisional intranet was introduced covering the most important facts and news about the soon-to-happen fusion of the two companies. When the current intranet was finally launched, it did not receive a special implementation, but Internal Communications disseminated a short video highlighting the changes, for example new features allowing employees to personalise the intranet.

In fact, as the project manager emphasised, the possibility to personalise one's starting page was considered a main feature of the new intranet since it promised to meet distinct users' needs. For instance, it allows employees to subscribe individually to different "news channels" which cover specific information beyond one's departmental belonging. Another important feature concerned the daily canteen menu which employees were now able to adjust to their own location. The feedback and commentary section, now accompanying almost all content on the intranet, was also a novel feature. However, I want to highlight that the setting permitted users to like an article by clicking on a specific button, but a comment was automatically presented as a dislike. Hence, the setup of the intranet did not feature a separate dislike button and comments were registered and presented as negative, which some of my informants in fact criticised.

When I first asked how both the chief editor and the project manager relate to the intranet, the chief editor described her position as being responsible for the general content (text and images) on the intranet. The project manager replied that he "take[s] care of the medium intranet" and in the context of the "brand changeover" he was responsible for the intranet's further development and all the applications that relate to the "medium". Indeed, the term 'medium' was invoked several times when talking about the intranet:

> The intranet is the central, actually the most important medium of Internal Communications. I don't think that one should expect the intranet to evoke a cultural change; it can only support this through several measures. We are just about to develop a media strategy to coordinate our internal media and exactly this common-, through this cultural change, to encourage the wish of a consistent, coherent culture and here, well, we are about to define the relevant elements.

As can be seen, the project manager describes the intranet as very important to the Internal Communications department, in fact as a property of it. Furthermore, the notion of the intranet being a "medium" of Internal Communications illustrates the intranet as a vehicle for sending out messages from Internal Communications to employees. This is remarkable as it frames the intranet as a transmitter, simply disseminating messages to a somewhat passive audience and without adding anything to these messages. The second part of the statement provides insight into the strategic considerations the intranet is part of; in fact, I experienced a variety of media such as posters and advertisements in magazines and on various screens in hallways and elevators featuring ads of the company's internal branding campaign. But even though the project manager denies that the intranet has magic powers, he nevertheless describes it as an instrument able to induce change. Apparently, a shared and as he says "consistent" culture across the company is desirable and can be achieved among employees with the help of the intranet.

Indeed, the steering attitude of the project manager resembles managerial literature and statements about organisational change, highlighting the ability of technologies to change work procedures or the culture of a whole company. This is not astonishing as he, as the project manager of the intranet, was responsible for the strategic setup of the intranet. In the interview, he continued to explain the Internal Communication's strategy that in particular focussed on increasing employees' commitment to the new company:

> There are several strategies, on the one hand via identification, for orientation, working with role models, this is very substantial now, we plan to make a magazine that is partly available online, too, this is in any case very, very difficult. As I said at the beginning, the intranet is always a reflection of the corporate culture.

The quote makes apparent that the intranet was embedded in a larger campaign which included different type of media. When I continued my visits in the company as part of the second phase of my fieldwork, the above-mentioned magazine had been introduced and I was able to examine the fabrication of "role models" as a means of "identification" and "orientation" among staff members. In fact, the project manager's narrative hints at the construction of the so-called "Einfach Macher", which describes the ideal employee who is dedicated to his or her work and who stands out due to her hands-on work attitude. As will be shown, it aims to create cohesion among employees by promoting a specific idea of membership in the company. However, the concluding idea of the intranet being a reflection of the company's culture makes again apparent that the intranet is understood as an (online) reflection of the (offline) company, without adding to or interfering in work processes.

4.3.1 Beyond the intranet: Constructing the "Einfach Macher"

The notion of the ideal worker is a concept that emerged in the 19th century in light of the increasing industrialisation of work. It created a subordinated employee who is devoted to his or her work and whose "faithfulness [is] rewarded by promotions" (Davies and Frink, 2014: 26). As the authors show, only because of the strict separation between work and home and a female partner in the background, the ideal worker was able to follow his career where personal sacrifice is construed as a confirmation of one's career success. Back then, women in offices were rather occupied with menial work. Today, the separation of work and home increasingly blurs, not least because of a variety of technological devices that allow employees' constant availability; nevertheless, the devoted, masculine worker as an ideal norm has stayed in place (Kelly et al., 2010; Perlow, 2012).

Especially since the emergence of the post-industrial economy and the turn towards understanding organisations as cultures in the 1980s, increasing efforts towards managing employees in favour of efficiency and competitiveness have taken place, as illuminated earlier (Barley and Kunda, 1992). Furthermore, as already described above, a general demand to identify with one's work and company has become a standard, too. Submitting to these principles defines today's ideal worker norms and has led to managerial approaches of identity regulation, that is, of controlling and determining how employees identify with and commit to their company (e.g. Alvesson and Willmott, 2002; Cushen, 2009; Nair, 2010). Likewise, understanding work as an individual project that rests on constantly disciplining and optimising oneself describes another ideal worker norm of the post-industrial economy (Bröckling 2015).

The above-described ideologies also underpin the concept of the "Einfach Macher" which was introduced by Internal Communications about a year after the official merger. I first became aware of it on the intranet, but only when reading the internal employee magazine "X-Team" did the whole campaign became apparent. In fact, the notion of "Einfach Macher" translates into "Easy doer" or "Easy maker", emphasising the handling of things straightforwardly and without delay. In the editorial, the Head of Department of Internal Communications explains the campaign as deliberately opposing the Austrian and Bavarian phrase "Schau ma mal". The notion "Schau ma mal" describes a rather hesitant attitude, close to the term "let's see" in response to another person's suggestion and is often used in Austria and Bavaria as a polite way of rejecting such a request. It usually defers any decision to a later point in time, if at all.

In the editorial, the Head of Internal Communications, therefore asks: "Is it so difficult to speak out the small word 'yes!'? Or even 'yes, I simply do it'?" Obviously, in this manner, she opposes the "yes" to the hesitant attitude of "Schau ma mal", her rhetorical question being rather an appeal to employees to change their behaviour in favour of a more proactive stance. In the remainder of the text, she outlines the campaign and announces that the magazine already presents colleagues who "admit to this slogan". As she further explains, "[t]hey do not discuss, they simply say yes and do it." A few pages later, at the centre of the magazine, these employees occur on a page-wide advertisement. Each of them is quoted explaining the slogan and its meaning in the context of his or her work:

Figure 4: Employee magazine "Yes, I'm simply doing it!"

The page features employees' portraits inserted in smartphone screens accompanied by their name and department. A statement in green letters is positioned below explaining how and why they consider themselves as "Easy doers". For instance, P. P. working in Business Sales says: "I'm an 'Easy doer' because new, innovative ideas make me find solutions for Management and Sales. These simple approaches enable reducing administrative efforts and thereby increase efficiency." Making use of the omnipresent narratives in business management and consultancy – that of 'efficiency', 'innovation' and 'solution' –, this statement outlines an employee that commits straightforwardly to the campaign's objective, namely showing a proactive, hands-on work attitude. At the top left corner, a distinct square says "Yes, I'm simply doing it". It is accompanied by the statement: "Many Easy doers already do it. And each day they become more. Experience how easy it is to think positively. **Send a 'Yes' to** [number]. And we get closer still to our vision."

Obviously, the campaign tries to assemble employees around the notion of the "Einfach Macher" by describing it as an elected circle united by common thinking. The concept conforms to the notion of the ideal worker in the way it configures a dedicated employee, devoted to his or her work and the intention to tie employees around a predetermined attitude everyone has to share and that assigns employees their membership in the company. In fact, the campaign's narratives remind of the 'new spirit of capitalism' Boltanski and Chiapello have pointed out in relation to the changes in the management literature since the 1980s (2005).[3] As said, these changes emphasise employees' self-responsibility, emancipation and individual fulfilment and orient towards flexible and 'creative' employment relations. In addition, especially the appeal "to think positively" reminds of the forms of subjectification that are characteristic to today's post-industrial economy. In fact, as Andreas Reckwitz has outlined, intrinsic motivation and striving for self-fulfilment rests on ideas from the so-called positive psychology that underlines a "culture of positive emotions" (2020: 215, own translation) which nowadays extends to people's working life.

However, I want to highlight that deliberately linked to the Austrian/ Bavarian phrase of "Schau ma mal", the notion of the "Einfach Macher" conforms in particular to the work attitude emphasised by my informants formerly part of Mobile-X. To recall, one of my informants used the phrase *simply making things possible* in order to differentiate between the mind-set of people within Mobile-X and the presumably bureaucratic work attitude of people formerly working in Phone-Y. Following such an understanding, the fabrication of the ideal worker – the "Einfach Macher" – seems to rather support the separation in the company. Other than that, the phrase can also be understood as a critique of a very common and traditional attitude

---

3   In 2012, the internal employee magazine "Inside-X" was awarded a prize that acknowledged the „commitment to a constructive dialogue with its staff members". It received the first place because of the "handwriting of a professional editorial team. The corporate identity of the company is noticeable across the whole magazine, thematically creative and at the same time consistently implemented" (all my own translation). For reasons of anonymity, I omit the online source as it mentions the company's name.

in Austria and Bavaria. It is therefore questionable to what extent such an approach is successful.

Nevertheless, it is obvious that the idea of the "Einfach Macher" attempts to impose certain normative understandings on employees regarding how work has to be done within Telecompany-X. It underlines the fabrication of subjectivity that is characteristic to contemporary knowledge work: The normative prescription of a committed employee that dedicates herself to the company and that finds self-fulfilment at his or her work. These measures are forms of subjectivation that exercise normative control on employees' behaviour. As will be further shown, not just the internal magazine, but also the intranet distributed the managerial idea of a desired employee that commits to the company's goals and objectives.

4.3.2   The intranet as 'integration' and 'change' agent

Following the branding efforts described above, the new intranet was primarily understood to set an example of the new company culture and to function as an extension of these branding measures. In fact, this orientation constituted a central expectation towards the intranet. As the project manager underlined, "[...] right now, we've got to kind of model it and pull people along, this is what we can do to live the new culture and also demonstrate it for others." Accordingly, the "Einfach Macher", but also the overall campaign was intended to positively attach employees to the new company and brand by affirmatively presenting the merits of the desired new company culture. In this context, the intranet was understood as a means to bring the new culture and brand as close as possible to employees' desks and, by doing so, make them learn about and follow the new agenda.

However, conforming to the company's new brand and culture was also associated with a coherent appearance of the intranet. As the project manager emphasised: "the user should not see whether he opens a content page or clicks on the daily menu". Actually, at the time of the interview, system integration of applications was not finished yet; some applications were taken over from the previous intranets so that the new intranet simply linked to these 'old' applications and interfaces. Still, a vital concern was to create a coherent interface, or 'façade', implying the appearance of a homogenous intranet, thereby integrating employees through shared identification.

But in addition to these functional and visual issues, the project manager was also concerned about the department's overall strategy and the distinct logics the intranet assembles. As he explained:

> Well, our main goal is to increasingly synchronise things, that is, the intranet as the medium of Internal Communications, that's us, we have several objectives we would like to achieve, and, on the other hand, the intranet is very well also an employee-portal, that is the central online entry point for all employees, if you want the operating system [*laughing*] of the company. Certainly, it's also a task to access as fast as possible the various other applications. And we have the strategy to integrate things better, the different applications [...]. However, the bottom line is to make the intranet more homogenous and efficient at the end of the day.

As can be seen, when talking about the intranet, the project manager refers again to the term "medium" and refines the strategy of Internal Communications. This involves, as he says, an increasing coordination ("synchronisation") of different media, namely of the internal employee magazine and the company newsletter, but also the intranet. Furthermore, besides implementing the strategic purposes of the Internal Communications department, the project manager considers the intranet to also serve employees – this becomes evident in his terminology describing the intranet as an "employee-portal", a "central online entry point for all employees" and the overall "operating system of the company". Apparently, the intranet not only serves Internal Communications' strategic objectives, but is involved on a functional and very fundamental level in employees' everyday work. Thus, navigating between these two dimensions, the project manager points out an important difference between managerial objectives and employees' interests.

In this manner, the quote sheds light on a tension the intranet embodies with reference to its particular setup in Telecompany-X. The intranet brings together both managerial objectives and strategies and also is the main working tool, obviously relevant for employees' everyday work. The project manager points very clearly at these two dimensions while describing it as a problem from the point of view of bringing these differences together on the intranet: "That's the challenge; on the one hand, the company wants to reach its goals, and on the other, each and every employee has to find what he [or she] needs. And these two things can be very, very different." The quote first of all highlights a fundamental division between company management and employees and their different interests in the company. Furthermore, apparently, those involved in setting up the intranet are aware of this difference and the related tensions. However, in the context of the intranet being repeatedly described as a medium of Internal Communications, it seems that the intranet is not only understood to integrate or mediate both interests, but that the perspective on the intranet sending out messages designed in the Internal Communications department is rather prevalent.

As will be shown in the following, instead of integrating the different interests, the 'divided intranet', as I call it, creates a tension in employees' appreciation of it, eventually leading to an ambivalent relation to the intranet. In particular, employees tend to prioritise work-related content and applications and, thereby, devalue the managerial efforts of corporate and internal branding. It divides the intranet into an 'important' and 'less significant' part, that is, one that is associated with work and one that is designated as useless playing around. However, I am going to develop these insights step by step in the following.

4.4   A "tool of purpose": The intranet as part of everyday work

Coming back to how the new company and brand was internally advertised to employees, the new interface and setup of the intranet played a significant part – not only from the perspective of Internal Communications. It also resonated with employees, but not necessarily as expected. As one of my informants working in the Customer Service division told me, the new intranet was introduced, in fact "promoted", describing it as "our new intranet" and the "Internet-home of our new brand", i.e. being especially recognisable in relation to the new brand. This new design and layout of the brand and the intranet was described by my informant as self-evident since this, she said, was a necessary condition in order for employees to identify with the new brand. Another employee, Manuel, who worked in Business Sales, explained that from the beginning, the intranet was considered "the pioneer of the shared world", illustrating the new company and the new brand. In particular, as Manuel framed it, Internal Communications followed a certain kind of thinking, a "mind-set" he said, which directs how topics and articles were presented. When I explicitly asked him whether this thinking has been taken up by people in the company, he answered:

> Well, surely it was a part, which, without making it now too big, contributed that one develops such a mind-set. It's rather subtle, [...] because you use it regularly and you look at it regularly, and when things are framed in such a way, like this, it has worked quite well. Well, I can't say that it has been **the** [*emphasis in original*] integration-positive driver, but it surely has contributed a positive part. [...] it's a playground, the intranet, of Internal Communications, they can live it all up there and make their messages public among employees, of course, it should be that way. It's certainly a mind-set-forge, that's obvious. Whether you want it or not.

The quote stands out because of its somewhat reflexive approach describing Internal Communications' efforts on the intranet. First of all, he points out a certain "mind-set", a specific way of thinking that is being put forth through the intranet and the Internal Communications department. In fact, as he said just before the quote, the intranet was considered to set an example of the new company that employees may follow. Furthermore, the notion of mind-set-forge (which is in German "Mind-set-Schmiede") conveys the impression that the mind-set, that is, a specific thinking, is being manufactured, in fact 'bent' into the appropriate shape, in the Internal Communications department.

Obviously, this type of bending concerns a certain attitude about and towards the company. According to Manuel, these measures have received a response from employees since they have to look at these messages in form of the new interface every time they use the intranet. Following his description, it seems that the fabrication of thinking has been successful and contributed to a shared understanding of the new company. His statement resonates well with the project manager above who described the intranet as a medium of Internal Communications that is intended to promote a coherent company culture.

Altogether, describing the intranet as a "playground of Internal Communications" creates the impression of the Internal Communications department as a somewhat separate sphere where messages, slogans and applications are developed and tried out just for themselves, in alignment with managerial goals and less with the rest of the company. It appears as likewise detached and at the same time confined to the understandings of the department itself. Nevertheless, Manuel somewhat approves or almost defends this activity in front of me by saying "it should be that way". Apparently, employees are unavoidably exposed to these efforts on a daily basis.

However, the rather subtle exposure becomes also obvious in relation to the campaign of the "Einfach Macher" which appeared at the time of my second phase of fieldwork, about a year after the official merger, on the intranet starting page:

Figure 5: Intranet starting page: "This way to the world of the 'Einfach Macher'!"

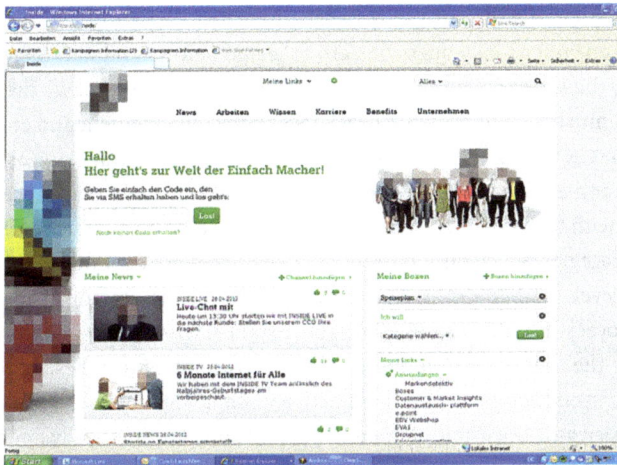

The green slogan greets the employee and addresses her by saying: "This way to the world of the Easy doers!". It prompts her to enter a code she has received on her mobile phone. In this manner, the starting page corresponds with the advertisement in the internal magazine I have described above which asked employees to send a text message saying "Yes" to a number. On the right side, an image of a group of people is shown, one of them carrying the company and brand logo, presumably indicating the group of "Einfach Macher" in the company. Below, the page features the section "My Boxes" which the employee can adjust individually. The current version has selected the daily menu. In the middle, the headline "My News" announces a live-chat with one of the chief executives, calling upon employees to take part and ask "their questions". The section is called "Inside Live", referring to the internal TV channel "Inside-TV". The ad below carries the headline "6 months Internet for everybody" which refers to the company's programme educating children in the area of media and digitalisation. It announces a video and report on these workshops.

As can be seen, the starting page of the intranet aims to engage employees in different ways. Both live-chat and company TV as part of the newsfeed, but also the campaign prominently on top try to involve employees and to participate in particular in the campaign of the ideal worker. Furthermore, the company and its activities (i.e. children's education) are positively highlighted, while a seemingly close contact to the management, that is, the chief commercial officer (CCO), is suggested through the live-chat. In fact, as I was told by the chief editor of the intranet, these 'live chats' are less immediate than it appears; usually questions are collected beforehand and then pre-selected by the Internal Communications department. Nevertheless, these chats give the impression of transparency between the management and employees (cf. Mishra et al., 2014). In the described manner, the starting page assembles formats and enables employee activities that are intended to advance identification with the company. Thus, it can be understood as a carrier of management strategies which aim to promote a positive work attitude.

However, as I found out, these strategies on the starting page appeal to employees in only limited ways. For instance, when asking Viktoria, who works in the Customer Communication department, about these efforts, she said that even though she does not actively use it, she necessarily has the intranet open and looks at it. Remember the intranet automatically opens when one logs on to the computer and uses Internet Explorer:

> [...] ok, it can happen that you quickly glance over it, I mean for example there could be something, that I'll get a text with a code, and then I keep working, and there are also things that – even if I don't actively look for them, I still **see them** [*emphasis in original*]. So, in that way, yes.

In fact, this is the only time one of my interview partners refers to the campaign of the "Einfach Macher" and the sending of text messages involved; but the way she talks about it, the campaign does not receive her full attention, only a quick glance before she continues her work. In fact, in this quote we learn how Viktoria engages with the intranet's starting page; she only glances over, that is, she takes a look but it seems that she immediately is about to engage with another work task. Nevertheless, even though she does not actively look at it, she notices it as it presumably disrupts her work. As can be seen, the efforts of culture management in the form of the "Einfach Macher" or possibly other ads and activities appear as being imposed on employees as they use the intranet, without their active consent and attention. Apparently, they indeed leave a trace, at least this is what her afterthought suggests, realising the campaign's impact on her awareness: "I see it, yes. Well, if you look at it like this, yes". Her "yes" confirms that she indeed takes notice without actually actively engaging with it.

The two quotes by Manuel and Viktoria above describe the somewhat subtle working of the internal branding activities put forward by the Internal Communications department with the intention of increasing identification with the company among employees. As can be seen, even though employees do not deliberately engage with the messages and applications on the intranet, they do take notice of them and also recognise a certain impact of them. However, I consider Manuel's statement on the intranet being a "mindset forge" and his generally affirming attitude towards the efforts of Internal Communications also as a form of explaining and explicating, perhaps even rationalising, these activities to me as an outsider and researcher. In fact, his somewhat positive and straightforward statement ("it should be that way") does not correspond to how I experienced employees' engagement with the intranet.

Rather, as I found out, work-related content and applications on the intranet receive employees' far more deliberate attention. Furthermore, as will become evident, this attention was accompanied by a general devaluation of the efforts of corporate and internal branding existing on the intranet. In fact, the following quote by Manuel from Business Sales shows his rather distant engagement with the intranet and how he actually focusses on the work-related part of the intranet:

> Well, personally, I use the intranet in the default standard version, and I didn't have the feeling, the need for myself personally, to adjust, to set it up. It's not that I have a feeling towards the intranet and would like to be at home there and make it comfortable for me, it's rather a tool of purpose for me, I use it like the others, I have a lot of information at first sight when I enter the starting page so that I have the company news on all areas here [...].

The notion "tool of purpose" stands at the centre of this statement; following this framing, the intranet appears as a neutral instrument that simply serves to reach a given aim. Moreover, my informant puts this understanding in contrast to developing feelings towards the intranet which he does not have. For him, this lack of emotional attachment is also the reason why he did not personalise or adjust the starting page. We also learn that the default version of the starting page provides an overview of a set of internal news which is apparently a widespread setting among employees. In fact, he creates a commonality among employees in the way they apparently share the same default starting page and set of internal news.

From the perspective of the intranet project manager and chief editor who understand the intranet as representing the new company and brand, such a statement would probably be a disappointment since Manuel denies having any emotions towards the intranet and hence refrains from engaging with it. But from his perspective, the intranet seems to work quite well since it enables him to use it in ways he considers necessary, that is, as a "tool of purpose" that facilitates certain work processes and lists the news he considers as relevant.

But what does the notion of "tool of purpose" actually mean in the context of employees' everyday work? As I am going to show in the following sections, it means that, first of all, employees do not read the newsfeed for its own sake, that is, they do not scroll around the different news entries because of the time constraints they experience during their work. Secondly, employees distinguish between content and applications relevant for their work and those that relate to the corporate and internal branding and overall culture management efforts which, as will be shown, they in fact dismiss. As I argue, they display a specific 'framework of instrumentality' in relation to their evaluation of the intranet. Finally, insights from a conversation among the technicians in which they make fun of the culture management measures indicate a likewise limited appreciation of these efforts beyond the intranet. Against this backdrop, the chapter lays bare how the starting page in the current version configures a user in ways that do not correspond with the existing work settings, that is, the reported conditions of work and related understandings that accompany the intranet-in-use.

4.4.1   Un-reading the newsfeed: "You would need time to read through it"

As presented above, the intranet contains a newsfeed which is prominently placed in the middle on the starting page. During my investigation into how employees engage with the intranet, I experienced that the daily menu, located on the right side on the starting page, usually receives employees' first attention on a work day. As Stephanie from Customer Service noted,

> Well, the very first look goes to the daily menu [*laughing*], you have to know, whether you should keep the lunch break free, indeed, in my case this is always the first thing I look at – I have to admit; here, the information, the news there [*points at the news section*], it gets lost sometimes, well, it depends how fast I click away from the intranet, but I like reading them, here and there I take a look [*scrolling*].

Apparently, the daily menu is the first application Stephanie looks at; it seems to structure the workday as it helps her to decide whether to take her lunch break in the canteen. In contrast, the daily news section tends to be over-looked; as she says, it "gets lost sometimes". Apparently, whether she looks at it depends on how much time she has ("how fast I click away from the intranet"). This becomes even more evident as she explains:

> But when I have time, I look into the intranet, for instance, and I see what kind of news, what has been added, ah ok [*she scrolls through the news section*], I haven't read this one, I'll look at it. And then I find it useful again.

Again, whether or not she looks at the starting page seems to depend on her time schedule. During our conversation, she indicates that she did not have time to read the very recent news entry and says she plans to read it later. I also want to underline that she refers to "the intranet" which she apparently associates with the newsfeed. A similar association becomes apparent in the next quote which is from Viktoria in the Customer Service department. Once more, a positive attitude towards the news section becomes evident, but she also notes the amount of entries and information available as well as her lack of time to read them during a workday:

> [...] for example, these are news channels [*clicks on it*], I mean, this is in-teresting, but you would need also time to read through it and this is sim-ply, I think, there is so much information which is interesting, but actually the time is missing when working, well, you'd say it's good that it's there, it's good that it is saved there, because, perhaps I have time and can read through it, or I need it and it's still there, but that I inform myself through this on a daily basis – [...], no, simply because I don't have the time [...].

As can be seen, the lack of time, but also the number of entries in the news sec-tion seems to prevent Viktoria from reading the entries and from subscribing to specific news channels. Moreover, she refers to the storage of news, which she appreciates since it enables her to read the articles at a later time. But in connection with the quote above we may also say that the storage of data enables her to constantly postpone the reading- "when needed", "perhaps I have time" or, as Stephanie said, "I'll look at it". Thus, at first glance, the storage of data appears as a solution to the number of entries and the regular, daily update, but looking more closely, in association with employees' lack of time, reading the newsfeed is constantly deferred and rarely happens. Indeed, the lack of time was apparent in other employees' accounts as well, usually mentioned as a side note which made it appear even more self-evident to my informants. For instance, Katrin, a Service Team Manager in the Customer Service department discussed the intranet not being important for her work, only if "you have an extra five minutes" might she have a look.

The least regular reading of the news section occurred among the technicians in the Operations Support Systems (OSS) department; when I asked Thomas how he actually receives information about the company, he answered that important news is mostly sent directly via email, especially those communicated by the management, and they usually comprise a link that directly transfers to the intranet. Pointing to the newsfeed, he further explicated:

> [...] and the rest − not at all, because, unfortunately, it just gets lost in the masses there [*scrolls through the news section*], and I don't look into it that often, I mean I don't look every day to see what's happening, just on the 21st there were already two [entries], one, two, and on the 22nd, I probably always look once a week, I open it [the starting page] all the time, but only up here at the top [*points at the search for people*], I rarely have the time to actually really look through what's there, so that somehow it all just goes under.

Apparently, Thomas has the intranet starting page open regularly, but without looking at the newsfeed every day. As said before, employees automatically access and open the intranet; thus, the intranet opens without deliberate consent. But my informant's attention is obviously selective; despite using and looking at the starting page and the newsfeed, he does not engage with it. Moreover, this quote makes apparent that the archival function of the newsfeed in the sense of storing all entries does not solve the problem of not reading, it simply postpones it. During a week, entries add up so that in the end, numerous entries take too much time, hence preventing him again from looking at it. But the quote also shows that important information and especially statements by the company management are sent out via emails or a regular newsletter. Only through the message that features a direct link to an intranet page, he accesses the intranet. In this manner, Internal Communications does not encourage consulting the newsfeed, since important messages are sent out regularly and entries on the newsfeed are often a little late, I was told.

As can be seen, the entanglement of the material feature of the newsfeed, that is, its archival function, with employees' time constraints encourages users to constantly defer the reading of entries. Also, the routine of sending out company news via email undermines the importance of the news section on the intranet starting page. At first glance, the storage of news items seems to make up for the lack of time as it enables employees to read at a later stage. However, employees' accounts suggest that they constantly defer reading the news. But let me now turn to another insight we actually receive from the data; as Thomas said above, instead of reading the newsfeed, he prefers to use the search box at the top corner. While Chapter 6 examines the practices around the search function, for the time being I concentrate on employees' distinct appreciation of content and applications on the starting page, in particular the orientation to work-related tools and content.

4.4.2   Hierarchising content and applications: "This is playing around"

As illustrated above, several applications and content areas on the intranet are thought to increase identification with the new company and to communicate the ideal worker attitude to employees. For example, giving employees the ability to design their own company logos and asking employees to participate in the "Einfach Macher" campaign, as well as the more general presentation of employee role models, were some of the efforts of the Internal Communications department on the intranet. When I visited Stephanie, who worked in the Customer Communication department where she was responsible for the training of call centre agents, she explained to me how she is able to design her own company logo. In fact, while doing so, she described it as "totally cute" and as a way to create one's own brand, as was being emphasised repeatedly by the Internal Communications department. As she further illustrated the application, she characterised it as follows:

> Yes, you can play around a lot, there is an infinite number of-, there are so so many interface prototypes [...] well, these are fun things, and then when I have my [name of the logo], I of course can use it as my background, then I always know it's my [name of logo]!

Apparently, Stephanie has used the application and designed her own company logo, which she is able to demonstrate. But she also associates the application with playing around and designates it as "fun". It is remarkable how her words, subsequent to the quote, resemble the messages sent out by the Internal Communications department when she describes the application as a way to identify with the brand and to bring in one's "individuality" and "creativity" since this is "what the new brand stands for". In fact, my informant Gloria, who was involved in the brand development process, used exactly the same words for describing the new company brand. Initially, the application was only intended as an incentive during the brand introduction period, but since it resonated so well with employees, it was even upgraded and kept as a fixed application on the intranet.

While these observations suggest that Internal Communications' messages have been taken up and obtained acceptance by employees, upon closer examination of how the application and other content is part of everyday work, this impression changes. In fact, this became already discernible in Stephanie's notion of "playing around" and "fun things". For instance, when talking about the logo application, my informant Viktoria, also from Customer Communication, commented:

> I mean, this is playing around [*clicks and scrolls, shows the application*], I could generate one [a logo] and could say I'd like to have this as a background there, yes. Well, the intranet is actually good for, in order to know a procedure, I'd say I have a special rate for staff members or a work phone, how do I have to proceed with certain things. And this is all saved here.

Again, the intranet and especially the application for designing one's own company logo is associated with the notion of "playing around". In contrast to Stephanie, Viktoria did not design her own company logo. Furthermore, she contrasts the application with what she thinks is good, that is, relevant for her work, namely stored information on how certain procedures in the company take place. The notion of play conveys the impression that she ascribes a different relevance to an application that allows her to design her own version of the company logo than a work-related application that, for instance, enables her to send messages or to call up company procedures. In addition, the quote makes also clear that because of her work load, she is not able to afford spending time on generating her own company logo.

However, prioritising the work-related content on the starting page occurred more often among my informants. Coming back to Stephanie who I quoted above, she noted while looking over the newsfeed and pointing to the section "My Boxes": "But there are indeed things that are also very applicable, for instance the HR/SAP-portal, these are very relevant things, and I have a look here." Despite her earlier enthusiasm for the logo application, she also contrasts two types of content on the starting page: one affects the logo application and the other relates to applications that are described as useful and therefore considered of different value. In this regard, it is not surprising that the section "My Boxes" often received attention among the employees I visited; it links to applications that directly refer to company procedures such as time management, managed through a Human Resources application which is an SAP software. My informant Katrin, a Service Team Manager in the Customer Service department, similarly underlined that she indeed shifted the applications "My Links" and "My Boxes" further up the page. But apart from that, she did not personalise the starting page "because I need it relatively less for my daily work."

This lack of personalisation and the overall preference for the standard version of the starting page and news section occurred in many settings I visited. Most of my informants had the default setup without subscribing to specific news channels. Some did not even know about the option to individually receive issue-specific news. Only a few, as in Stephanie's case, adjusted the starting page by moving around the applications relevant for their work. In fact, the lack of personalisation echoes the statement by Manuel cited earlier who described the intranet as a "tool of purpose", that is, a device he has no emotional attachment to and which he only uses, for instance, to look something up (instead of, for example, reading the newsfeed for its own sake). It is another version of employees' disregard of specific content and applications that are considered as "playing around", in this case the possibility to adjust one's starting page. In addition, customising the intranet obviously takes time which employees, as described above, do not have. Nevertheless, this specific disregard is remarkable since the project manager of the intranet described the individual adjustment of the starting page as an important new feature. It was understood to take care of individual user needs and hence to increase acceptance among employees.

Obviously, the prioritisation of work-related applications and content is not neutral; rather, it was accompanied by a devaluation of intranet features contributing to culture management. For instance, Thomas in the OSS department referred to the announcement of an internal contest by stating: "all these prize vouchers, this reminds me more of a newspaper than a company portal, even though perhaps others use it, but I don't need it for my daily work." Likewise, Viktoria from Costumer Communication described explicitly a hierarchy between the different types of content:

> [...] but I'm more interested in the professional information, more than — I don't know, when there is a lottery somewhere, where I perhaps participate in a football game, it's nice that the company is offering this to me, but I'm not really interested in it, well, I don't think this is actually relevant for me as much as when new tariffs emerge, well, it's rather the professional content that's relevant [...].

Once again, the focus on work-related content on the intranet in contrast to the measures of culture management becomes apparent in the quote. As stated above, employees in the company receive gift vouchers or specific discounts for various companies, which are part of the efforts to increase company identification. Also, several contests were held in order to increase team building and commitment among employees. As outlined in the previous chapter, these are all activities that aim to positively attach employees to the new company and brand and hence control employees' behaviour, attitude and emotions towards the company. Even though these managerial strategies were understood as particularly relevant after the merger, especially the technicians apparently refuse to take them up.

In fact, my informants' statements actually make apparent that by bringing together Internal Communications' messages and applications with work-related content and tools, the intranet exposes the measures of internal branding and culture management in a rather negative way. That is, contrasting work-related content and tools with Internal Communications' messages and applications, the intranet exposes the measures of culture management and their character becomes even more evident in contrast to the necessities of everyday work. In fact, this juxtaposition recalls the two interests the intranet is understood to bring together: the notion of the medium that promotes messages by Internal Communications, and the idea of an employee portal that serves employees' concerns in relation to their everyday work. But, from the employees' perspective, the efforts of culture management are irrelevant, and in fact they are perceived as distracting and preventing employees from engaging with the "professional information" that is stored on the intranet and perceived to be relevant to their work. Thus, the intranet does not integrate, but instead puts these different interests at odds with one another, despite the new interface and a homogenous appearance which was considered as one of the main concerns by the project manager.

As I am going to show next, the intranet's appeal for employees to interact with specific content such as management's video messages not only caused refusal among the technicians, it also shows that the internal branding and culture management efforts on the intranet challenge what is understood as work. As will become apparent, while the company TV is considered as a means to address employees, it instead contributes to further distancing the management from employees. Let me make this clear by referring to a conversation I experienced among the technicians in the OSS department.

4.4.3   Making fun of identification and team building efforts: "But we rarely watch TV, only at home"

As presented earlier, the starting page of the intranet showed a video statement by the CEO on the company's business results and the status of the current investigation into the allegations of corruption. To recall, the intranet contains a section called Inside-TV which is the internal video channel of the company. As I learned during my fieldwork, the company channel shows short clips on company activities as well as statements and live events with people from the management. In light of the managerial efforts of the Internal Communications department, such live chats and videos correspond well to the idea of the intranet as a medium sending out messages to employees. But when I asked Frederik in the technicians department about the different formats that distribute news and information in the company and especially the company TV, his colleague joined our conversation saying:

> Colleague: [...] And concerning X-TV, it's not so much used, the TV.
> KS: Ok.
> Colleague: It's nice, but we rarely watch TV, only at home [*laughing*].
> Frederik: Only at home [*laughing*], indeed, you are right, yes.
> Colleague: But we wonder that we are really – really forced via the intranet, to watch TV in the company.
> Frederik: Indeed, ahh, yes, when our top management, there are video recordings, partly also live broadcast – [*he interrupts as a colleague enters the room, introducing himself to me*]
> [...]

Frederik: And you can either attend live, or watch it delayed, that's also possible.

Colleague: On "[...]" [country wide news programme, *laughing*]

Frederik: On "[...]", yes, with subheadings [*all laughing*]

KS: And what does one listen to? The top manager speaks to the company, what has changed, what is going well?

Frederik: Press conferences, you can partly –

Colleague: [*simultaneously, partly incomprehensible*] ... he often says "No, we are not to blame! The management is not to blame!"

Frederik: Yes, that's the first sentence! [*all laughing*]

This humorous conversation displays the technicians' rather distanced attitude towards company management and towards watching company TV. This becomes evident in the amusing tone and the way the management is made fun of. As we learn, the videos feature members of the management but they are not always explicitly directed towards employees, as in the form of the live chat; sometimes they are simply recordings from a press conference. Thus, these videos are also publicly broadcasted, as employees have also watched them as part of the country-wide news programme in the evening. It is therefore not surprising that Frederik described these 'live events' as "Well, quite strange, yes [...] well, in reality, more or less they talk to us, but partly also more what you can see on '[...]' [the country-wide news programme on TV], we see sequences of it also there."

As can be seen, while these 'live events' are presented as a form of internal communication of the management to employees, they are likewise directed towards the wider public. Frederik's description of them being "quite strange" points at their ambiguous character; put on the intranet, they address employees inside the company, but when shown on the public news programme, they likewise speak to the wider public. Moreover, as said earlier, in cases when they feature a chat and involve employees only, questions are preselected so that the interaction is arranged, I was told by the chief editor. Hence, they rather seem to be a public undertaking where emphasis is put on the management's performance. Overall, the character of such an event is also ambiguous and the presumed intent to establish a connection between company management and employees rather fades into the background.

Again, as indicated earlier, some content on the intranet starting page appears as indeed indecisive when it comes to whom it actually intends to address; that is, the measures of internal branding and culture management

– the newsfeed and its content, several applications – make the intranet appear as a website intended not for the company's internal communications only, but likewise as directed towards the public. In light of the presented findings, this is problematic since it creates a rather hesitant, even ambiguous relation to the intranet among employees. Especially the example of the video message highlights the intranet's indecisiveness which seems to move the intranet further away from employees.

Moreover, the interaction above also points to the fact that Internal Communications' appeal to watch company TV at work confuses what is considered as work among employees. As one of the technicians in the conversation put it, employees are requested or even "forced" to watch these videos. But they do not do so because watching TV is an activity understood to be done in leisure time. In fact, a little later Frederik notes: "I'm here, so primarily, I concentrate on my work". Apparently, watching TV interrupts his work and also contradicts his understanding of what he does in the office. The application of the company TV questions this understanding.

In addition, in the conversation above the technicians make fun of how the management addresses them through the company TV application. As literature on employee resistance has shown, humour is a way of distancing oneself from managerial control (e.g. Mumby, 2005; Ybema and Horvers, 2017). Thus, the conversation shows how humour gives employees space to disengage from the managerial strategies of pretending to engage in a conversation with employees and instead brings about cohesion and solidarity among the technicians. This becomes also evident in the quotation at the end "we are not to blame" which similarly makes fun of company management as it refers to the company's suspected involvement in a corruption scandal, which was at the time of my visits being repeatedly discussed and unravelled in the media.

In fact, the neglect of culture management initiatives among the technicians went beyond content and applications on the intranet; so-called "social events", regularly held in the company, were similarly discussed and made fun of. When referring to one of these events, my informant Frederik searched his email account, but he had difficulties finding the message that announced the event. His colleague nearby commented jokingly that it is probably "put on an index", implying that someone secretly has removed the information so that he, Frederik, would not find the email. As I learned, this time the social event was a talk by Tim Berners-Lee (founder of the World Wide Web), discussing the future of the Internet. Not having heard the name before, the colleague further explained to me that attendees had to be selected, as part of an internal nomination process by one's team: "Apparently, in order to emphasise the group dynamic, you can nominate someone in the group who will be invited so that he can [*reading*] 'meet the speaker'." Only afterwards, I was told, they were allowed to join, or rather, as he said, "have to" join, emphasising the constraining character of the process.

Obviously, so-called "social events" are intended to encourage exchange and communication in the company and thereby initiate processes of team building. As one of the technicians humorously stated above, the nomination process is considered to encourage group dynamic processes since participants have to be selected by their respective group. The event was announced on posters in hallways and staircases calling upon employees to participate. When the technicians make fun of the nomination process and the fact that some information might be put on the index, i.e. is only given to a selected circle of employees, they devalue the company's intent to create community and playfully turn around the idea of being part of the chosen few. From the technicians' perspective, employees are forced to participate in such activities. Furthermore, the colleague's expectation that the event will happen "in front of cameras" where primarily the management will be involved recalls the feel of a public talk directed towards an audience outside the company rather than an (internal) event for employees. Altogether, the cynical tone underlying the episode exposes the technicians' hesitation towards the efforts of Internal Communications to promote organisation and team building in the company.

To sum up, the efforts to install employee identification with the company – of which the company TV is part of – again did not meet a positive resonance among my informants, especially among the technicians. In fact, the Inside-TV application reinforced the ambivalence of the intranet when combining internal and external content, as I also discussed in relation to the intranet starting page. Furthermore, the application and the related appeal to watch these videos actually create the impression that the measures of culture management are not only devalued and considered as "playing around", but altogether question what is understood as work. In this manner, they further increase employees' ambivalence towards the intranet.

4.5   A divided intranet that engages the 'many' users

This chapter began by examining the intranet's starting page; at first glance, it appeared to be an external website promoting company ads and information. Only at closer inspection, it became apparent that it indeed assembles applications and content addressing internal company matters and work processes. This impression relates to the intranet being a carrier of so-called corporate branding efforts, that is, marketing measures applied to company members. As I further illuminated, by bringing together these different types of content, the intranet seems 'divided', namely on the one hand making available content and applications linked to the branding and culture management efforts and, on the other hand, providing tools and content which relate to specific work processes. In this manner, I argue, the intranet assembles contradictory logics which create an ambivalent relation to the intranet among employees. But nevertheless, while doing so, it engages the 'many' users. Let me discuss these insights one by one.

First of all, employees' identifying with the new company and brand stood at the centre of the conceptualisation and introduction of the new intranet. In particular, the new coherent interface adapted to the new company brand was understood to set an example of the new company. Within this framework, the intranet was considered as a "medium" of the Internal Communications department sending out messages that align with the department's agenda. At the same time, the project manager described the intranet also as an "employee-portal", that is, a portal that enables access to a variety of tools and applications related to everyday work. In this manner, the intranet was designated both a change and an integration agent; that is, by initiating a shared identification with the new company brand, it was understood to install a form of togetherness among employees and, likewise, to mysteriously integrate both company management's and employees' interest.

As the analysis has shown, the new appearance was recognised by employees, but nevertheless a fragmentation occurred along content and applications that relate to everyday work in contrast to the internal branding efforts. While research in internal brand management underlines the correlation between employees' individual behaviour, their internalisation of brand messages and organisational identification, this perspective in fact misses examining the work setting employees are actually part of (cf. Löhndorf and Diamantopoulos, 2014). That is, even though existing research investigates employees' perspectives in terms of attitudes towards internal branding efforts, such a conception tends to overlook the work practices that bind certain understandings, specific technologies, tasks and the employees themselves.

The chapter's second part addresses these shortcomings; building upon above-described insights, it analysed how employees describe and use the intranet. Overall, as has become apparent, employees consider the intranet in the sense of a "tool of purpose", namely an instrument that primarily enables employees to complete work processes. This framing somewhat contradicts Internal Communications' idea of the intranet as a change agent that gathers employees around the new company brand.

Furthermore, examining employees' handling of the newsfeed on the starting page has shown that also specific conditions of work affect how employees engage with the intranet. That is, employees constantly postpone reading the newsfeed because of reported time constraints. Also, the storage of news entries did not initiate a later reading, as possibly intended, but instead caused a further deferral. Thus, this case is a paradigmatic example for the "constitutive entanglement of the social and the material" in practice (Orlikowski, 2007: 1440); that is, the content of the newsfeed and the specific materiality of the archive in connection with regular updates and employees' time constraints encourage in fact a limited engagement with it.

A similar sociomaterial association became evident in relation to employees' rather instrumental understanding of the intranet, namely how they appreciate content and applications relevant for their work to a greater extent than the internal branding efforts of the Internal Communications department. In fact, certain applications are work-relevant and hence prioritised since their technical or material features enable specific work processes. In contrast, employees devalued the efforts of culture management and the features that come along with them. As I argue, this devaluation relates to the specific situation of the "divided intranet": it exposes the efforts of culture management even more because it constantly contrasts the two. In this manner, the measures of internal branding and the wider culture management efforts on the intranet do not find much resonance among employees.

The final section analysed how the technicians relate to the company TV and unravelled how this application contradicts established understandings of work. That is, watching company TV lies outside of what is considered as work, as the technicians humorously pointed out. This understanding also underpins the devaluation of content described as "playing around": most employees considered the playful logo application not as part of their work. Furthermore, technicians' rather hesitant and depreciating attitude became also apparent in relation to so-called 'live chats' which are intended to increase exchange with the management. As outlined above, these chats are less direct and rather pre-arranged; moreover, the videos do not primarily address employees, but rather the general public. As the conversation among the technicians made obvious, these characteristics contribute to the technicians' distance towards the application.

In light of the analysis, I argue that the engagement with specific brand messages through the intranet rather fails since the current version of the intranet prompts employees to constantly reflect on and evaluate the different types of content. As stated, in the way these two compete, the branding and culture management efforts come off badly, so to speak, so that they are degraded and, in the case of the technicians, made fun of. That is, the comparison of content encourages a distant attitude towards these efforts and an overall ambivalent relation to the intranet. Ambivalent since, on the one hand, the intranet indeed proves itself as useful and relevant to employees' everyday work; on the other hand, within the framework of instrumentality, the measures of corporate and internal branding are considered as not relevant or a waste of time. Thus, the aim to normatively control and increase employees' identification with the company and brand through applications and content on the intranet appears as somewhat limited.

Consequently, in its current setup, especially the branding content seems detached from employees and the reported conditions of work so that the partial dismissal of the intranet is not surprising. But this describes also the quality of the intranet; it allows employees to overlook the branding content and hence engages the 'many' users in relation to the work-relevant content and applications. Thus, the intranet's script is 'loose' enough to allow employees to concentrate on what they consider as relevant to their work. From this follows that one of the main characteristics of the intranet is less the way in which it determines work processes, but its 'structure of availability' that provides access to various contents and applications.

In contrast, the branding content configures a user that, first of all, has a great amount of time to, for instance, design one's own company logo, and secondly, to watch company TV or to engage with the campaign of the "Einfach Macher". Likewise, the newsfeed presupposes a user that has time to read the entries every day since they add up on a daily basis. Against this background, it is not surprising that most of my informants said that they had never commented on an entry. Just to recall, almost all written content on the intranet may be commented on. But, the lack of time and, as I learned, the related understanding that too much commenting on the intranet actually indicates laziness, prevent employees from commenting. In a similar manner, the logo application relies on employees' having enough time, but is also based on employees that consider designing one's individual company logo or watching company TV as belonging to his or her work. As can be seen, preferring and engaging with a certain type of content is apparently also based on existing understandings about and the reported conditions of work.

Especially the branding efforts on the intranet presuppose users that are open to and want to identify with the new company and brand. But the idea of the intranet as a "tool of purpose" contradicts this configuration. Such instrumental appreciation was especially present among the technicians; indeed, despite the prevalent devaluation across departments, I want to underline that employees from the Customer Service division were somewhat more open to internal branding efforts and to giving attention to the new company design and interface of the intranet. For instance, some had designed their own company logo which I did not see among the technicians. Also, they appeared much closer to the new brand in the way they were able to report on the new design and conception. Within the managerial framework of corporate and internal branding, these employees are closer to what is understood as change since change is predominantly associated with the branding efforts and less with the functionality of the intranet.

Indeed, when talking about the internal branding efforts, one of my informants from Customer Service described information on the intranet as echoing the management's perspective and standpoint, which she found useful when facing a discussion with friends outside of work. This resembles findings I have described at the beginning under the notion "brand-centred control" (Müller, 2017); employees become brand messengers and identify with the company also when not at work. But, in relation to my own findings, I assume that the identification with the company does not relate to the intranet exclusively, but to other internal branding measures happening offline, especially those that people from Customer Service are faced with as part of their training programme. Nevertheless, such findings underline that creating the inside of a company through internal branding measures is increasingly realised by means of controlling how employees relate to the outside (cf. Schein, 2015: 160).

Overall, the focus on the company brand as a means to create a shared identification among employees and the reported absence of employee involvement gives the impression that company management has put primarily emphasis on culture management measures. As the analysis of metaphors and narratives in the field of internal and corporate branding has shown, the focus on branding efforts in contemporary management indicates a "hidden value system" (Müller, 2018: 59) where brands are rated superior to employees and employees are increasingly considered as exchangeable (ibid.).

The different types of content on the intranet's starting page, in particular how employees engage with them, were taken into account by neither the project manager nor the chief editor of the intranet. Rather, as illustrated, the idea of the intranet being a "mouthpiece" of the Internal Communications department was given priority, even though the project manager described the intranet as intended to mediate both the interests of company management and of employees. This understanding overlooks the fact that a workable technology is not only a matter of balancing or integrating 'interests', but of comprehending work practices and related understandings and the processes employees are part of. It is all the more surprising since both the chief editor and the project manager are similarly employees in the company, hence they may themselves experience time constraints and participate in the social and cultural understandings of the company. However, it seems likely that their department's agenda was more relevant in this case.

To conclude, I want to stress that this chapter's analysis has discussed the internal and corporate branding measures in relation to foremost content and applications on the intranet; unfortunately, it does not provide insights about the internal branding campaign that was also happening offline. As illustrated, the intranet was considered an important part, but other media, events and activities were involved, too. These went beyond my data generation. I can only assume that ads and clips distributed across the company and the larger introductory events indeed impacted how employees experienced the new company and brand. This became at least apparent in how some of my informants reflected on Internal Communications creating and distributing a certain mind-set and how the regular use of the newly designed intranet already had an impact on at least grasping the new company and brand.

The subsequent chapters move away from the corporate branding campaign and zoom in on the work-related content, that is, the handling of specific applications on the intranet as part of everyday work. In doing so, the chapters take up topics that have only been touched upon so far; Chapter 6 investigates the practices around the corporate directory and organigram on the intranet and how they inform and mediate employees' interaction at work. It asks: How can we understand the interplay of different technologies and how does the intranet contribute to upholding a specific interaction order at work? It develops the notion of 'mundane' knowledge work in order to highlight that contemporary knowledge work does not only involve expert knowledge but knowledge emerging from 'mundane' communication practices that constitute a large part of my informants' everyday work. Chapter 5 focuses on the practices around the search function on the intranet and discusses its shortcomings in relation to notions of usability and technology acceptance and adoption. Underlying questions are: What kind of characteristics configure a successful software technology? How can we further understand employees' (dis-)engagement with the intranet and specific applications? Let me start outlining respective answers in the following chapter.

5 "This has to be coordinated": Interacting with one another as part of 'mundane' knowledge work

The previous chapter has shown how the setup of the intranet starting pages engages employees in contradictory ways. That is, while work-related content received employees' attention, the corporate branding content was rather disregarded and considered as irrelevant to their work. As I have pointed out, the branding content questioned established understandings about work and did not meet employees' current working conditions that are first and foremost permeated by time constraints. While this has nurtured an overall ambivalent relation to the intranet among employees that, one may think, undermines the technology, I have highlighted the fact that employees were able to overlook and leave aside this layer. In fact, I have described this as the advantage of the intranet and its starting page: it makes available various applications and content and hence engages the 'many' users.

Against this backdrop, this chapter zooms in on another handling of a specific application on the intranet, namely the corporate directory and the organigram, and analyses how both are used in employees' daily work. Thus, the chapter further touches upon both the formal prescription of work and communication processes through technologies and the actual, somewhat informal and non-intended use of the intranet as part of specific work practices. As will become apparent, the two applications are involved on a very basic level in employees' daily communication practices and thereby sustain a specific way of interaction among employees in the company.

When it comes to the notion of interaction, one obviously has to look into the work of Erving Goffman and the ways in which he analyses how people interact with one another. Goffman directs our attention towards the immediate encounter between two or more individuals which he calls the "social situation" and which, as he says, is the main unit of microanalysis (1983: 3). As he argues, participants of a social situation gain insight through the bodily presence of themselves and of others, that is, through directly observing and reacting to one another. Thus, the direct encounter in which people are in each other's "response presence" must be understood as a form of revelation: participants expose each other through their bodily presence, that is their physical engagement in the moment. But this "revealment", as Goffman says, does not happen arbitrarily; the mutual orientation enables a specific form of exchange among participants, in fact of *coordinated action*, which he describes as the "interaction order" (ibid.).

In fact, according to Goffman, two ways of identifying one another inform our face-to-face encounters; one relates to "social categories", such as gender and race, and the other to the "individual", meaning specific characteristics, such as voice and physical appearance, distinct to that person (Goffman, 1983: 3). Thus, identifying each other in this sense provides insight into the other person and informs how people interact with one another. Against this background, it is not astonishing that my informants reported using the corporate directory and the organigram several times a day in order to search for and identify colleagues they had only been in contact with via email, mobile or landline telephone. As Frederik, software technician in the Operations Support Systems department (OSS) underlined, "To be honest, I'd like to know what my counterpart looks like", adding "It's more comfortable, in case you call someone". Likewise, his supervisor Walter, team leader of the group in the OSS department, explained in more detail:

> [...] in case you call someone more often, you would like to have an image of what that person looks like, to whom are you actually talking, because you don't see these people, some people you know only from calling or through email [...]. Actually, it is also an advantage, in case you see these people somewhere again, you may say something.

According to my informants, the image on the directory adds information that is missing in the communication through landline or mobile telephone and email. While phone calls or email communication enable the exchange of information and work directives, the person's image adds a revealing layer usually only available through face-to-face meetings. It seems the image hints at the other person's presence, as if ready to be identified. In fact, searching for colleagues on the directory and looking up the image resembles the widespread custom of searching for people one does not know on the World

Wide Web. As research on identity performance and interpretation on Facebook has shown, participants looking at profile pictures for only a few minutes subsequently think they can report in quite some detail on the person's personality (Farquhar, 2013). However, while on Facebook profile pictures are often specifically illuminating, for instance when someone wears a t-shirt of his or her favourite sports club, even a standard profile image on the directory seems to convey insights that enable employees to recognise an unfamiliar colleague. Thus, the image on the directory apparently installs a moment of identification and recognition otherwise missing in the communication via email or telephone.

In addition to identifying someone's appearance, Walter also mentioned that knowing how someone looks is important in order to adequately address a colleague when indeed meeting face-to-face, offline. In this way, he said, a possible embarrassment of not noticing each other and of confusing how to approach one another is avoided. In fact, as Goffman has illustrated, embarrassment in a social encounter leads to disruption; the established arrangement people have built up through their interaction is threatened when participants do not fulfil each other's expectations (Goffman, 1956: 268). Thus, the image on the directory ensures tactful behaviour through the adequate way of addressing each other and thereby enables the maintenance of a specific way of interacting with one another. In this manner, a 'synchronisation' between the offline and online sphere takes place since the image on the directory informs possible face-to-face meetings in the future.

In light of Goffman's analysis on the interaction order, it is not astonishing that communication via email or mobile and landline telephone seems to lack information my informants consider necessary for interacting with one another. Indeed, it misses the moment of immediate presence which is sometimes deferred; communication is rather limited to the verbal or written transfer of information. For this reason, the directory and in particular the image can be understood as supplements that add insights about the other colleague. These findings confirm Goffman's analysis of the social situation in which a specific interaction order is upheld through the bodily presence of both (or more) participants. Against this background, it is not a surprise that in Goffman's work interacting via email and telephone receive only a remark in brackets in which he considers them as "reduced versions of the primordial real thing" (1983: 2). Only the 'original' social situation in which structures and processes happen immediately, is worth being analysed.

However, the idea of the face-to-face situation as being the *original* social encounter obviously contradicts today's increasingly technology-mediated interactions, especially when it comes to contemporary businesses and the everyday work happening therein. In fact, the quote presented above hints at the fact that for my informants, communication via email and telephone are primary work activities ("some people you know only from calling or through email"). As this chapter shows, the directory and organigram are essentially constituent of communication via email, landline or mobile telephone: By providing detailed information not only about the appearance, but also the physical location and departmental belonging of a colleague, employees are able to identify the other colleague. These insights are relevant to interpreting requests and inquiries sent via email and the internal company network. Moreover, illuminating the involved rules and techniques employees make use of when referring to the corporate directory and organigram, it becomes apparent that the applications sustain a specific way of interacting with one another, one that is informed by existing hierarchies as well as departmental belonging in the company. Overall, while the analysis shows that employees' encounters through these devices constitute a great deal of their everyday work, it nevertheless becomes apparent that the face-to-face encounter still appears as most natural to them.

Starting point for the analysis has been the observation that, contrary to the narrative described in Chapter 3 that outlines a contrast between the two former distinct companies and their working cultures, employees follow a specific *interaction order* which is informed by the hierarchical, but also departmental structure of the company. To recall the narrative, subsequent to the merger, a contested issue has been the different ways in which employees of the former two companies approach each other. Employees from the former mobile part supposedly relied on very informal ways of getting in contact, in contrast to employees from the landline division that were used to a formal as well as hierarchical approach. However, despite this narrative, the deployment of the directory and organigram show a somewhat different picture; employees from both former companies have quite coherently set up a system of how to approach one another that resorts to the hierarchical as well as departmental structuring of the company.

As Erving Goffman has emphasised, examining how people interact with one another provides insight into the social and cultural rules people establish among each other. It is therefore of great interest not only for understanding how employees utilise the internet, but also when aiming to comprehend the post-merger organisation. Against this background, the chapter focusses on the interaction at work emerging through different technologies and applications, such as email, mobile and landline telephone, which is supported by the corporate directory and organigram on the intranet. Thus, the practices around the directory and organigram do not only compensate for the limitations of email and telephone communication, but must be understood as an arrangement of specific sociomaterial practices that employees enact as part of their everyday work and which is specific to the work context and the organisation. Against this backdrop, the chapter argues that today's knowledge work does not only involve expert knowledge, but a knowledge that emerges from these everyday communication practices which I therefore describe as 'mundane' knowledge work.

5.1 Mediated communication as central characteristic of 'mundane' knowledge work

The increasing implementation of information and communication technologies since the 1980s has been described by concepts such as "information society" or "knowledge society" which emphasise the changing conditions of work in today's post-industrial societies, as I have already outlined in the introduction. In relation to these developments, the growing importance of knowledge, or information respectively, has been described as the main characteristic. For instance, Nico Stehr centres the economy's dependency on knowledge, spreading into cultural and political spheres so that "knowledge as a productive force constitutes the 'material' basis and justification for designating advanced modern society as a 'knowledge society'" (Stehr, 2007: 147). He describes the different ways in which knowledge determines societal developments, for instance the growing importance of educational degrees on the labour market, generating value for business profits. His concept differs from Manuel Castell's idea of the "Network Society" (2003) which emphasises the interplay between digital technologies and society, in particular the logic of networks that are conceptualised as the basis for the global economy. In a similar manner, Carl Shapiro's notion of the "Network Economy" highlights the immediate and rapid access to information, challenging companies to find new strategic orientations (Shapiro and Varian, 1998).

These concepts have been criticised especially with regard to the level of generalisation and because of their insufficiency for small-scale analyses (cf.

Soeffner et al., 2006). This is in particular remarkable since most of these concepts understand organisations as the site where the transformation from an industrial to a post-industrial era becomes most visible. Moreover, to what extent the application of knowledge within organisations differs from former industrial work practices is difficult to state; most authors within the discourse on knowledge society admit that the significance of knowledge is not something genuinely new, but has been relevant in the past, too (Drucker, 2012). In fact, the focus on knowledge involving more intellectual and less bodily work has been questioned especially within research undertaken in the framework of theories of practice (e.g. Gherardi, 2012; Nicolini et al., 2003). As already mentioned in the introduction, this field of research has shown that knowledge is less an abstract asset that may be transferred from one place to another, but very much situated in the sense that it emerges "in action", that is, as part of certain work practices (Knorr Cetina, 1999: 3). Hence, knowledge is not conceptualised as an exclusive cognitive or intellectual product, but involves the body (and the material) as the site of active knowledge generation (Schmidt, 2008: 283; Reckwitz, 2003: 292; see also Laube, 2012).

Similarly, the notion of "information society" has been critiqued as a rather vague concept; utilised as a socio-structural description, it refers to the category of so-called information work in order to compare occupational structures and the specific work tasks employees perform (Knoblauch, 1996: 348). But, as Knoblauch explains, it leaves blank how to quantitatively determine the amount of information, that is, the degree of informatisation, of a society or specific work settings. In fact, the concept overlooks the fact that this work is accompanied by new forms of work organisation and changing conditions of work (ibid.). Most often, the application of information and communication technologies occurs in association with increasingly distributed work which indeed implicates more interaction among employees and new forms of communicative activities (Knoblauch, 1996: 354; see also Suchman, 1997). This is why Knoblauch refers to the notion of "Kommunikationsarbeit" ("communication work") which underlines that communication is not an additive part of this kind of work, but constitutive and essential for technology-mediated work processes (Knoblauch, 1996: 358).

The perspective on "Kommunikationsarbeit" highlights that interacting with one another is essential for accomplishing contemporary work tasks that are increasingly mediated by information and communication technologies. In fact, as this chapter shows, communicating with one another is a central work activity in Telecompany-X, often involving people that are located elsewhere. Thus, orienting towards each other happens by means of orienting towards technologies. As Knoblauch underlines, only through increasing communication are employees able to cooperate and coordinate their work under these circumstances (1996: 359). However, while researchers in the field of "Workplace Studies" use the notion of interaction, he prefers the term "Kommunikationsarbeit" for describing the technology-mediated interaction. As he says, it emphasises the specific social and communicative capabilities as well as the practical knowledge employees have to develop in order to react to and deal with their routine work, in particular in relation to technologies and the ways in which they often insufficiently align with existing work processes. Thus, in addition to the term interaction, the notion of "Kommunikationsarbeit" makes evident the communicative character of so-called service or knowledge work that mostly happens through conversation by email, mobile and landline telephone and by taking part in meetings.[1]

Against this background, the intranet can be understood as an 'outgrowth' of this amount of communicative work and, furthermore, an attempt to structure and mediate the various communicative exchanges in the company. Following this idea, the chapter unravels how the application of the corporate directory in connection with the organigram take part, shape and thereby enable a specific communication among employees in Telecompany-X. As I will show, these applications are part of employees' daily routine communication via email, the company network or landline and mobile telephone in ways my informants consider essential: By providing detailed information on the physical location, the appearance as well as the departmental belonging of a colleague, employees are able to identify a colleague and, furthermore, understand requests and inquiries sent via email and the internal company network. Moreover, recognising the formal, that is, hierarchical status of a colleague through the organigram puts forward a specific interaction order among employees which directs how they approach one another.[2]

In this manner, the chapter adds to research on today's technology-laden work settings. It takes into account the alignment of various technologies and

---

1   The different terms also highlight the distinct vocabulary that is being used in the Anglo-Saxon and German academia (cf. Knoblauch, 1996: 358).

2   In a similar manner, Lucy Suchman highlights the "mundane, practical aspects" (2000: 30) of everyday work in order to question the distinction between knowledge and routine work. As she says, analysing types of professional work involves moving beyond such categories since the two go together, they in fact inform each other.

specific applications which is indeed a characteristic of today's knowledge work. In doing so, it shows that knowledge work does not only involve expert knowledge, but also relies on 'mundane' communication practices that predominantly involve telephone or mobile calling and email writing. It confirms earlier research on knowledge work that describes it as foremost oriented towards objects and specific technologies (cf. Knorr Cetina, 1997, 2001). But while this research has focused on the specialised knowledge emerging from these engagements, the type of knowledge work my research refers to is characterised by a materiality-mix of different 'mundane' technologies and devices that align with one another into workable configurations. Only these workable alignments enable employees to interpret and contextualise the email-messages they receive.

Examining today's technology-laden work settings, existing research has detected the technological environment as contributing to a general work overload. As scholars have pointed out, the assembly of technologies and applications leads to another level of the interweaving of work tasks which becomes apparent in a "frenzy of activity" that is often accompanied by a growing demand to be available and to send and receive instant replies (Jäckel, 2008: 137). This observation stands in contrast to research by Judy Wajcman and Emily Rose who found that while interacting through a variety of technologies, employees actively configure the interaction through these devices and must therefore be considered as less passive towards these technologies (2011: 950–1; see also Rose, 2015). Despite these findings, my research in this chapter questions whether today's 'mundane' knowledge worker can be described as indeed autonomous in the way he or she is tied to these devices and the specific requirements that come along with it.

To recall, as in the previous chapters, the interactions I recount stem from visits in the technicians' Operations Support Systems (OSS) department and from the second phase of research in different work settings. As described in the methodology chapter, my informants during the second phase were all but one related to Customer Service; they either had worked or were still working in the department or sub-divisions of Customer Service.

5.2   The corporate directory and the organigram

All my informants referred repeatedly to the corporate directory and the organigram, despite their different work settings and company divisions. They described it as the "main functionality" or the "hot application" of the intranet, meaning it was used often and extensively in the company. Let me explain both applications in more detail.

As outlined in Chapter 5, the intranet allows users to search within three different categories: "content", "people" and "all". When searching for staff members, employees usually restrict the search field to "people" and type in either a person's name, telephone number or the domain username employees inhabit as part of the internal company network. Pushing enter on the key board or clicking on the search button, another page opens and displays a list of names featuring the selected detail(s). Clicking on one of these names, the page of the corporate directory opens, showing the colleague's personal details. This is an example of the directory page of one of my informants:

Figure 6: Corporate Directory

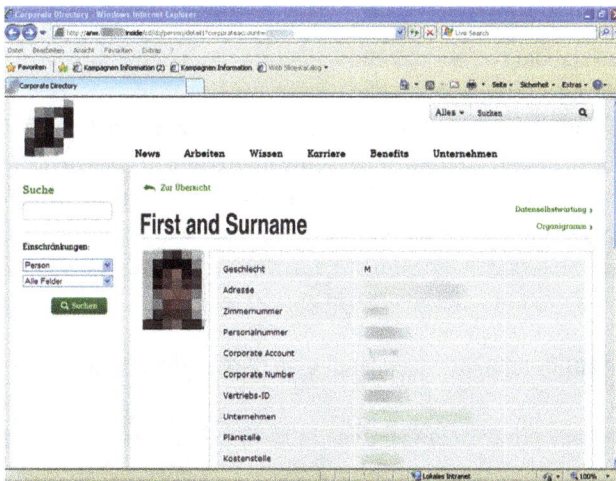

As can be seen, the page displays on top the employee's first and family name and below his or her image. The list of personal details presents at first the person's gender and then the company location where he or she works, the room number, the corporate account and the corporate number as well as the company division the employee is part of. At the bottom, the list indicates another number associated with the person's post and the related cost centre. As I learned, this field stays empty in case of external employees, i.e. those not holding a permanent contract. Accordingly, people can see immediately whether the person is an external or internal employee. Also, employees have different corporate numbers according to where they previously belonged to; members of the former landline division featured at first an "Q", while those of the mobile division an "M". Surprisingly, none of my informants referred to these different numbers in order to differentiate colleagues according to their former organisational belonging. As I learned from informal conversations, usually employees had enough insights offline – clothes, the different ways of addressing one another – that disclosed a colleague's former affiliation, that apparently the directory was not necessary in this regard. At the very end, the list displays employees' organisational unit which is not covered by the image, but was repeatedly referred to as it allowed users to connect the employee to a specific department.

Examining how my informants made use of the directory, only specific information on this page turned out to be relevant: the person's work location and the image, but also the link to the organigram at the right side (green). While the first link – "Datenselbstwartung" – enables the administration of one's personal data on the directory, the second link directly connects to the organigram. Clicking on the link, another page opened – the organigram – which displayed the person in association with the wider formal and hierarchical structure of the company. As my informants emphasised, the list of details on the directory and the possibility of locating the colleague in the context of the company when viewing the organigram made these two applications so important. I am going to describe the related practices and show the implications of these activities in greater length in the following.

5.2.1   Identifying another colleague as part of the company

First of all, my informants mentioned the directory mostly *in connection with* the organigram. As illustrated above, the directory provides a direct link to the organigram which my informants used regularly in order to get an overview of where other employees are located in the company. In fact, as the technicians' group leader in the OSS department, Walter, framed it, the organigram shows "where people are at home in the company." Thus, when investigating how the organigram was part of my informants' work, it became soon apparent that it is an important device so as to identify and locate another colleague and, while doing so, to get a sense of the whole of the company. In fact, especially the organigram made apparent how employees, departments and work tasks hang together. However, both applications, the organigram and the directory, configure the whole of the company in relation to its hierarchical and departmental structure, thereby orienting employees' interaction towards departments, hierarchies and respective work tasks.

Explaining to me how he uses the corporate directory and organigram, Walter emphasised three characteristics he wants to get to know in relation to his colleague: "A. where does he sit, B. what does he look like and C. where does he belong to and where is he located in the organisation." Thus, the directory and the organigram provide three essential characteristics for identifying another colleague: first of all, information about a colleague's physical location, furthermore, how he or she looks and, finally, where the person is located in the company in relation to the formal, departmental and hierarchical structure. In fact, these three characteristics are reminiscent of Goffman's social and individual categories he described as informing our face-to-face encounters and which are, in this case, slightly adjusted to the technology-mediated work setting. However, let me focus on the first two characteristics, that is, the physical location and the image, which are both important for interacting with one another through email as well as mobile and landline telephone. When it comes to the first category, the physical location, my informant explained that this is also of particular relevance,

> [b]ecause, in case I call someone und cannot reach him and it is nevertheless urgent, I need to find out where he belongs to; next, I can call a colleague, if he also does not answer, I may call his boss and ask where his people are, [tell him] I need something, this is how you can move forward quite well.

As can be seen, referring to the organigram, Walter is able to identify and approach the direct work environment of the person he is trying to get in contact with. In fact, this information is only given through the organigram on the intranet. By calling the person's colleague or the manager, he (possibly) receives information on why the person is not available or when he or she will be back at his or her desk. Landline and mobile telephone appear once more as central devices in this statement as they promise an immediate response. As can be seen, when getting in contact, my informant follows the hierarchical order: first, he approaches the employees' colleague and afterwards the manager. In this manner, the organigram allows an employee to 'zero in' on his or her colleague by contacting his work environment. Overall, the statement also suggests that work conditions demand availability and prompt response;

the way my informant expects the colleague to be available and to otherwise contact his or her superior sheds light on a relatively tight work structuring.

The second form of identifying another colleague apparently happens through the image; as already illustrated in the beginning of the chapter, it adds an understanding about the colleague's physical presence that is usually only gained when meeting face-to-face. As Goffman has pointed out, identifying the other involves getting to know one another's bodily presence. It serves as a "revealment" to each other (1983: 3). Hence, the image complements the communication happening through phone conversation and email exchange, even though in a very limited way. Moreover, as we learned earlier, in case employees have only had contact through telephone or email, the image allows them to recognise the colleague face-to-face again, hence preventing a possible embarrassment when part of meetings or other gatherings.

5.2.2   Departmental belonging as a 'knowledge device' for understanding email messages

Another category my informant cited above referred to was described as "where does a colleague belong to" and "where is he [or she] located in the organisation". The notion of belonging in this context refers to the departmental affiliation of a colleague while the location denotes the hierarchical status of a colleague. In fact, as I am going to show, this information not only provides insight about another colleague's affiliation, but specifically serves as a 'knowledge device' for understanding email messages. But let me explain these insights in greater detail in the following.

Besides the primary work tasks around the so-called Cramer application, the work in the technicians' department also covered the maintenance of the internal company network. Mostly, this involved allocating access to employees for specific company drives or applications. In case someone requested access or reported a problem, my informants received a message with only the abbreviation of the employee's user name. In these cases, the technicians used the directory in order to find out who actually sent the request. As said before, the directory enables users to also search for employees by means of their domain user names only. Describing how he uses the directory and the organigram, Frederik, one of the software technicians in the OSS department, emphasised:

> Perhaps you receive an email from someone, who wants something from you, and you don't have the affiliation ["Zuordnung" in German], where he belongs to, because the more you know about him, in which context he works, the better you may answer the request.

And his supervisor, Walter, while talking about inquiries send by email, further explained to me:

> In addition, you can also find out, in case someone asks a question [in an email], where does it actually come from, because it makes a difference whether I give an answer to someone from marketing or from the IT department, since what I write down, or **how** [*emphasis in original*] I write it down, is, to put it simply, different [...].

According to my informants, the organigram provides necessary information such as the employee's departmental and group affiliation which is missing in the email or the message sent through the internal company network. In fact, as Frederik's statement makes evident, this information provides a form of 'ordering' or even of classification of the email and its content, as the notion of 'Zuordnung' in German emphasises. In this manner, it helps in interpreting the request and answering it appropriately. Furthermore, communicating via email or the internal company network necessitates consulting the organigram. But, as Walter underlines, it does not only provide the relevant information for understanding and interpreting, it also informs the message he sends back. As can be seen, in the way the organigram is part of the practice of email communication, it serves as a knowledge device: it enables employees to understand the message as well as to send back an appropriate answer.

As described in the methodology chapter, the second phase of my visits in Telecompany-X took place four months after the initial period of my investigation. In the meantime, the integration of different software systems had progressed; as I learned, this change affected in particular the organigram and its design. Just to recall; this time, the employees I visited were mostly located in the headquarters and had all but one been engaged in the Customer Service department, now mostly working in different organisational sub-divisions. However, while similar ways of using the organigram became evident, my informants now predominantly complained about it. Some even tried to avoid it or had developed additional ways of getting the information on a colleague's departmental and hierarchical affiliation.

Let me now move beyond the technicians' open plan office and include Viktoria from Customer Communication in the analysis. She referred to the organigram complaining that because of its new interface, the "relations" ("Zusammenhänge" in German) within the company were not identifiable anymore, though she relied on them when answering messages. As she explains:

> [...] we get a lot of feedbacks [messages] from employees and when we're dealing with them it's important, since a lot of times someone just wrote it in a hurry, to understand the background, why someone wrote it the way they did – it's different if it comes from accounting or IT, [...] or from a totally different department [...].

The statement makes apparent that the messages Viktoria received – in this case via the internal company network, here in fact she terms them as "Feedbacks" in the original – lack background information on the colleague who sent the message. But this information is important for understanding the inquiry and for writing an appropriate answer. In fact, Viktoria's work involves the administration of the "X-Coach", an information tool primarily used in Customer Service. The messages she gets concern the information on the coach that needs to be modified or updated. But since everyone, not only employees working in Customer Service, may access the X-Coach, she could possibly get messages from employees across the whole company. Similar to the technicians, the organigram enables Viktoria to understand messages she receives via the company network. Furthermore, the notion of "in a hurry" sheds again light on the time constraints that employees apparently experience and which affects their work; it has been mentioned before in the technicians' statements, too. Thus, while on the one hand the technology seems to compensate for the shortcomings of the messages sent through the internal network, it may also increase time pressure on the other hand as it demands employees to be constantly available and to answer messages instantly.

This section has shown how the organigram in connection with the corporate directory proves itself as a knowledge device since it informs and thereby sustains the technology-mediated communication among employees. Let me describe in the following how the two applications also configure a specific way of interacting with one another in the company.

5.2.3 Hierarchy as a coordinating principle in everyday interaction: "This is what it's all about!"

Interaction in Telecompany-X mainly happens through email as well as mobile and landline telephone. In fact, these devices are central for everyday work in Telecompany-X. As illustrated, these applications enable users to identify the employee they do not know – by locating the colleague in the context of the company and by recognising him or her through the image. Through these insights my informants get a 'taste' of whom they are or are going to be involved with. Indeed, while in face-to-face encounters identification happens *in* the moment, in case of the mediated interaction in Telecompany-X it is a little delayed or occurs in advance with the help of the corporate directory and the organigram on the intranet.

Moreover, we have also learned that the hierarchical order plays a part when, for instance, one of my informants described how he proceeded trying to get a hold of a colleague. To recall, Walter said he contacts the colleague's direct environment and in the end his or her manager in order to get in touch. While in this example hierarchy stays rather implicit, it has also been explicitly mentioned in various accounts of my informants. Surprisingly, while in the context of the merger, corporate hierarchy has been a characteristic of distinction between the formerly separate companies (as reported in Chapter 3), when it comes to interacting with one another, it turns out to be a unifying principle. As will be shown, the orientation towards the hierarchical order is a fundamental organising mechanism, shaping how people interact with each other in the company, both offline and online.

Such orientation became particularly apparent when I visited Stephanie, a team leader in the Quality Management division of the Customer Service department, when the organigram had been changed and employees complained about it. Explaining to me the organigram, Stephanie highlighted its modification by pointing out her difficulties getting information on the hierarchical status of a colleague:

> Stephanie: [...] previously, it [the organigram] has been very nice, you could see very well, but when I call it up now, this is a mid-size catastrophe, because, simply, from an optical point of view, I mean, I don't need to say much about it, this can't do anything, yes, or can you see who is the boss here?
> KS: Nope.

Stephanie: And this is what it's all about! The team is called Quality Assurance, it's attached there, and one may click on it and sees, there are still staff members attached below, so you actually ask yourself, why are they attached below, well, because these colleagues [*pointing at the names*] – those, this is me, and this a colleague – we all work in Quality Assurance, yes, even though, this isn't even existent anymore, yes, because it is now called Quality Management, and this is our boss, but no one can actually recognise that this is our boss, this is what I mean when I say the background information is partly not useful anymore.

KS: Ok, but this seems to be related to the presentation in –

Stephanie: This is because of this organigram-thing, it's the program, horrible! [*laughing*]. This is a catastrophe, I hate this thing!! Before, I liked looking at it, because you could actually move it around, I could in effect recognise the top-level and the lowest level and also specific divisions, and this is not possible anymore.

In the first quote of the conversation, Stephanie underlines how well the organigram worked before, meaning the company's formal structure was visible and easily accessible to her. But the second part addresses the organigram now being a "mid-size catastrophe" since, apparently, the way it displays the formal structure of the company had changed. As she explained to me, there were various situations in which the "background information" on the organigram was necessary for her work. For instance, when allocating employees working in Customer Service to further training, she usually relied on the organigram in order to divide them into groups according to their work division. But also for looking up telephone numbers or for simply locating the colleague it was relevant to her work.

As I learned, the initial organigram was a java-script application and displayed in a tree-like structure the different company divisions and departments, easily accessible at first glance. In the second version, employees could always see only a limited section since the new design made it necessary to scroll down or upward in order to grasp the next reference. Indeed, in the course of the integration of systems from the formerly separate businesses, the organigram had changed – not just in relation to its design, but also when it comes to its functionality. SAP, the above-mentioned enterprise software program for managing business operations, had been integrated and hence the organigram looked and worked completely different now. While previously the organigram allowed an overview of where people are located in the context of their department and the wider company division, now the organigram captured a lot of blank space while showing marginal information. It was now necessary to scroll in and out without being able to actually see and recognise the formal structure of departments, groups and teams and how they relate to one another.

In this manner, the new organigram is considered a failure because Stephanie is not able to easily recognise the manager of her company division anymore. As can be seen, she puts emphasis on the formal, hierarchical structure of the company ("And this is what it's all about!"). Furthermore, we also learn that apparently the internal reorganisation and renaming of departments and subdivisions had not been finished yet, or had not been integrated into the organigram. But why, apart from grasping the overall hierarchical and departmental structure of the company, is the information on the organigram so relevant? We get an answer in relation to an explanation by Katrin, the Service Team Manager in the Customer Service department, who I already introduced in the previous chapter.

As she told me, her main tasks are to accompany and coordinate the department's larger projects and thereby, to be available as a contact person. She likewise underlined the importance of the directory in order to call a colleague and to clarify things by telephone, but also to identify who is a manager, as this is important in order to know

> [...] whether I can approach them directly, or should I contact the manager beforehand, because, I cannot simply show up there and say 'you stop calling, because I need something from you!', this has to be coordinated [...].

Her statement makes evident that the formal, hierarchical structure directs how she interacts with employees she does not know and has not been in contact with so far. Thus, instead of simply calling, she first finds out on which hierarchical level the person is located in order to move along the appropriate hierarchical lines. In fact, her quote resembles the team leader's statement in the technicians department cited earlier that referred to the hierarchical order when attempting to approach the direct environment of a colleague he tried to get in contact with. As can be seen, contacting another person in Telecompany-X is obviously a *coordinated* activity, i.e. very much informed by the company's formal, hierarchical order. It sheds light on the specific interaction order employees enact when approaching one another in the company.

This specific *ordering* was also mentioned by other informants in the technician's group. Frederik and his colleagues highlighted the directory and the organigram being relevant in order to figure out "where is he located in the hierarchy – am I allowed to say 'Du', or rather not." Immediately adding: "Well, this is not always the case, usually, the younger ones, we all say 'Du'". Even though the second sentence limits the message of his statement, I want to underline that he explicitly referred to the different ways in which people approach each other in the company. And these two ways orient towards the hierarchical order; the distanced German 'Sie' appears to be used when addressing colleagues ranked higher, while the colloquial 'Du' is utilised when approaching regular employees as well as it is common among younger colleagues.

At this point I want to emphasise that the technicians were located in a former landline business site, away from the headquarters; as said in the methodology chapter, they described themselves as belonging to the former landline business, but initially, they were taken over from one of the company's suppliers shortly before the business integration. But it is not surprising that they refer to the hierarchical order and the different ways of addressing one another which inform whether to turn to the colloquial 'Du' or the formal 'Sie'. As described in Chapter 3, the different styles of employees approaching one another has been outlined as a characteristic that differentiates the former two companies. Indeed, as I experienced, people from the former mobile division mostly offered me the colloquial "Du", while those formerly part of the landline part kept the formal "Sie". As explained in the chapter on my research methodology, I got confused as in the beginning I usually did not know to which of the two companies my informant previously belonged. This insight corresponds to my informants' 'stories of difference' I have described in Chapter 3. However, Frederik's statement above indicates another cultural divide running through the company, namely between old and young employees and their preference when addressing another staff member.

As can be seen, the directory in connection with the organigram informs and guides how employees approach each other in Telecompany-X: When trying to get in contact with an unfamiliar member of the company, employees follow the formal, hierarchical structure of the organisation with the help of the directory and the organigram on the intranet. In doing so, employees have built up a system that contributes to maintaining a specific interaction order; in fact, this was not restricted to one department or former division of the company, but turned out to be a (unifying) principle across the organisation.

5.3   Mundane communication practices

As outlined in the beginning, Erving Goffman describes our social encounters as situated and likewise coordinated since they happen in one another's
physical presence. This presence enables us to observe each other and, as a
consequence, adjust our expectations and behaviour accordingly. In particular, we recognise our counterpart in relation to so-called "social categories"
(Goffman, 1983: 3) such as a person's gender, but also concerning individual
characteristics which include how the other looks, his or her voice and the
overall appearance. However, while Goffman assumes our social encounters
to fundamentally happen face-to-face, today we can think of numerous examples in which orienting one another is mediated by technologies. Especially contemporary work settings are permeated by various technologies and
applications that mediate people's social encounters and that are very much
original in the sense that they constitute employees' everyday work.

In fact, research has often referred to Goffman's work in order to point
out how technologies have become a symbolic opponent, that is, another
participant, in technology-mediated interactions (Knorr Cetina, 1997, 2009;
Einspänner-Pflock and Reichmann, 2014: 57). In contrast, this work has
discussed Goffman's analysis on the interaction order so as to illuminate the
interplay of various devices and applications as part of employees' everyday
communication practices in Telecompany-X. As I have shown, communicating via telephone and email is central to my informants' everyday work which
I have described as 'mundane' knowledge work in order to emphasise the
everyday character of these communication practices. In fact, using the directory and the organigram is part of an interplay of technologies (mobile and
landline telephone, the internal company network) and applications (email,
corporate directory and organigram) which all contribute to interacting with
one another in specific ways.

Just to recall, the corporate directory and the image enables employees,
first of all, to identify the other colleague one does not know in relation to his
or her appearance, but also concerning one's location and hierarchical status
in the company. It provides, as my informants put it, so-called "background
information" which enriches telephone and email communication that lacks
people's physical presence. In fact, as Goffman has pointed out, participants'
"statuses and relationships" (1983: 3) become apparent when being physically
present, this information is – in alignment with the work setting – displayed
in the directory and organigram. Moreover, as one of my informants pointed

out, this form of identification also ensures appropriate behaviour and avoids a possible embarrassment when meeting colleagues offline again.

I want to stress that while it may appear as a minor incident, one has to bear in mind that the company employs about 10,000 people and, as my informant in Business Sales underlined, "We are a big company, you get constantly new contacts, lots of new ways, always new processes where new people are involved." Thus, it is not astonishing that the practice of searching for employees is central to the everyday work of my informants. Moreover, by identifying employees and their characteristics such as their physical appearance, their work location, but also their departmental affiliation and hierarchical position, a recognition of the employee as part of the wider company becomes possible. In this manner, the directory and the organigram allow my informants to get a perspective on the whole of the company; as one of my informants put it, it makes apparent where employees are "at home". Thus, in this manner, both devices can be seen as "media of relation" (Goll, 2008: 143, own translation), or rather 'applications of relation', since they support a sense of the new company – but not by exchanging personal information, as in the case of email communication analysed by Michaela Goll, but by (simply) locating employees in the post-merger company. That is, the analysis suggests that the directory and organigram contribute to a 'sense of togetherness' – not only by connecting employees across departments and divisions on the level of work cooperation, but also by allowing employees to grasp the company as a coherent whole through these applications.

In addition to coordinating how employees approach each other, the two applications are also important for specific work practices. In particular, they are relevant to email communication and messages sent via the internal network that miss information on the sender. As scholars in organisation studies have pointed out, formalising work processes in the context of technology implementation involves the sequencing of procedures which is often accompanied by an increasing decontextualisation and an emptying of meaning (Schulz-Schaeffer and Funken, 2008: 18; 27). Against this background, both applications can be understood as resources that sustain the technology-mediated communication in distinct ways; first of all, they enable employees to locate and thereby *contextualise* messages that cover only limited information on the sender, especially when it comes to messages sent via the internal network (a partly automatised, predetermined function), but also email messages that do not feature information on the sender. As I have argued, in this manner, the organigram serves as a knowledge device; by resorting to the directory and organigram, employees are able to understand and interpret the information meaningfully and write the appropriate message in return.

Secondly, when trying to get in contact with a colleague, the directory in connection with the organigram was used to approach the direct work environment of a colleague in order to increase the chance of getting hold of the colleague. Proceeding like this increases the pressure on employees' availability which is, apparently, to a great extent taken for granted in Telecompany-X. In fact, employees' time constraints have been part of the previous chapter and implicitly been touched upon in various comments of my informants in this chapter, too. For instance, my informants frequently said that messages are often written "in a hurry" or that approaching another colleague by telephone often happens when it is "urgent". While my research did not focus on this topic in particular, I still want to point out that these comments shed light on a culture of availability that is actively sustained through these and other technologies. For instance, the frequent use of the so-called "SMS-Tool" on the intranet supported this impression; the application enables employees to send text messages directly from the intranet starting page to a colleague's mobile. As I was told, it is often used in order to contact a (familiar) colleague who takes part in a meeting.

Overall, when it comes to technology-mediated communication, Goffman's response presence seems to happen by answering (as promptly as possible) messages or calls. However, interacting with one another through different technologies has shown that response presence is somewhat more complex than that since specific technologies are used for particular ways of getting a response (the example of approaching the direct work environment through calling or of using the mobile phone when in need of a prompt response, of using the SMS-Tool when an already familiar colleague is in a meeting).

Accordingly, whether or not these different devices interrupt or fragment employees' workday and put them under time pressure, as often discussed in organisation studies, must also be investigated from the perspective of employees' communication work that in fact constitutes most of their 'actual work' (Wajcman and Rose, 2011: 942). That is, technology-mediated communication must not be considered as exceptional, but constitutes employees' everyday work (ibid.: 958). Likewise, it does not only involve being available, but trying to get in contact with other employees, an activity employees carry out themselves. Nevertheless, my research suggests that employees still consider the face-to-face encounter with their colleagues as the 'original' social situation. Moreover, the perspective on the alignment of different technologies into workable configurations – which I understand as characteristic of contemporary 'mundane' knowledge work – suggest an increasing density of work employees experience. This perspective brings us closer to understanding the kind of work employees actually perform in relation to the different technologies at hand, but also underlines the importance of a further investigation into the handling of the different devices in relation to availability and time pressure (e.g. Mullan and Wajcman, 2019; Gershuny, 2001).

However, the analysis has also shown that the corporate directory and the organigram are not simply representation devices, they are integral to the practice of interacting with one another and thereby actively configure how employees approach each other in the company. They guide both how to identify the other colleague as well as how to address him or her. While doing so, existing understandings and routines such as the formal, hierarchical order are upheld and shape how people approach each other in the company. This is, first of all, relevant in the context of implementing new technologies that are often understood to undermine hierarchies and instead promote team-building in groups or departments (cf. Jäckel, 2008: 120). In contrast, the case of the directory and organigram shows once more how users develop their own ways of handling an application or technology and which possibly contrasts with managerial efforts that aim to move beyond, for instance, hierarchical or departmental divisions in the company.

Secondly, this insight is also relevant in relation to the discussion about the former distinct companies where hierarchy was treated as a separating characteristic, attributed to the former landline business only. Surprisingly, the hierarchical order turns out to be a unifying principle, enabling a specific way of interacting with one another as well as ensuring work cooperation and exchange among the different work sites and employees, previously part of distinct companies. In fact, the practice of searching for colleagues on the directory and the organigram with the aim to get in contact with one another did not happen only in one department, but, as I experienced, extended across the different work settings I visited. In this sense, the organigram enables and shapes work cooperation and thereby contributes to the integration of the company – even though this entails separating employees according to the formal and hierarchical structure of the company.

Overall, the modification of the organigram has shown that the established routine of identifying and recognising a colleague was obstructed. It led to various complaints and protest; in fact, as presented, some of my in-

formants became quite emotional about the modification and the related in-
terruption of practices. This was quite astounding to me since usually, my
informants showed little emotional attachment towards the intranet. As described in Chapter 4, they predominantly designated it as a "tool of purpose"
("Zwecktool" in German), understood to provide access to specific information
and applications, simply serving as a means to a particular end. However, the
modification and employees' reactions highlight that, suddenly, the specific
use of the organigram in relation to email and telephone communication was
not possible anymore. Thus, it shows that changing the technology and the
specific design of the organigram causes practical changes in the use of the
artefact and hence has further implications for the network of practices associated with it.

This understanding brings us back to the debate in management and business studies about the implementation of technologies intended to initiate
work collaboration and team building (cf. Cardon, 2016; Cardon and Marshall, 2015). First of all, it is not so much one single technology that has to be
taken into account in order to understand the contemporary workplace, but
the interplay and arrangement of the different devices and applications which
shape specific work practices. Thus, when aiming to understand processes of
technology implementation, it is therefore of significance, as said before, to
consider the wider technological infrastructure of the respective work setting, that is, how technologies and specific applications work together as part
of specific practices. Secondly, the case of the new intranet and the application of the directory and the organigram show how established ways of doing
in the organisation – e.g. in relation to the hierarchical order – are indeed
manifested with the help of these devices. In fact, contrary to the business
literature and the expectations of the management described in Chapter 4,
these findings underline that the introduction of a new technology does not
easily change, but rather sustains established routines and ways of doing in
the organisation.

This chapter has illuminated the ways in which the corporate directory
and the organigram ensure work collaboration. Thereby, a specific interaction order among employees is maintained that very much aligns with existing understandings and ways of doing, such as employees' hierarchical status
and a formal form of address in the company. In doing so, the directory in
connection with the organigram enable identification and recognition among
employees and hence contribute to a *sense of togetherness* in the company –
through interacting with one another as part of employees' everyday work.

The next chapter further explores contemporary 'mundane' knowledge work, but with regard to the intranet's search function and related questions about technology use and adoption.

6 Searching "our internal Google": Working around and towards the intranet

The search function on the intranet is one of its central functionalities; in addition to the website's navigation menu, it serves as an entrance into the intranet and its applications. It therefore receives great attention, not only from the users' perspective, but also when it comes to software design and development more generally. When using the search function, one has to type in a term and, subsequently, the intranet's search engine queries its database. Doing so, it goes through all indexed websites, that is, content such as text-documents and applications, but also stored media. With reference to the sorting algorithm, it presents a ranking of search results. In fact, the sorting algorithm awards distinct importance to different content and possibly formats. It is therefore one of the elements that may be adjusted when thinking about improving its performance. Examining a search engine in closer detail, one may differentiate between four different layers: the gathering of data, the engine's index, the specific characteristics of the search and the engine's overall maintenance (Stenmark, 1999: 3; see also Quirmbach, 2012: 21).

Precisely, data gathering concerns the way the engine collects its data which is mostly done through a so-called "spider", a specific crawler technology that goes through the internal company net, adding new pages and relevant links to the index (Stenmark, 1999: 1). This index constitutes another important component; for instance, when using the search engine, it is relevant how the content is indexed (the whole of a text or just parts of it, does it recognise numbers and specific characters) and how often the index is updated (cf. Mangold, 2007: 27). Thirdly, the specific characteristics of the search are relevant, too, since they determine how search queries have to be submitted and how results may be restricted (does the search engine allow one to confine the output, that is, differentiate between distinct categories such as general search or search for documents and applications only). As mentioned above, the sorting algorithm is another important element as it organises the ranking of results with regard to pre-set requirements. In addition, the user interface impacts how search results are presented to the user, it obviously receives great attention in software programming and development. Finally, the search engine's maintenance describes the technical requirements necessary for running it and touches upon questions such as who is responsible for the engine and who provides support (cf. Stenmark, 1999: 3).

As can be seen, from the perspective of software design and development, a seemingly simple function such as the intranet's search offers various parts that may be adjusted in case of poor performance. In fact, in the context of the increasing digitalisation of work processes within companies, the searching of various documents and content has become a popular endeavour. Enterprise search, as it is called, enables a user to examine all digital content within a company, across different applications (Bahrs, 2009; Bahrs et al., 2008). However, in addition to the technical aspects of software, the user is awarded a central role when thinking about the success and failure of software. For instance, analysing and evaluating query logs as a way to understand user behaviour is one of the preferred modes of research (Vu et al., 2017; Stenmark, 2008). Furthermore, so-called usability testing remains an important way of inspecting how users interact with the software's interface or a specific application (cf. Gould and Lewis, 1985). Overall, generating the ideal 'user experience' is one of the central aims of such research, which is preferably done by focusing on needs and wants of specific user groups (Quirmbach, 2012: 57).

6.1   The notion of "Google"

By the time of my fieldwork, Google as a new type of search engine was already a prominent web application, but it was ill-reputed for its long list of results. Google's algorithm, called *PageRank*, is a hyperlink analysis algorithm that organises the ranking of a page with reference to a set of pages, i.e. hyperlinks that indicate to other pages as well as those that recursively link back to it. Thus, it rates the relative importance of a page not only in terms of quantity measures, but of a qualitative understanding of links and hence promises more refined search results (Gerlitz and Helmond, 2013: 1350). It is not astonishing that in the beginning, when the algorithm was still at an early stage, its list of results was perceived by users as too long and confusing. When I visited the Operations Support Systems (OSS) department in Telecompany-X, my informants repeatedly referred to the notion of "Google" in order to describe the intranet and in particular its search function. But also employees with a background in Customer Service mentioned the term. For instance, while guiding me through the intranet, Katrin, the Service Team Manager in Customer Service, stated laughingly: "I always say, the intranet is our internal Google, we operate an internal Google" and she explained that the intranet and its pages often feature many links where she is led elsewhere without actually finding the information she was looking for. Likewise, Walter, the team leader in the OSS department, stated:

> Well, in general, searching for people works well, searching for content I have difficulties with – for example, what was I looking for last time [*typing*], it was not about travelling in particular, I think, but about visa regulations, I didn't get anywhere.

And he further explained:

> Searching for content, it finds many documents but less so pages, that's my impression. There are many PDFs somehow attached behind but which you wouldn't like seeing first, you would actually like to search, to find this page, perhaps this can be improved in the sort door.

In these statements, my informant differentiates between two modes of searching; while he considers the search function for looking up people to work well, he describes the general search function as rather troublesome. This becomes evident in his illustration in which he explains how he did not find the specific information on visa regulations he was looking for. As becomes apparent in the second quote, the search for content tends to present attached PDF documents rather than the websites that link to them or that provide the respective information. But since specific information on a topic is usually presented on an intranet-website, he was not interested in a form, i.e. a PDF document, but in a website. As a consequence, he suggested adjusting the sorting algorithm, that is, to award different importance to the distinct formats in the index.

When I was looking at this situation at first glance, the problem seemed pretty clear to me; my informants dislike the search function because it does not work properly. Thomas, the freelance technician I visited in the OSS department, similarly explicated his disregard for the search function with the result of a general neglect:

> What I actually use less is the general search function, well, I'd like to, in case I look for documents or something, but I get too many results using the search function [...] that's like Google, it's insane too much what I get [...] so that I actually don't try 'search-all' anymore.

Again, the term "Google" is utilised indicating the long list of results the general search presented. Apparently, the long list of results resembling (back then) the results of Google's search engine prevents him from turning to the intranet's general search at all. Thomas further explains that it is hard for him to identify the relevant content so that he does not know how to get the information he is looking for. As already said, the intranet's search function allows to filter the results according to 'content', 'people' and 'application'. Obviously, these categories do not correspond to my informants' differentiation between websites and PDF documents. Thus, from the point of view of my informants, when searching for a particular information or application, a certain preference concerning the different types of information on the intranet exists, namely one that prefers websites to documents. Thus, at the time of my fieldwork, my informants' preferences did not correspond to the setup of the search function.

In fact, so-called user preferences and defining these beforehand in order to build the appropriate software counterpart are fundamental for software programming and development. Overall, users' attitude towards a particular technology or application as well as the general acceptance and perceived usefulness are considered as decisive factors for successful technology development and implementation. Following these understandings, the solution to the above-described problem is evident: the intranet's search function has to be changed in terms of adjusting the sorting algorithm so that it differentiates between a PDF and a website and hence matches my informants' needs and preferences. However, another mention of the term Google slightly changed my understanding; this time, Walter was browsing and clicking through the intranet in order to give an overview on the different features, and said:

> Well, and I hope it's not going to change again soon. Because, with these things, you don't really occupy yourself with it on a regular basis, or actively try to learn with it, well, it would be similar to the Google starting page changing every day, you'd get a problem. Or the news page, I don't know, if the "Standard" [name of newspaper] changes, I'm not really happy, usually, because first of all you have to try to find the things you've been finding up until now. Yes.

In this quote, Walter describes his difficulties interacting with a website or application once they are newly designed or constantly updated. As his description underlines, from the perspective of the person referring to a particular web page, a new layout or algorithm disrupts well-established ways of reading and searching for information. Furthermore, he also provides insights into his level of engagement with the intranet and its setup: The intranet is apparently not something he is busy with on a regular basis or that he actively pays attention to. In fact, he conceptualises the intranet search function as a service that works invisibly in the background. This invisibility resonates with Google in that it enables access to specific information and services based on the web. Likewise, the intranet in Telecompany-X delivers a list with relevant links to PDF documents, websites or applications by resorting to the portal's index. Thus, both Google and the intranet search function are not applications in and of themselves; rather, they organise and enable access to data and applications and are therefore part of my informants 'working background'. This working background apparently distinguishes itself from the foreground in the way it involves a limited level of engagement.

However, in addition to the level of engagement, I want to highlight another aspect that illuminates my informant's dealing with the intranet search function. Subsequent to the quote above, he continued:

> Yeah, it's like a desktop, when you open it and you don't find anything, you don't wanna see it anymore. Yeah, and then you ask somebody else. Then a colleague has to go look [*laughing*].

Apart from underlining again his disregard of a changing website or application, he provides insight into his way of dealing with the search function; in case he cannot find a specific piece of information, he asks a colleague and delegates it to one of his team members. Obviously, as a team leader he is able to do so. But what is more remarkable is the overall involvement of his team members. As will become evident, the routine of involving a colleague is not restricted to him as a team leader, but is also practised by his colleagues. In fact, it constitutes a well-established routine among employees dealing with the search function. Thus, the two quotes above make evident that, first of all, the intranet and especially the search function is related to a certain type of engagement, namely one that is apparently less aware, but very much part of my informant's everyday routines. Actually, the technicians expect the intranet to work in the background since they have other applications that are more central to their work and that involve a more conscious engagement.

Furthermore, the two quotes indicate that in the event that problems occur, my informants involve their colleagues. As will be shown, these routines are decisive for understanding how employees in Telecompany-X deal with the search function.

Analysing more closely the different routines especially of the technicians in the Operations Support Systems (OSS) department, this chapter shows that considering employees' disregard of the search function exclusively as a 'technical' problem is misleading. As will become apparent, the different routines my informants have developed when circumventing the intranet's search function do not only compensate for the intranet, i.e. its technical deficits, they are also specific to their work setting and therefore relevant for understanding how my informants engage with the intranet. In fact, the routines of saving links in the browser, of interacting with colleagues through office and email conversation and of setting up an email archive are part of the existing work setting and culture among the technicians. This became also evident in comparison to my informants in other work settings who had similar strategies to work around the search function, but showed a more, as I term it, active approach towards the intranet. In contrast, the technicians' routines keep their engagement with the intranet to a minimum.

As I am going to illustrate, existing concepts such as "usability" (Gould and Lewis, 1985) or, more specifically, the "technology acceptance model" (Davis, 1993) which aims to determine how and under what circumstances humans engage with technologies, only provide a limited account for explaining how my informants deal with the search function of the intranet. These concepts proceed on the assumption that both humans and technologies can be 'matched' successfully, so that their needs and wants on the one hand and technical properties on the other correlate to one another. Criticising this conception, I refer to the notion of the "workaround" which is described in the information technology and computer science literature as how users, as part of their ongoing work, circumvent certain features of a software (cf. Wibisono et al., 2019; Büchner, 2018: 340). The notion of a workaround serves as an analytical-empirical concept to analyse and interpret my informants' handling of the intranet. Doing so, I propose that we consider workarounds not as something that has to be eliminated, as the literature suggests, but as insightful for understanding how the software (dis-)integrates into specific work settings and everyday work routines.[1]

The central concern of this chapter is twofold: First of all, it aims to explain how employees in Telecompany-X engage with the search function on the intranet. While doing so, it adds to existing concepts in software development and business communication explaining human-technology relations. As outlined before, the presented research approach on sociomaterial practices does not take 'preferences', 'needs', 'wants', or technical properties for granted, but rather asks how they are configured as part of everyday work and how these configurations differ in distinct work settings. It therefore moves beyond the human-technology divide and looks at the work setting itself for understanding the everyday use of software technologies. As I am going to show, this perspective is largely neglected within software development and business communication fields more broadly, since these fields tend to favour the idea of achieving a successful match between humans and technologies.

6.2 'Matching' humans and technologies: Ideas in business communication and software programming

How and under what circumstances information technologies and specific software applications work in practice is a pressing question in the realm of software design and development. But in order to forecast the practical applicability of software, research and development typically turn to either the human or the technical aspect of software use as being decisive for success or failure. As already mentioned, research on information technologies across a variety of social sciences focuses on people's attitudes towards technologies or certain media. In contrast, scholars in the realm of computer science and software programming predominantly concentrate on the technical part of the interface in order to design potentially successful tools (e.g. Carroll, 2003; Jacko, 2012).

---

1   In fact, while I came across the notion of the workaround as part of my interviews with software developers, the call for an examination of workarounds so as to interrogate what makes a "workable" technology has been already articulated by other scholars (Orlikowski and Yates, 2006: 128–9; Wagner and Newell, 2016). However, one should obviously not finish by researching failures, but also look into the solutions in order to recognise what needs to be done so that information systems indeed meet the requirements of the respective work setting (cf. Schabacher, 2017).

Despite these ideas and approaches that intend to explain humans and technologies and how they 'meet', the involvement of technologies as part of everyday work often takes place differently than expected; specific tools get used in ways that have not been taken into account by their developers, and technologies can also be neglected and not taken up at all by their intended users (Star and Ruhleder, 1996; Oudshoorn and Pinch, 2003; see also Hirsch and Silverstone, 1994). As this work argues, the gap between the development of software technologies and their practical applicability also sheds light on the limitations of existing concepts that intend to describe and determine human-technology relations.

6.2.1   Acceptance and diffusion

A missing return on investment in new technologies has fostered an especially large amount of case studies in business communication and management studies in order to determine the relevant variables for successful technology implementation (Damsgaard and Scheepers, 2000). For instance, the so-called technology acceptance model (TAM) aims to explain why users accept or reject a certain technology by investigating a person's attitude towards a specific object (e.g. Davis, 1993; Venkatesh and Davis, 2000). Variables that effect this attitude and, as a consequence, impact a person's behaviour, and his or her belief are at the centre of this type of investigation (Davis, 1993: 476). In particular, in order to determine acceptance, criteria such as "perceived usefulness" and "perceived ease of use" are considered important as they – according to the model – underpin the individual's evaluation of a specific object or technology (Davis, 1993: 477). Research in this area happens mostly through questionnaires as well as interviews. Following the TAM-model, these variables and criteria are considered to be central categories for determining the success or failure of a technology (e.g. Park et al., 2006; Tarhini et al., 2015).

Another strand of research in the social sciences focusses on the characteristics of specific user groups, such as age, education or gender, in order to predict who is more or less prone to applying certain kinds of technologies. For instance, in the German literature, the notion of "technikaffin" (having an affinity for technology or being a technophile) and its counterpart "technikfern" (being technology averse or a technophobe) are often referred to in order to explain user behaviour and develop implementing measures that address different groups of people (Jakobs et al., 2008). In a similar manner,

Rogers' "diffusion model" describes how specific groups of people take up or reject a new technology and hence aims to define the different stages in which innovations disseminate through a population (Rogers, 2003; see also Kappelman, 1995). In particular, the diffusion model illuminates the characteristics of certain 'adopters' and their willingness to take over a new idea or technology over a certain time period. Key to this understanding is the individual possessing certain needs and wants in relation to his or her educational background, age, socio-economic status, etc. which are understood to determine whether one adopts or rejects a new technology (cf. Beal and Bohlen, 1981).

Following such understanding, defining these key variables becomes central in order to predict and determine the acceptance or adoption of a new technology. Methods used in this context predominantly refer to survey research in order to collect and correlate these variables. For instance, collecting data on whether or not people are in their mid-30s and at the same time acquainted with social media can be used as co-variables in order to determine whether specific features on the intranet, for instance a so-called "like-button", might be taken up or ignored. Again, in connection with these methods and models, people are configured as individuals who either resist or willingly employ a technology.

As critics have pointed out, such thinking largely omits "user-situational factors" (Dillon, 2001: 5), that is, conditions and resulting dynamics that stem from the actual work context. These are existing routines and the specific work culture of a team or department and the technologies that are part of this network. In fact, as will be shown, these are equal or even more decisive factors than the individual characteristics of people or their attitudes alone when it comes to understanding individuals' engagement with technologies at the workplace (Carstensen and Schmidt, 1999, see also Oudshoorn et al., 2004).

6.2.2   Usability testing

Within the design tradition of human-computer interaction (HCI), technology acceptance is understood as being the result of specific characteristics of the software. For instance, terms such as 'intuitive' or 'transparent' as quality criteria were repeatedly mentioned by software developers and programmers I interviewed. Likewise, the notion of 'usability' assembles such characteristics by serving as a determining variable that describes how a potential user experiences the software. It has been utilised since the 1980s in software programming and stands in contrast to earlier software design approaches that side-lined the user by emphasising the role of the developer and specific properties of a technology. Today, usability testing is part of most development processes. In order to determine the usability of software, designers and developers measure "user satisfaction" or the "speed of learning" involved when users interact with a website or application (Preece, 2001: 352; see also Nielsen, 1999). As can be seen, these categories resemble those of the TAM model, they likewise aim to develop universal assessment criteria in order to ensure the software is taken up by its intended users.

My interviewee in a technology consulting company told me that, first of all, they conduct so-called "expert reviews" which involve their in-house "expert on usability" going through the respective website. In fact, my interviewee Maria was such an expert and explained that as a first step, she checks the website for certain criteria the company has defined as user-friendly and considers essential for every website. In a second step, she said, usability tests with relevant "subject groups" are conducted. This involves, first, research in the form of questionnaires, but also interviews with prospective users. Secondly, her team makes use of the method of creating so-called "personas": Based on preceding research, these are imagined people with an individual biography, understood to carry specific interests and preferences a software has to match (Massanari, 2010). Subsequently, a specific "use case" is defined; it is a situation in which the imagined person searches for particular information or aims for a specific activity on the website, for instance subscribing to a newsletter (Mulder and Yaar, 2007). As I was told, narrowing down the range of people and their activities helps to identify the essential features of a website. Only afterwards, in a third step, will her team invite three to ten people representing the target group to use the new website or application. These user navigations through the website are recorded and evaluated, and sometimes interviews are conducted, too.

As can be seen, the method of creating personas defines prospective users in the sense of a target group that the website has to address. In fact, usability testing and especially the method of creating personas prompts the design team to adjust the technology to somewhat concrete, but imagined, people in relation to a set of specific activities it facilitates (Massanari, 2010: 407–8). In this manner, creating personas makes a website's intended users tangible to the programmers. Furthermore, it also illuminates the level of abstraction that is involved in software development, which is evident in the list of predefined "universal characteristics", the construction of fictional personas, and when website prototypes are tested by "human prototypes", as Maria framed it.[2]

Following this understanding, users have certain characteristics, desires and needs that the software has to match. These preferences must be collected in order to translate them into the technical properties and the software's interface as part of the development process. As can be seen, this approach complements the first research strand around the notion of acceptance, wherein people are understood as individuals who act in goal-oriented (or goal driven) ways and whose aims motivate using or even ignoring the software. It relies on determining relevant variables, that is, properties of technologies and characteristics of individual people, in order to define and forecast whether a technology will be taken up. From this perspective, software development and its methodologies follow the human/technology dichotomy and pursue the idea of a perfect match between software technologies and their intended users.

6.3   The concept of the "workaround"

The conceptualisation and abstraction of needs and preferences on the one hand and of matching technological properties on the other develop a rather static image of human-technology relations. Indeed, usability testing has been criticised for emphasising the theoretical conception of abstract people while at the same time departing from actual users (cf. Massanari, 2010: 410). It also resonates with the forms of social and technological determinism I have described in the introduction as characterising widespread approaches towards technologies in organisations. Predominant to this understanding is either one as being the determining factor: technological properties or solely human interaction. As discussed before, both are understood as somewhat solid and stable and as being fundamentally distinct from one another (Orlikowski, 2007: 1436–7).

---

2   Following this description, software development appears to be a foremost cognitive activity involving designer's imaginations while reconstructing prospective user's motivations, preference and desires. As research in the realm of theories of practice has shown, in this sense software programming is part of a widespread misunderstanding about knowledge work being foremost a mental activity (Schmidt, 2008).

However, as I was told by one of my informants in a technology consulting business, the recording of how specific "target groups" navigate through a website often shows that users do not follow a rational plan, but are successful by "muddling through" the website or specific applications. Indeed, research in science and technology studies (STS) has shown that technologies do not embody just one script, that is, one plan that prescribes and configure users' activities in a one-way direction; rather, different enactments of a technological script are possible and they in turn define the relevant properties of a technology (e.g. Akrich, 1994; Jarzabkowski and Pinch, 2014; Oudshoorn and Pinch, 2003; Woolgar, 1991). This is why within software development, people have advanced so-called "agile methods" that include feedback-loops into the development process, as I have outlined earlier. This approach takes into account that the technology and the user mutually shape one another (cf. Beck et al., 2001).

A concept that in fact turns to the different enactments of a software is the notion of a "workaround," which is quite prominent in the area of business communication and system design. By definition, a workaround is a "goal-driven adaptation, improvisation or other change" to a work process or a specific set of practices in order to bypass certain elements that hinder people from performing a specific work task (Alter, 2014: 1044). Thus, it describes activities deviating from a prescribed work process which, according to the theory, should be prevented (Malaurent and Avison, 2016). As research has shown, workarounds increase in the context of software standardisation; for instance, when work tasks are handed over to a software that is not adequately aligned with the work setting (Debono et al., 2012).

However, while in the literature workarounds are considered a sign of a deficiency, within software programming they constitute a reasonable source for successful design and development as they provide insights into the actual handling of a technology (Pollock, 2005; Büchner, 2018: 340). In line with this idea, I want to acknowledge workarounds as a source of information for the researcher; in fact, by illuminating these 'detours', we get valuable insights into what is actually done in practice with a specific technology (cf. Star, 2002). Thus, taking workarounds as a point of entry enables one to research what I have above cited as "user-situational factors" that tend to be excluded or black-boxed in concepts such as the technology acceptance model. As will become evident, it allows one to shed light on the mutual shaping – that is, the reciprocal configuration of humans and technologies – and how they assemble as part of work practices (Law, 1992; see also Latour, 2005).

6.4   The search function

Against this backdrop, the chapter objects to the idea of a perfect match between humans and technologies, especially the belief that the two can be adjusted to result in a smoothly operating work process. As I show, when it comes to the intranet's search function, my informants have developed a set of daily routines that indeed work around this application. But while resorting to similar routines, my informants from different departments and work settings show distinct degrees of engagement with the intranet. That is, the technicians engage with the intranet from a distance, and thus keep the intranet excluded as much as possible from their everyday work practices, while my informants with a background in Customer Service engage more regularly and show a more active approach towards the intranet.

As I argue, these differences are rooted in the interplay of the intranet, other technologies at hand, and the established and ongoing routines of the respective work setting. Thus, I hesitate to consider it exclusively the result of a failed match between the technology and my informants. In fact, the insights show that accepting a technology moves beyond the individual that either adopts or rejects the technology. The technicians in the OSS department certainly belong to the category of being open to technologies ("technology affinity"), but, as my research shows, they keep their engagement with the intranet to a minimum. As will become evident, it is the specific configuration of the search function in this setting which makes its usage negligible. Overall, the chapter shows that it is less a question of whether or not a technology is accepted, but of how the technology is configured as part of an interwoven net of different sociomaterial practices that exist in the respective work setting (cf. Suchman, 1997; Suchman et al., 1999). Furthermore, the findings also suggest to conceive of technologies and humans not as being solid and finished, but as emergent and distinct in different contexts.

6.4.1   Saving links in the browser: "I would never search for [it]"

When searching on the intranet, my informants typed in a keyword and possibly selected a filter – 'people', 'content' or 'application' – so as to limit the results upfront. As outlined before, if no filter is applied, the search engine browses through all categories and presents an accordingly longer list. This list features different data formats, such as PDF documents describing certain applications, links to websites or applications themselves. One of the central applications my informants mentioned regularly was the time management tool which was accessible through the intranet search or through navigating the headlines. Documenting one's working hours is obligatory for all employees; only self-employed staff members were sometimes subject to different time documentation policies. However, as the following section will show, instead of consulting the intranet, my informants usually turned to the autofill function of the web browser in order to use the application.

One of my informants doing so was Thomas, the self-employed technician in the OSS department I quoted at the beginning of the chapter. He sat in another room down the corridor from the open plan office I had visited before. He is part of the inventory and provisioning team, but works with other teams in the OSS department, too. His position is called "roll out and delivery management", meaning he is responsible for the last step in the development process, when software products are tested and released before being installed in the telecommunication system. Explaining the different header sections on the intranet to me and discussing the search function, he pointed at the time management tool and referred to the address line of his browser. As he explained:

> Thomas: Exactly, in my case everything is saved, too; that is, for example "TIME" [name of the time documentation tool] I would never search for.
> KS: You wouldn't access it via the intranet –?
> Thomas: I type in "TIME" [*types the word into the address line of the browser*] on top and it is loaded automatically, it doesn't matter where it is within the word, and I'm in there, that is, I need the intranet and its hundred thousand links very little because I can address things directly. Yes, similarly, the daily menu, look, everything is there. One gets to the intranet page anyway, to the respective one, but I would never click through WORK – FOOD – DRINK [*reads the intranet header*]."

In the above quote, my informant describes how he prefers typing the name of the time management tool into the browser instead of accessing it through the intranet. In doing so, he takes advantage of the technical property of the browser that automatically completes a web page accessed before. In doing so, he is able to disregard the intranet: "I need the intranet and its hundred thousand links very little", he says. Again, the Google-reference resonates in this description, as the *large amount* of links, not the links themselves (websites, applications, etc.), are negligible. In fact, from the perspective of my informant, the intranet, with its numerous links and need to navigate through the headlines, seems to be a detour he avoids. Instead, he makes use of the browser's address line that completes pages he has accessed before. In this manner, the browser allows a more 'direct' access.

The described routine is somewhat astonishing since the starting page of the intranet allows its users to define so-called 'quicklinks' that directly lead to a certain page or application. But, as became evident, my informant was not even aware of this function, as he stated at a later stage during my visit: "What's interesting, but I haven't used it so far, I only see it now, you can define your own 'quicklinks' here, I've always done it via standard favourites, on the Internet Explorer." Thus, the automatic function of the browser and the option of setting standard favourites in fact makes the quicklinks application on the intranet obsolete. In doing so, the intranet, with its starting page and search function, is omitted from Thomas' information accessing practices.

In fact, the routine of typing the name of an application or webpage into the web browser's address line was a central practice among my informants – not just in the technicians' department, but also in other work settings. As said, using the web browser's autofill function enables a direct access to applications on the intranet. At the same time, this routine works around, or circumvents, the intranet, its menu, and the long list of results it often presents. One might question whether this is indeed a workaround in the sense of the definition being a "goal-oriented adaptation" to a prescribed work process. While it does seem that my informant did develop this workaround because it provided him with a speedy and direct route to the information he frequently accessed, this example also highlights the materiality of the web browser, its ready-at-hand availability, and employees' overall orientation towards the browser. Moreover, my informant's neglect to define quicklinks also supports the idea that users are less deliberate or rational beings in the way they handle a software. Instead, we see evidence of an employee attending to the software as part of his ongoing of (work) practices, a process that in fact unfolds its own dynamic.

The somewhat 'competitive' situation of the browser and the intranet – both allow one to save links – shows that, again, the context, that is, existing routines and devices or applications, in which the software is put plays an important role in understanding how users refer to a software. Thus, not just the specific service on a website or the location of a link on a page is decisive. Instead, the entanglement of existing routines, such as referring to the web browser, as well as its material availability and the habitual manifestation in people's search routines, contributes to whether or not specific functions of the intranet are taken up.

6.4.2   Office conversation and exchanging emails: "That's the Google effect"

The statements I presented in the beginning stemmed from the technicians' team leader, Walter, and the self-employed technician Thomas, both located in offices along the same corridor. Let me now introduce the technicians' open plan office, a fairly large room comprised of two rows of tables next to each other in the middle of the room, which provided space for about six to eight people. The walls were fitted with posters and charts, for instance explaining methods of agile software development and scheduling projects the team currently works on.

When we entered the room, I was at first surprised at the amount of people sitting in the office. Offering me a seat next to his desk, my informant Frederik put down his mobile and finished something by typing into the keyboard. His desk featured two screens connected to a CPU (central processing unit) tower, another laptop, a landline telephone and some sheets of paper. When we started to focus on the intranet and I asked my first question, the atmosphere went rather quiet and a little tense as it seemed his colleagues listened to our conversation. However, after some time, his colleagues increasingly joined our conversation and the atmosphere became more lively and chatty. This became also evident when transcribing the record which featured his colleagues' voices, their whistling as well as door slamming in the background.

The first fifteen minutes of the interview concentrated intensively on my informant's everyday work in the OSS department. The "Cramer application" is the central software application he and his team refer to on a day-to-day basis. As discussed in the methodology chapter, this is a so-called "Inventorysystem" which assembles information from other software systems and thereby maps the inventory of the telecommunications network (switch points, cables, routers) in relation to customer data and orders. It illustrates sequences of work activities for the OSS team and thereby provides an overview on the remaining tasks involved in each customer order. My informant's primary work task was called "configuration management", which is the adjustment of relevant parts (such as switch points, cables, routers, and the like) through software programming as well as general system support. This support encompasses especially the integration of different online environments used in the company.

At first, my informant Frederik mentioned the intranet's search function in relation to the intranet header which he said he usually disregards since it is "too varied". Apparently, navigating through the headlines is not accessible to him. Later in the interview, he explained a situation in which he was looking, that is searching, for specific information on the intranet:

> Frederik: What I've also looked for recently, information about the WLAN in the company.
> Colleague 1: [*commenting*] But you won't find it anymore! [*colleagues laughing*]
> Frederik: Exactly! [*more laughing*] Well, this was –
> Colleague 2: [*addressing the interviewer*] What an impression, please don't get the impression – [*colleagues laughing*]
> Frederik: Well, it's about how we work with it! But this was actually the case, a colleague pointed out, hey, there is something, you should have a look, and then I received an email with a link, this is communication-wise the easiest way, before one probably starts searching, at least this is how it is for me, and we would have used it again, but it suddenly didn't exist anymore. It had been moved elsewhere.
> KS: Ok, the link didn't exist anymore.
> Frederik: The page didn't exist anymore.
> [...]
> Frederik: Yes, it was about the WLAN. There is an own WLAN-network for mobile phones.
> KS: And you wanted to get information on that?
> Frederik: Yes, exactly. We have two, I think we have two WLAN-networks, I don't really know how it works, but one of them, you have to get access every day through 'Webend', this is a homepage, and the other one, you don't have to do this, you always get on the Internet and this is for mobile phones primarily. But you won't get access to the intranet. This is the Internet.
> Colleague 1: Well. This has actually changed, again! One finds it again via search, simply 'WLAN' and you'll find it. First on search. It works again. [*incomprehensible, referring to the 'old version'*] ... you certainly searched –
> Frederik: [*insisting*] No, but this was without chance.
> [*More interaction among colleagues while another colleague enters the room, more chatting*].
> Frederik: There, 'WLAN mobile', now I see it.

KS: Ah, that's the one.

Frederik: Probably ... This is a PDF. It is sometimes difficult when using the search function, well, actually to figure out what you are actually looking for. That's the "Google effect", yes. But this is actually, well, in Google mostly, it requires getting used to, you need some time, in order to see what you want to see. I have troubles doing so, obviously, as I don't use it intensively.

The interview sequence describes how my informant searches for information on the intranet about the WLAN company network. Apparently, two internal company networks exist, one of them is open and intended for mobile phones, but does not connect to the intranet. The other one requires employees to log in and afterwards enables them to access the intranet. Thus, aiming to get on the intranet on the mobile phone involves knowing about the requirements for getting access. But following the conversation among my informant and his colleagues, we learn even more, namely about the challenges involved when searching for information, both websites and applications, on the intranet: often, a website is suddenly gone and/or updated and not available anymore. For my informant, the website in fact does not exist any longer. While explaining the case, we also get to know how my informant proceeds in order to find the information he is looking for. But let me discuss these insights in greater detail.

First of all, the excerpt shows that communication offline as well as online through sending back and forth emails allows my informant to also work around the search function. In fact, this is not only what he reports on, also during the interview sequence we experience how his colleague joins the conversation and provides input on how to find the information Frederik is looking for. As explained in the methodology chapter, the interview can be understood as an opportunity to observe how interviewees re-enact what they describe, either staged or in situ (Hirschauer et al., 2015). Thus, the sequence illustrates how the technicians interact with each other and, while Frederik re-enacts his search for information on the internal WLAN network, we experience him finding the solution: he asks his colleagues and gets instant feedback on his request. As I learned, this is a regular routine among the technicians.

In fact, the notion of the "Google effect" refers to this routine, or, to put it differently, it points at the lack of usage among the technicians. That is, as a consequence of the immediate exchange among the technicians, Frederik is not used to read straight away the list of results, an experience he has apparently made in relation to Google's search engine and which he also associates with the intranet's search function. Thus, not only is he irritated by the different formats (websites and PDFs), but, as he says, one has to learn what one "wants to see", meaning one has to become familiar with what kind of and, more importantly, *how* information is actually presented on the intranet. Therefore, his ability to successfully work with the intranet, that is, to read the search results, is not something that is simply given, but it emerges in relation to engaging with the intranet. But since the technicians seem to prefer the immediate exchange, he does not make use of the search function on a regular basis and has therefore difficulties identifying, or making sense of, the search results. As can be seen, the notion of the "Google effect" also makes apparent that making use of software technologies is an emerging quality that might not be given and which has consequences for thinking about the entanglement of employees, the technology at hand and the specific workplace culture.

Another important element in this situation is apparently the constant update of the intranet and the different formats (websites and PDF documents) which also makes it difficult for my informant to establish a regular routine he can rely on. In fact, based on this experience, he does not even refer to the intranet's search function anymore, he says, he prefers to send an email. In fact, the exchange of emails among employees was a regular form of information distribution which also enabled them to set up an email archive that could be consulted whenever necessary. As my informant added in another statement, he would rather search his archive than refer to the search function on the intranet. I also want to mention that, in general, email communication in Telecompany-X was still very central, since a great amount of internal information was sent out by the Internal Communication department as a regular newsletter and/or extra emails whenever necessary.

Apparently, technical properties, such as the different formats on the intranet (namely webpages, PDF documents and distinct applications) as well as the constant updates and changes to the intranet are reasons for working around the search function. At the same time, routine talk among team members offline as well as through email exchange plays a part, too. The discussion with colleagues enables my informants to instantly get feedback when looking for particular information on the intranet and, when sending back and forth emails, to subsequently store this information in one's email archive. Indeed, I repeatedly experienced Frederik asking his nearby colleagues for information or discussing an application with them. In addition, previous experiences with the intranet, but also other search engines such as Google actually configure how my informants (dis-)engage with the search function. Overall, the illustrated entanglement of technical applications, existing routines and past experiences is constitutive for the practice of searching and finding specific information on the intranet. In this manner, making sense of the intranet and the search function in particular appears not as an individual, but as a collective capacity and is shared in relation to specific software technologies, that is, the intranet's search function as well as the web browser.

The sequence presented above shows that a software application such as the search function on the intranet demands that users learn and get familiar with how it presents certain information. It is not something given, but rather evolves as one engages with it. But, obviously, the technicians appear somewhat persistent in the way they undermine this objective, which allows them to refrain from constantly experiencing the "Google effect". In fact, other situations bear witness to this persistence, too; for instance, as my informant Frederik noted, he considers the time management application to be the one used most frequently on the intranet because "we have to use it". Thus, the policy to document one's working time forces him and his colleagues to use the time management application. But, again, he does not access it through the intranet, but through the browser. As can be seen, the technicians display a consistent resistance not engaging with the intranet.

As I am going to show next, this stands in contrast to other employees I visited; while exchanging links through sending emails was a widespread practice used to circumvent the search function, other employees tended to use offline talk and email exchange to get 'closer' to the intranet, meaning to become familiar and to engage with the intranet. Let me give some examples in order to illustrate and explain these findings.

6.4.3   Working towards the intranet:
Differences between technicians and Customer Service

Examining the different workarounds has given insight into the ways my informants deal with the search function. As explained above, they are very much rooted in the daily work routine of my informants, who referred to the web browser numerous times a day. Moreover, colleagues in the open plan office also interacted with one another and discussed possible paths to find the information – mostly links to websites and documents – they were looking for. Through this talk, my informants dealt with the constantly changing intranet, stemming from updates and rearrangements that happen regularly or that were still part of the system integration activities following the merger. Finally, continuing this exchange through email and setting up an archive allowed them save this information so they could refer to it again at a later stage (as it was the case during the reported conversation above).

As stated earlier, these routines did not only occur in the OSS department; my informants with a background in Customer Service also told me they either sent an email or asked a colleague for help when searching for information or an application on the intranet. But the main difference I noted was their closer or more active engagement with the intranet, meaning they were more open to turning to the intranet instead of setting up an email archive that kept the status quo, that is, a *disengagement* with the intranet. For instance, when I visited Stephanie, the Service Design Manager with a background in Customer Service, she explained her recent search for the facility management application and underlined:

> Definitely, yes, I'm a Self-Admin[istration]-Fan, everything I can do by myself, I rather do it myself; today, when I heard you can do the Facility Management-story yourself online, I asked my colleague since she said one can do it there, I said please show me quickly how this is done, and I did it immediately by myself and next time, I don't need anybody, and I can do it straight away on my own.

In a similar manner, she referred to the starting page of the intranet:

> Well, I can change anything here, I can change my logo, my background, my links, likewise my news, as we have just seen, I can adjust my data, well, when I notice something is not stored well, or, like the other day, there was an ancient photo in there I found awful, then I simply kick it out!

These two statements stand out in the way they convey a very active approach towards the intranet; in the first quote, Stephanie reports having asked her colleague how to find the facility management application on the intranet, describing it as a "story" since it involves filling out a document and sending it to the department. While doing so, she underlines that she did so in order to be able to do it on her own next time. In the second quote, she attends to the starting page of the intranet and illustrates how she is able to adjust the surface and applications as well as the content of her personal data. As I experienced during my visit, her colleague sat diagonally opposite her desk. But in contrast to the lively environment of the technicians' open plan office, this office fulfilled the expectation of a rather quiet room, featuring a conference table and some chairs as well as separated desks for both employees. In fact, almost no interaction between her colleague and Stephanie took place while I was there.

Likewise, my informant Gloria with a background in Customer Service, too, and located in the Residential & Business Sales department, showed a similarly active approach towards the intranet. While her primary job was to promote the company's sales activities to small businesses, part of her job also entailed putting information on the company's sales activities on the intranet. During my visit, she wanted to show me a video in which the company's new shop design was presented since she was involved in these activities as part of her previous job post. But searching on the intranet, she did not find the video anymore, and she stated apologetically:

> Gloria: Well, this is embarrassing, basically, that we have links leading nowhere –
> KS: This is probably so much information –
> Gloria: Yes, maintenance is really a challenge, here we had all posts from previously –, this does not exist anymore, this I would actually look at right now. These things, if I notice, I save it and report it to the relevant editor, these are posts from 2010, this is terrible [*she clicks and saves the page in a file*].

It is quite evident that in this sequence, Gloria presents herself as a spokesperson for the intranet in the way she tries to present a functioning intranet to me, an intranet that is up to date in the way it features 'active' links leading to websites or applications. But, apparently, this is not always the case and she says that if she finds these "dead links", she reports them to the editor responsible for the respective content or application. In comparison to what I learned in the technicians' department, this stands out in the way she feels responsible for the content on the intranet. Up until this point, I visited people that had only written a comment or expressed approval by clicking the like-button of a post on the intranet. But in relation to her work that involves editing content for the intranet, this is perhaps less astounding since maintaining content is a regular work task for her.

Also, I want to underline that Gloria hints at an important issue that is often underestimated when it comes to the implementation of software technologies: the maintenance of content which is an ongoing and time-consuming task. In fact, the case of the disappearing website in the technicians' department shows that content is updated and maintenance does happen. On the other hand, the example above illustrates that there is also a lack of maintenance in the way the intranet features links that are conceived of as dead ends. Apparently, as both cases show, the work is not done by simply maintaining the content when it is not clear to people where to find the up-dated information afterwards. Thus, maintenance not only involves system administration, but measures that work towards integrating the content into existing work processes and practices. As this chapter is trying to show, the software 'being accessible' to users is a complex endeavour that is not easily achieved.

As discussed in Chapter 4, my informants with a background in Customer Service located at the headquarters appeared to me more open to and also fa-miliar with the new company brand that was introduced and promoted after the merger. Likewise, the intranet, understood as representing the new brand as a means to unite the company after the merger, appealed to my informants with a background in the area of Customer Service more so than to the tech-nicians in the OSS department. For example, they were more open to design-ing their own company logo and watching company TV and related videos on the intranet, whereas the technicians distanced themselves by making fun of these features, as described in Chapter 4. As can be seen, these different ways of appreciating the new brand and hence the intranet also play a part in helping us understand employees' different engagements with the intranet and its search function.

6.5   Keeping the workflow going: On the (dis-)integration of the intranet into existing work settings

I have started this chapter by describing the search function as a central en-trance into the intranet. Furthermore, I have outlined the complex of technical properties that underpin search engines more generally in order to illustrate and explain the different layers of the search engine and its long list of re-sults. In fact, my informants' recurrent reference to this list in connection with the notion of "Google" called attention not only to the fact that they dis-regard it, that is, work around the search function, but also to the intricate ways in which the search function is embedded into the existing work set-ting. Illuminating how the technicians in the open plan office circumvent the search function, I started to question their disengagement with the intranet as an exclusively technical problem, that is as a case of 'mismatch' between my informants' search criteria and the software not adequately mirroring these criteria. As illustrated, such a view is proposed and rooted in software de-velopment methodologies and information technology research. Departing from this understanding, I have turned to the notion of the workaround as an empirical-analytical concept in order to analyse the different cases in which people work around the search function.

Doing so, I have discovered several practices to be important: the imme-diate communication among my informants in the form of talking and email exchange, and, in relation to this, the setup of an email archive. Moreover, the routine of using the web browser's automatic function to complete a web page was another practice that circumvents the search function and the nav-igation menu of the intranet. Overall, comparing the technicians and people working in the area of Customer Service has shown that specific work tasks and the respective setting of the office also play a part; in particular, different degrees of engagement with the intranet became apparent in relation to my informants' work tasks. In fact, these differences underline that dealing with a software or technology is not something ready at hand and simply given, but also emerges in relation to the specific work context it is part of.

The findings indicate that theories about user involvement such as the "technology acceptance model" (TAM) as well as socio-structural categories, for example defining people as 'early adopters' or as possessing 'technology affinity', are insufficient for describing and understanding human-technol-ogy relations. Likewise, usability testing investigates how people engage with the user interface, but leaves other elements that impact this engagement largely aside. These theories and methods overlook the complex sociomaterial entanglement the software becomes part of. In fact, as I argue, this arrange-ment very much decides how and whether or not a technology is taken up, partly overlooked or simply ignored. But let me discuss these insights one by one.

First of all, the analysis of how my informants work around the search function makes apparent that the perceived shortcomings or deficiencies of the intranet's search engine must be seen in the context of existing work routines in the respective work setting. That is, the sorting algorithm of the search function generating a long list of results as well as the constant up-date of the intranet do not occur in a vacuum, but in connection with specific ways of communicating in the office, both offline and online, and of turning to the functionality of the web browser as a central application. Thus, asking a colleague sitting next to oneself and getting immediate feedback to one's re-quest is a preferred way of searching for specific information on the intranet in the technicians' open plan office. Furthermore, writing emails back and forth with the respective link allows one to set up an email archive that may be consulted again later. In fact, this email archive was the most consequent form of disengagement with the search function, predominantly created by the technicians in the OSS department.

However, apart from shedding light on the communicative practices among my informants, these workarounds also highlight the material arrangement in the respective work setting that appears to be important; properties of the software, e.g. the browser completing a web page, but also the email archive, all play part and configure how work is done and how the intranet (dis-)integrates into the setting. But especially the technicians' open plan office and the regular routine of discussing properties of the intranet collectively was different from the offices I visited in the headquarters where people tended to work on their own. This became most obvious in the case of Stephanie, who described herself as the "Self-Admin-Fan", referring to the various standardised parts of the intranet that allow employees to process administrative work tasks individually. Looking at the physical setting of her workplace, I noted that she was not part of a lively, chatty environment, as was the case with the technicians. I also did not experience her asking a colleague in order to explain the most relevant applications on the intranet, as was done in the technicians' office. She only reported having asked her colleague about the facility management application on the intranet in order to do this on her own next time. Unlike the technicians, who mostly accessed applications through the web browser's address line, she was browsing through the intranet and was very much aware of how the intranet was structured.

In fact, while the technicians considered the intranet as working in the background, hence demanding a limited way of engagement, most of my informants coming from Customer Service seemed to at least enjoy working with some applications on the intranet. As I have already outlined in Chapter 4, in contrast to the technicians, who completely overlooked these activities, people with a background in Customer Service were more open to participating in the initiative to design one's own company logo or to adjusting the starting page and to defining the so-called 'quicklinks'. My informant Gloria, who initially also came from Customer Service, even made herself an advocate of the intranet and declared responsibility for its content by defending its maintenance as a demanding task. But Gloria's job also included putting together information on the company's sales activities on the intranet. Hence, whether or not parts of the intranet or specific applications are taken up also happens in relation to people's regular work tasks.

Such an approach was far from what I experienced in the technicians' office. Rather, as described, their workarounds underlined a strong resistance towards regularly engaging with the intranet and kept the intranet at a distance, that is, reduced the engagement to a minimum. But these differences must not be understood as a deliberate decision. As one of the technicians stated while going through a list of search results he generated: "That's what Walter [the team manager] actually said, when taking part [in the research], you incidentally also learn something about the intranet." While this quote tells us how my initial contact was trying to get his team members involved in my research and that my approach was indeed able to make the rather hidden uses of the intranet evident, it also shows that my informant is somewhat open to getting new insights about the intranet by participating in the research. Hence, the analysis of the various workarounds and his statement suggest that it is less a reflected, rational decision, but emerges from the existing work culture, that is, the communication and work practices, and the properties of the technology in connection with the perceived failure of the search function.

With regard to these observations, I want to suggest that 'preferences' are not only a matter of individual characteristics or technical features, but as well of the respective work setting. As outlined in the beginning, categories such as 'technology acceptance' rely on enquiring the 'perceived ease of use' as well as prospective users' attitudes towards a new technology. Thus, they proceed on the assumption that acceptance is located in the individual. This is similar to the development of personas in software programming that assume 'preferences' to be associated with the individual, somewhat existing independently from the context. Also, methods of usability testing focus exclusively on the individual interacting with the interface. As I argue, these concepts and methods overlook the existing complex sociomaterial entanglement of which the individual and the technology are a part, i.e. specific technologies and their properties, existing routines and the kind of work people attend to as part of specific work tasks. In fact, all these elements contribute to configuring the technology and its users. As a consequence, this research suggests to developers and researchers on information technologies to examine more closely the work settings and respective practices and to analyse the variety of elements that play part, such as people's routines as well as the technology at hand and the physical setting of the office.

These findings also question social-structural characteristics such as 'technology affinity', 'technophobe' or 'early adopters' as termed in innovation and diffusion theory for defining certain groups of people in order to forecast their engagement with a new technology. Comparing how the technicians work around the search function with how people with a background in Customer Service approach the search function (and the intranet more generally) has, perhaps surprisingly, shown that the technicians display a somewhat stable disengagement with the intranet. Resorting to socio-structural characteristics, they would probably be attributed an enthusiasm or at least openness towards new technologies. But when it comes to the search function in particular and the intranet in general, they keep their engagement to a minimum. In doing so, they also resist the normative objective in the company, which implies that employees should engage with the intranet on a regular basis, in particular concerning the reading of the newsfeed. But instead of attributing this disengagement exclusively to the individual, I want to emphasise again that this analysis suggests that we should think of characteristics as stemming from the respective work setting, the specific practices and the more general work culture that is apparently different in the technicians' OSS department from people with a background in Customer Service (cf. Shove et al., 2012: 12).

I also want to highlight that these insights question theories of technology adoption and diffusion in another manner: while these approaches tend to take into account the individual technology in the present, they mostly disregard how new and old technologies in fact overlap. Indeed, as the different workarounds show, as part of practices, new and old technologies such as email communication and web browser functionalities occur simultaneously and are less separated than innovations theory often frames them to be. Furthermore, assuming technologies and humans to be solid once and for all and ready to match in stable conditions is misleading; rather, how email communication is used to find and store information on the intranet, it makes evident that the array of technologies enables to adapt practices in the course of time and in relation to specific work tasks. That is, the example of the search function shows that implementing a new intranet means engaging with a possible future, but also present practices and related previous experiences that likewise interweave and configure a 'new' intranet.

This, in fact, becomes evident in the notion of "Google" and the "Google effect"; it has first of all called attention to the perceived deficiencies of the search function, but, in doing so, also highlighted the specific practices that allow employees to work around this function and hence has provided insight into how work is done in the settings I visited. Furthermore, the term "Google effect" has illustrated that "meanings and materialities are enacted together in everyday practice" (Orlikowski, 2010: 135) and the two do not, I want to add, exist on their own. But they are not somewhat stable once and for all, even though this chapter has perhaps nurtured the impression that well-established, already existing narratives and routines are somewhat stable and resist change. As one of my informants put it, handling a software or a particular application is also an emergent process that allows one to gradually "see what you want to see". That is, the transparency of a software or its intuitive accessibility, which are often described as criteria of quality in the literature and repeatedly mentioned in my interviews with software developers and programmers, are not simply given, but emerge in relation to the sociomaterial entanglement they are part of and hence (dis)-integrate into the work process (Suchman, 1997; see also Conrad, 2017: 21).

These observations stand in contrast to the literature that highlights one right way of handling a technology, initiated by its 'script', and that might be undermined by a workaround. But there is not just one abstract right track in handling a technology; it emerges in association with the work context and the respective work setting. Hence, the success of software is not only a question of system administration and maintenance, an issue often wrongfully underestimated, but also of learning and being accessible as part of work practices in different settings. This understanding, in fact, challenges the development and implementation of technologies and software applications because it emphasises that not alone one individual feature of the intranet's search function is decisive. As this work suggests, only by expanding our perspective in this manner may we begin to acknowledge the different aspects that make a workable technology.

7 Conclusion: More than a machine for doing business

This dissertation has set out to investigate managerial and work practices around corporate intranet technology that is, by now, self-evidently part of today's working world. As the introduction has outlined, intranets are a paradigmatic example for the one-sided praise of technologies; management literature and the consulting industry frames intranets as 'tools' that solve certain problems, but they nevertheless often fail to live up to these expectations. This has fostered the emergence of various case studies that investigate and further theorise how intranets are implemented and made use of (e.g. Clarke and Preece, 2005; Damsgaard and Scheepers, 2000; Martini et al., 2009; Neil and Richard, 2012; Ruppel and Harrington, 2001).

In addition, I have described the wider societal developments of the emergence of intranet technology and in particular of my case of the intranet; in fact, the post-industrial economy differs from industrialisation in the way it relies on forms of 'immaterial' labour that focus on the cultural-symbolic appreciation of goods and products, but also of work itself (Boltanski and Chiapello, 2005; Lazzarato, 2006). Especially knowledge work does not only rely on an increasing use of technologies, but on creating a symbolic value of work by addressing employees' affective attachments (cf. Reckwitz, 2020: 213). This is most often executed by means of culture management, in particular corporate and internal branding. These measures aim at exercising organisational control by determining and manipulating a company's culture and employees' identities, especially their subjective experiences, in order to install commitment and compliance (Costas and Kärreman, 2015). Overall, within the framework of the post-industrial economy, work is considered as an individual project that should be subjectively satisfying, providing people's individual fulfilment (cf. Bröckling, 2015; Lohr, 2003).

Against this backdrop, the dissertation has utilised the specific case of a company merger and the implementation of a new intranet in order to, first of all, illustrate the expectations towards the technology and, furthermore, investigate how the intranet is indeed part of everyday work in different settings of the company. Doing so, it has considered the intranet as configured by sociomaterial practices (cf. Suchman, 2012; Suchman et al., 1999; see also Orlikowski, 2007, 2010). Such a framework attends to the multiplicity of the intranet; that is, it investigates the different practices the intranet is part of, the accompanying narratives and logics, but also possible contradictions in the course of its implementation and utilisation.

Moreover, referring to theories of practice has been decisive also concerning the situation of the company merger; that is, analysing the intranet in the context of the merger has further refined the study's research framework and questions. Thus, I address not only questions about technology use and adoption, but also the ways in which the intranet is involved in the company's integration process. As outlined in the introduction, the perspective on practices resorts to a specific understanding of culture, namely one that does not only refer to 'immaterial' layers of meaning, but that includes the material dimension of social life (cf. Reckwitz, 2002a). Accordingly, my perspective on practices disengages from the predominant understanding in organisational studies that frames a company's culture as an all-encompassing system and, when it comes to merger processes, tends to differentiate groups of people in a homogenous fashion. Instead, the study has looked into the different practice-arrangements in the company that bring specific cultures about. As can be seen, this understanding of culture underlines the plural of organisational cultures and their possible divergences and tension (Knorr Cetina, 1999: 10–1). Furthermore, it encourages one to think about how connections are established in the post-merger company, especially in relation to the new intranet.

Altogether, the study has considered the case of the intranet as distinctive to today's post-industrial economy that centres the individual employee and his or her emotional commitment to the company. That is, the focus on the new company's brand as a connective fabric woven into the intranet disregards other conflicts in the company and instead emphasises the generation of a shared identity among employees. This is exemplary for approaching employees in the post-Fordist era: The brand is understood as an exclusive asset that awards the company a new identity, an identity employees are asked to identify with when taking part in training programmes, company events, internal competitions and promotion schemes (Reckwitz, 2017: 201 et seqq.; Kunda, 2006).

In this manner, this research has provided insight into the politics of intranet software, especially the informal practices surrounding intranet implementation and use (Winner, 1980; Kühl, 2011: 105). For instance, the analysis of how employees work around the search function and instead develop alternative strategies highlights how they continue using specific content without directly engaging with the intranet (cf. Büchner, 2018: 340). Likewise, I have shown how employees make use of the organigram and the directory in conjunction with other technologies in unintended ways so that meaningful communication in the company is possible. In so doing, the study has shed light on the "micropolitics" (Burns, 1961; see also Alt, 2005) in organisations; that is, the analysis of the intranet made apparent that power belongs not exclusively to upper management, but also to employees and the ways in which they enact the intranet as part of everyday work – and thereby (at least partly) reject the branding campaign (cf. Crozier and Friedberg, 1979; see also Kurz, 2012).

In the following, I discuss the implications of the study's main findings. I do so in relation to summarising the chapters and distil their contribution to the different academic debates. The implications concern (1.) the intranet and the *type of technology* it actually constitutes; I outline the reasons why the intranet is indeed worth researching, beyond merely examining use statistics. (2.) I highlight the study's main findings in relation to technology use and adoption; this concerns, first of all, *the intranet as an ambiguous carrier of practices of culture management, in particular internal and corporate branding.* (3.) the study also adds to thinking about *how technologies are integrated into workable configurations as part of contemporary 'mundane' knowledge work.* That is, it revises concepts such as technology acceptance and diffusion as well as the notion of usability by underlining the importance of the immediate work setting in which the intranet is put. In a nutshell, this study makes apparent that contemporary knowledge work relies not only on expert knowledge, but on knowledge emerging from the alignment of different technologies as part of coordinated mundane communication practices. The final section of this conclusion (4.) discusses the intranet as a designated 'change agent' or, as I frame it, a 'cultural integrator', thereby tackling the question *to what extent the intranet is indeed able to bring together the former two companies.*

7.1   The intranet: A 'multiple' technology by definition

One of the insights of this study concerns the *type of technology* the intranet actually constitutes; as I have outlined in the methodology chapter, in the beginning, my informants often stated that they do not use the intranet very much. In the course of my research, I found out that – despite my informants' possible intimidation by the research situation, as said – the statement also relates to the specific setup of the intranet. That is, the intranet is characterised by bringing together and enabling access to a great variety of applications and content, such as an input form for reporting a failure to Facility Management or for ordering a software program as well as it provides access to a messenger or simply shows the canteen's daily menu. In this manner, content and applications on the intranet slip into work practices which makes them rather unnoticeable to employees. Thus, as regards its setup, the intranet is not 'self-sufficient', it does not feature *one* specific identity among employees, but must be understood as a 'multiple' technology that provides access to various applications and content.[1]

Therefore, from the perspective of my informants, the intranet has a rather supportive character; that is, it enables employees to perform specific work tasks, but does not constitute employees' "actual work", as one of my informants put it. Hence, it has a predominantly ancillary character and rather runs in the background of employees' work. However, as the analysis has shown, despite this ancillary character, the intranet turned out to be central to my informants' work, in particular to their everyday communication practices. As a consequence, I argue that investigating the intranet brings necessarily to the forefront those work practices that are rather hidden and informal, often taken for granted and considered as self-evidently part of everyday work. For this reason, the study is also a call for further research into the diverse ways in which intranet technologies are involved in everyday work, beyond questions of internal communication and information distribution.

---

1   At this point, I refer to the notion of the 'multiple' not in the theoretic-methodological sense I have outlined in the methodology chapter (Mol, 2002), but to the actual manifoldness of the intranet being a platform that associates access to applications and content.

7.2   The intranet as an ambiguous carrier of internal and corporate branding practices

One of the central characteristics of the starting page concerned the different logics it assembles; that is, the starting page provides access to different applications and content such as the newsfeed, a messenger tool and the daily menu. But, as I have demonstrated, at the same time it also promotes measures of culture management in the form of corporate and internal branding which address employees' emotional commitment to the company. The application that allowed employees to design their own company logo, but also the starting page's newsfeed were relevant in this regard. But from the perspective of the employees I visited, these two layers of the intranet and the starting page contradicted each other. That is, one layer served employees to perform certain work tasks, therefore they entitled the intranet "a tool of purpose". In contrast, the other part of the intranet was considered the "mouthpiece of Internal Communications" as it featured especially measures of corporate cultural management, in particular content that promoted the new company brand. Employees associated with it the notion of 'play' because they considered this part as not relevant to their work. In fact, as I have underlined, they devaluated this part because it contradicted employees' understanding of work and the established distinction between work and leisure time.[2]

As a result, I have pointed out my informants' rather ambiguous relation to the intranet that was shaped by the different, indeed contradictory, layers. The ambiguity resulted from the fact that the starting page configured a user that, first of all, must be open to engaging with the branding content and hence considers this engagement as part of his or her work. Secondly, employees need time to do so. Both aspects did not match the reality of my informants. This, I have indicated, risks undermining the whole technology

---

2   This leads us to the question whether undermining this distinction is indeed useful from the perspective of strategic management. As Lucy Suchman and Libby Bishop (2000) point out, when it comes to the implementation of innovation and change projects, employee resistance may be understood as a "reasonable response[s]" (ibid.: 332) to such efforts. As they further underline, instead of investing in long-term programmes and joint activities, these projects often reinforce "existing organizational and economic orders" (ibid.: 331) and hence interfere with the potential for organisational transformation. Thus, from this point of view, defending the distinction may serve not just employees' interest, but possibly facilitates the company's successful performance in the long run.

as it is not clear what the technology actually 'is', so that the negative part of it may easily be put to the forefront. However, in the case of the intranet in Telecompany-X this was not the case since employees were simply able to overlook and indeed disregard this layer. To put it in other words, the 'script' of the starting page was 'open' or 'loose' enough so that it allowed employees to just concentrate on those applications they need for their daily work. In fact, even though the newsfeed features an archive that enables employees to read entries at a later stage, my findings suggest that the reading was constantly postponed, indicating again my informants' time constraints and related pressure they experience as part of their work.[3]

Altogether, the multiple character of the intranet turned out as likewise an advantage and disadvantage; that is, from the perspective of strategic management, the intranet seemed to not deliver expected results since content and applications featuring the corporate branding campaign were mostly overlooked and disregarded. In fact, staff members' limited engagement with this content indicates its failure to realise the reported managerial desire of company coherence. In contrast, as said above, the work-related part, that is, applications and content that assisted specific work processes such as looking up information on work procedures or staff members on the directory, indeed worked well and was considered relevant. This implies that the intranet's quality is less its deterministic character, but its loose 'availability structure', in particular of the starting page. In this way, the intranet offers access to multiple content and applications, thereby configuring the 'many' users. This is an advantage since these elements can – to a certain extent – be overlooked, as in the case of the branding campaign, e.g. the logo application, but also concerning the newsfeed.

Another insight concerns the different groups in the company that engaged indeed differently with the intranet. As I have explained, employees described the intranet as a means to an end – a "tool of purpose". This idea actually echoes the widespread understanding in business and communication management I have outlined in the introduction; it considers technologies as instruments that serve certain work processes, as in the quote of the intranet as "a machine for doing business" (Bayles Kalman, 2003: 684). This 'framework of instrumentality', as I have called it, apparently prevails so that

---

3   This idea resembles the notion of the "boundary object" (Star and Griesemer, 1989) which, because of its "weak structure", serves as an integrating device across different social groups.

attaching other purposes to the intranet – that of involving staff members into the branding campaign where the immediate contribution to one's work is not apparent – seems to fail.

Thus, when thinking about technologies, it may be useful to not only consider the determination of work processes, as mostly done in relation to software design and development, but also to reflect on the ways in which the technology is left open enough to engage the 'many' users. In fact, engaging the 'many' users also differs from personalising specific features on the intranet; as I learned, most of my informants did not even know about the personalising features of, for instance, the newsfeed since their disengagement with the intranet and the starting page started well before that. Rather, engaging the 'many' users also involves taking into account internal communication strategies and the overall working conditions, including employees' different 'frameworks of instrumentality' that may contradict management strategies.

For the time being, I want to further highlight that employees especially pointed out time constraints that prevented them from engaging with the starting page, in particular the newsfeed and the content of the branding campaign. Apparently, the conditions of work play a fairly big part for whether or not employees involve themselves in such a campaign, that is, use the applications and read the newsfeed and other types of content. This limitation was neither considered by company management nor Internal Communications; in fact, as mentioned, selected employees were involved in realising "the project intranet", as it was termed, but the overall implementation process did not include any investigation into employees' everyday work or the handling of the intranet.

As I have outlined above, authors in critical management studies point out that the focus on brands – which indeed is apparent in the branding campaign accompanying the merger – indicates a "hidden value system" (Müller, 2018: 59) where brands are rated superior to employees. My research on the intranet as a carrier of post-industrial management practices, in particular corporate and internal branding, suggests a similar orientation, one where employees' involvement and their interests are neglected, or at least subordinated.

7.3   The intranet as part of workable configurations in mundane knowledge work

The second part of my study has shown that the intranet is indeed part of the company's technological infrastructure and that specific applications work well and must be considered as central to staff members' everyday work. In the following, I am going to, first of all, describe the insights about contemporary knowledge work this study provides and, furthermore, illustrate how my research on the intranet also contributes to thinking about the implementation and integration of software technologies into existing work processes.

(a) The findings of this study suggest that contemporary knowledge work does not only involve expert knowledge, but knowledge emerging from 'mundane communication practices'. These practices rely on a sequence of activities which in my study foremost were email writing, telephone and mobile calling in connection with the intranet's corporate directory and organigram.

That is, the examination of the corporate directory and the organigram show that it is an array of different devices, a 'materiality-mix', which align one another into workable configurations. But these mediated 'mundane communication practices', as I call them, must not be considered as plain or trivial; as the focus on the notion of "communication work" ("Kommunikationsarbeit") (Knoblauch, 1996) has highlighted, the communicative capabilities employees have developed in relation to the different devices and applications – which they align in meaningful ways – are an integral part. Furthermore, while doing so, employees refer to and sustain existing principles, such as the departmental and hierarchical ordering, in the company.

These insights confirm earlier research on knowledge work that highlights the orientation towards technologies, or objects more generally, as characteristic of this type of work (Knorr Cetina, 2001, 1997). But while this research highlights the involvement of specific and individual objects in connection with academic expertise, my study shows that knowledge emerging from communication practices is (temporarily) shared with these rather mundane objects at the particular sites of work (e.g. Law, 2016: 350; Reckwitz, 2002a: 246; see also Mol, 2002). Moreover, my study also underlines that today's 'mundane' knowledge work, understood as communication work, especially involves employees to contextualise and interpret the information they receive and deal with, as the case of the exchange of messages in relation to the directory and organigram makes apparent (cf. Schulz-Schaeffer and Funken, 2008: 18). In fact, my research on the intranet and related work processes confirms that communication work, that is, dealing with and evaluating communication, constitutes a great deal of contemporary technologically mediated work (Wajcman and Rose, 2011: 944).

However, even though earlier studies found that employees apply strategies that negotiate their availability (Wajcman and Rose, 2011: 956), this study underlines the density of this type of work. That is, the ways in which employees have to contextualise and interpret messages by recognising another employee and identifying him or her as part of the organisation through the directory and organigram emphasises that technology-mediated communication work is a time-consuming and dense endeavour. It not only relies on well-aligned sequences of activities, but, as I experienced, also puts time pressure on employees. My informants did not feel able to read the newsfeed because of the time pressure they experienced. This was also not made up by the archive function since, as reported, it allowed employees to constantly postpone the reading. In fact, employees' time pressure actually pervaded almost all chapters of this study in one way or another.

Even though the analysis has described the use of the organigram and the directory not in terms of simply supplementing the 'original' encounter, but as a set of sociomaterial practices in their own right, I want to underline that, similar to Goffman, my informants apparently understand the offline, fact-to-face encounter with their colleagues as the 'original' social situation. That is, even though they deal with an array of different technologies on an everyday basis, the immediate exchange with colleagues still appears as most natural to them. It would be worth investigating whether nowadays this is still the case and to what extent this focus may have changed in the course of time and in relation to the implementation of new applications.

(b) Another insight from my study indicates that when it comes to technology implementation and adoption, we need to consider the immediate work setting. That is, existing routines and already present technological devices are important for understanding how technologies (dis-)integrate into the work process. This idea questions concepts that solely focus on the 'matching' of individual technologies with distinct users.

As illustrated, the phrase "our internal Google" was an expression used by employees to describe the intranet's search function that often featured too many results they were unable to identify. But while the notion of Google, at first glance, indicated to me a technological problem – that has to be solved by changing the search engine, its index, and the presentation of search results –, my investigation into how employees were used to *work around* the search function made apparent that it is a conglomerate of existing work routines, the physical setting of the office and the involved devices and applications that indeed contribute to its dis-use. Just to recall, in the technicians' office, my informants tended to save links in the browser, respectively the bookmarks menu, and to send back and forth emails that featured the relevant links to a website on the intranet. In doing so, they set up an archive in their email account which they could easily access when needed. Another way to circumvent the search function related to the local work culture among the technicians; they were used to a rather chatty atmosphere and hence preferred to involve a colleague nearby for answering a request.

These findings indicate once more the sociomaterial arrangement of existing routines and technological devices and applications that are important in contemporary 'mundane' knowledge work; properties of the software, for example the browser completing a web page, but also the email account and its archival function, all play part and configure how the intranet's search function (dis-)integrates into employees' work. In fact, the technicians' open plan office and the regular routine of collectively discussing properties of the intranet differed from some of the offices of employees with a background in Customer Service I visited in the headquarters. In these settings, employees tended to work on their own and they were more open to engaging, for example, with the self-service part of the intranet, such as reporting a failure to Facility Management or designing one's individual company logo. These insights confirm earlier research in the realm of theories of practice that has highlighted the materiality of the office for understanding the work that is happening there (e.g. Schmidt, 2008: 290; Conrad and Richter, 2013; see also Elsbach and Bechky, 2007). But they go beyond existing research as these insights underline the connections between office design, technology use, in particular of specific applications and functionalities, and work routines.

Altogether, my study shows that technologies and devices considered as 'old' and 'new' may overlap in unpredicted ways and thereby shape how one technology is taken up or rejected.[4] Thus, when it comes to the conceptualisation of software technologies and how they are appropriated, this research

---

4   This research locates the digitalisation of work within the interplay of these ‚old‘ and ‚new‘, increasingly digitalised technologies (Schulz-Schaeffer and Funken, 2008: 15).

shows that the quality of a technology does not only relate to its particular features, but emerges in relation to other technologies that are involved in the respective work setting. Likewise, the preferences of the individual must not be ascribed to the user only, but are also shaped by the same sociomaterial practices, that is, an array of technologies and possibly other involved materialities in connection with the specific work tasks and the local work culture.

Consequently, concepts such as technology acceptance (e.g. Davis, 1993; Burton-Jones and Hubona, 2005) and diffusion (e.g. Cooper and Zmud, 1990) that take into account the distinct user and the individual technology are insufficient as they overlook the specific characteristics that emerge from its situated use. For instance, one would consider the group of technicians I investigated as particularly open to new technologies, but they showed only little engagement with the intranet and even made fun of other measures of culture management existing in the company. In contrast, people with a background in Customer Service were more open, for instance, to design their own company logo. As illustrated, the differences in employees' engagement, respectively their rejection of the branding campaign, related to the setting of work and, it can be assumed, also to their previous training as agents in the call centre. Furthermore, as I experienced, communicating the different company products and brands constituted their daily business. Therefore, I argue that categories describing certain types of users such as 'technophobe' or 'technophile' must be treated with caution since they wrongly imply a solidity of preferences, independent from the situated and material setting of use and the involved practices there.

In a similar manner, the notion of usability aims at a successful 'match' between users and the respective technology, as described in Chapter 6, hence it rests on the assumption that both are somewhat stable entities that may be investigated in the isolated situation of usability testing (cf. Orlikowski, 2007, 2010). Such a perspective does not acknowledge how, for instance, the web browser and the routine of saving links in the bookmarks menu may indeed shape one's (dis-)interest in the search function. The present investigation also adds to research in STS, in particular to the notion of "script" (Akrich, 1994: 208) as analytical framework that rightly underlines how technologies limit the scope of users' possible actions, but that nevertheless assumes a somewhat stable 'message' or 'reading' of a technology (cf. Latour, 1994: 31; Woolgar, 1991: 70–1). Rather, my study suggests that the reading is precarious, an emergent one, as well as the technologies' 'message' must be understood as rather uncertain. Against this backdrop, the 'usability' of a software or technology is not a quality of the individual technology only, but possibly linked to other technologies and existing work routines which also involves the setting, i.e. the physical office, where it is being used.

From this follows that categories that evaluate software technologies such as the transparency or intuition of a software may not necessarily be universally applied, but must be developed in relation to the settings of use (Conrad, 2017). The example of the search function shows that implementing a new intranet means engaging with a possible future through moments of learning, as actually done in usability testing, but also with present practices and previous experiences that likewise interweave and configure the 'new' intranet.

7.4   Coming together while staying apart? The intranet as a 'cultural integrator' for (dis-)connected organisations

The literature describes business mergers as demanding endeavours, often leading to post-merger conflicts so that mergers and acquisitions frequently fail to deliver expected results, such as company efficiency or an increasing company value on the market (Cartwright and Schoenberg, 2006; Kansal and Chandani, 2014). When it comes to understanding post-merger conflicts, the duration of merger integration processes, the strategic or organisational fit between merging business as well as cultural differences have been described as decisive factors, amongst others (e.g. Buono and Bowditch, 2003; Datta, 1991; Oh and Johnston, 2020). Outlining a rather hesitant attitude towards the unquestioned use of the notion of 'cultural difference' in merger research, I responded to the call for a further incorporation of cultural theories into research on mergers by introducing the focus on practices as an alternative and more specific account on the concept of culture in organisation studies (Angwin and Vaara, 2005: 1448). As emphasised above and outlined in the introduction, a perspective on sociomaterial practices allows the researcher to analyse the different practice-arrangements in the post-merger company and to acknowledge possible fractions across these groups.

Following this agenda, I have analysed employees' different strategies of making sense of the merger which I recognised all as forms of identity work. As outlined, the notion of identity work describes employees' ongoing involvement in discussions and activities about who they are as part of the organisation they work for and identify with (Alvesson and Willmott, 2002: 626;

Langley et al., 2012: 138). My informants' sensemaking practices encompassed 'upholding', but also 'overlooking' and 'downplaying' the former two companies' differences. As I have pointed out, they echo the managerial desire of company coherence in the way they either resist that prescription or tend to ignore and try to distance themselves from it. Accordingly, this study confirms the observation that increasing identity work often results from "managerial identity regulation" (Alvesson and Willmott, 2002: 637), that is, from the pressure to take over another company's or an overall new identity.

Following this literature, I have described employees' strong advocacy for the former corporate values and culture at the time of the merger (i.e. one year ahead of my research) as making apparent the *previous* identity work and managerial regulation in both companies, especially in the former mobile division that was reportedly organised as a 'start up' business. According to employees, this manifested itself in different work routines and distinct clothing, but also an overall different attitude towards work. Secondly, in relation to the three practices of upholding, overlooking and downplaying the former companies' differences at the time of my research, I presented the perceived problem in the post-merger company, namely the still apparent (cultural) difference of the former two companies. Thirdly, I introduced company management's solution, namely Internal Communications' corporate branding campaign, especially the implementation of the new company brand and logo. I understand this campaign and related events as a form of managerial identity regulation that aimed to gather employees around the new company brand in order to initiate company coherence after the merger.

Even though company management has defined the former companies' differences as a problem, I have tried to describe how post-merger identity work may be integrated by emphasising the ways in which the new company is necessarily permeated by references to the two former companies, which relates, obviously, to their former products and services that were now processed in the same company. But instead of involving itself in reported conflicts, it seems that company management rather withdrew from its engagement and instead put emphasis on the branding campaign. As I have underlined, when it comes to research on identity change in organisations, ambiguity is described as a necessary step in this process which was somewhat prohibited by company management in Telecompany-X.

As described above, the intranet was considered as one of the significant parts in the corporate branding campaign, but the involvement of employees into the campaign on the intranet rather failed. Nevertheless, my findings suggest different degrees of (dis-) engagement, as described in relation to the technicians and employees with a background in Customer Service. Also, I obviously did not investigate the full picture of the campaign which included other events and advertisements, not only on the intranet, but on posters in hallways and in the employee magazine. I can only assume that this might also have contributed to employees' identification with the new company.

However, my observation in the technicians' group suggests that identification rather happens on the level of work cooperation and in relation to employees' immediate work setting. This, for instance, became apparent in the ways in which they made fun of team building efforts. In contrast, employees with a background in Customer Service were more open to engage with the branding campaign on the intranet. Overall, the preference of work-related content that all employees actually displayed underlines their focus on everyday work as a potential for identification. This finding implies that employees first and foremost identify with their work and, as became particularly apparent in relation to the technicians, their immediate working community. In fact, this insight confirms earlier research in the framework of theories of practices that emphasise the local communities to be decisive when it comes to employee identification and shared work cultures (Brown and Duguid, 2001: 202; see also Lave and Wenger, 1991).

Furthermore, as my research has shown, while enabling work collaboration in the various ways outlined in the previous chapters, the intranet indeed connects employees on the level of work collaboration. In addition, the directory and especially the organigram have been described by participants as at least providing a feeling for the company in the way both applications enabled employees to locate and recognise colleagues as part of the whole of the company. In this regard, one may indeed consider the intranet as providing a *sense of togetherness* – not in the manner as expected by the management, but as part of the ongoing work. Certainly, organigram applications are nowadays part of most company websites, but in the case of Telecompany-X, it is used in rather unintended ways. In fact, this usage stands in contrast to the culture management efforts, in particular the internal corporate branding campaign that intends to provide a sense of the new company and hence unify the company, but fails to do so – at least when it comes to the described disregard of this content on the starting page.

It is not surprising that the implementation of a technological device is not enough for inducing organisational change; rather, as I have just said, specific applications are used in ways not intended by the management and thereby possibly maintain existing orders. That is, as illuminated, organisational hierarchies have been part of the differentiating narrative of former mobile-employees that aimed to distinguish 'their' former business from the bureaucratic landline division. But the hierarchical and departmental structuring of the company again played a part when using the directory and organigram; in fact, in this context, these two ways of classifying employees turned out as *connecting principles* across the organisation that allowed employees to locate and recognise, that is, identify, unfamiliar employees in the company.

In fact, the continuous reference to company hierarchies stands in contrast to current ideas and trends in management literature and consultancy that emphasise flat hierarchies and competence-based work structures. For instance, the notion of "holacracy" calls for organisational structures that are built around collective decision making and role-specific work tasks with the aim of engaging employees in the management of the company and increasing their empowerment (Robertson, 2015). While this approach may align with the above-described work conditions in the post-industrial economy (cf. Daum, 2021: 39), one may nevertheless ask in relation to this study whether orienting towards organisational hierarchies also occurs as part of other work practices in Telecompany-X and, overall, whether this principle is typical for former, partially state-owned companies? Moreover, further research may take a temporal perspective by interrogating whether such an orientation changes over time.

Against this backdrop, one may question the campaign of the "Einfach Macher" that aimed to address employees beyond company hierarchies and the departmental structure by emphasising a hands-on work attitude which, in fact, may rather be associated with the former mobile division. In addition, as scholars in critical management studies have highlighted, the artificial construction of branding messages may stir up employee resistance, as in the case of the technicians (Cushen, 2009: 111; Müller, 2018: 45). Indeed, employees in Telecompany-X were confronted with the conflicting situation of being asked to eliminate old advertising and merchandising products while the new brand and company identity were promoted across the company. Following this incident, employees from the former landline business expressed their disagreement by wearing branded clothes of the company to which they previously belonged. In fact, these observations cast doubt on the integrating capacity of the overall branding campaign and call into question for whom the "Einfach Macher" is relevant and who indeed engages in such an endeavour.

Altogether, the efforts of corporate culture management were intended to create a somewhat homogenous group of employees that attend to their work in a similar fashion. But, as stated, such an approach actually misses the fact that difference is also relevant for expertise and processes of innovation. That is, local research communities and the know-how developed there are valuable for the company and risks being erased by a strong focus on branding as a way of initiating commitment to the company. Therefore, I have argued that differences in the company must not only be considered as problematic but can be seen as *shared points of reference* that are constitutive for the coordination of work in the new, post-merger organisation. Obviously, the new company is permeated by various traces of the two previous businesses in the form of distinct knowledge and forms of collaboration, different software applications and related work processes. Furthermore, the company now sells products and services of both, the green and the black world; thus, referring to the two previous businesses can also be understood as a pragmatic way of dealing with the new company and of referring to the respective areas of expertise, as my observations in particular in the call centre made apparent.

In addition, I have also suggested that these shared points of reference may serve as a starting point for a discussion of working conditions and how work should be done in the new company. They may assist in figuring out the advantages and disadvantages of certain work routines and forms of collabo-ration. In fact, this understanding leans on the idea of the so-called "Integra-tion Paradox" by Aladin El-Mafaalani (2018); describing the integration of im-migrants into German society, he underlines that integration processes need not necessarily proceed silently, but may be conflict-laden. In fact, he claims that conflicts actually indicate successful integration since, broadly speaking, people ask for their participation in society. Thinking of conflict in terms of participation allows one to see differences and conflicts in the company not only as obstacle. Obviously, a company that only engages in conflicts would not be able to survive, but the idea of participation brings us back to thinking about working conditions, forms of employee participation and the ways in which both, company management and employees, may be engaged in the merger.

As this research suggests, promoting the new company brand is not enough for a fruitful exchange or conversation between management and employees; in fact, the problem in relation to how people approached each other differently was not just that these incidents created confusion among employees. In fact, the problem was that the company's management took so long to intervene. Thus, perhaps surprisingly, this research questions the intranet as a (partial) carrier of managerial practices and instead underlines the importance of deliberate involvement by company management in the merger, in particular for configuring the integration process.

Bibliography

Adams, D.A., Nelson, R.R. and Todd, P.A. (1992) 'Perceived Usefulness, Ease of Use, and Usage of Information Technology: A Replication', *MIS Quarterly* 16(2): 227–47.

Akrich, M. (1994) 'The De-Scription of Technical Objects', pp. 205–24 in Bijker, W.E. and Law, J. (eds.), *Shaping Technology / Building Society: Studies in Sociotechnical Change*. Cambridge, Mass.: The MIT Press.

Alt, R. (2005) 'Mikropolitik', pp. 295–328 in Weik, E. and Lang, R. (eds.), *Moderne Organisationstheorien 1: Handlungsorientierte Ansätze*. Wiesbaden: Gabler Verlag.

Alter, S. (2014) 'Theory of Workarounds', *Communications of the Association for Information Systems* 34(55): 1041–66.

Alvesson, M., Ashcraft, K.L. and Thomas, R. (2008) 'Identity Matters: Reflections on the Construction of Identity Scholarship in Organization Studies', *Organization* 15(1): 5–28.

Alvesson, M. and Willmott, H. (2002) 'Identity Regulation as Organizational Control: Producing the Appropriate Individual', *Journal of Management Studies* 39(5): 619–44.

Amcoff Nyström, C. (2006) 'Design Rules for Intranets According to the Viable System Model', *Systemic Practice and Action Research* 19: 523–35.

Angwin, D. and Vaara, E. (2005) 'Introduction to the Special Issue "Connectivity" in Merging Organizations: Beyond Traditional Cultural Perspectives', *Organization Studies* 26(10): 1445–53.

Arvidsson, A. (2005a) 'Brands: A Critical Perspective', *Journal of Consumer Culture* 5(2): 235–58.

Arvidsson, A. (2005b) *Brands: Meaning and Value in Media Culture*. London; New York: Routledge.

Ayatollahi, H., Peter, A.B. and Goodacre, S. (2010) 'Factors Influencing the Use of IT in the Emergency Department: A Qualitative Study', *Health Informatics Journal* 16(3): 189–200.

Bahrs, J. (2009) 'Enterprise Search – Suchmaschinen für Inhalte im Unternehmen', pp. 329–55 in Lewandowski, D. (ed.), *Handbuch Internet-Suchmaschinen: Nutzerorientierung in Wissenschaft und Praxis*. Heidelberg: AKA, Akademische Verlagsgesellschaft.

Bahrs, J., Meutrath, B. and Peters, K. (2008) 'Selbstlernende Suchmaschine als zentraler Informationszugang bei heterogener Informationslandschaft', pp. 365–371 in Hegering, H.-G., Lehmann, A., Ohlbach, H.J. and Scheideler, C. (eds.), *INFORMATIK 2008. Beherrschbare Systeme – dank Informatik*. Volume 1. Bonn: Gesellschaft für Informatik e.V.

Balle, N. (2008) 'Hearts at Stake: A Theoretical and Practical Look at Communication in Connection with Mergers and Acquisitions', *Corporate Communications: An International Journal* 13(1): 56–67.

Barley, S.R. (1983) 'Semiotics and the Study of Occupational and Organizational Cultures', *Administrative Science Quarterly* 28(3): 393–413.

Barley, S.R. (1986) 'Technology as an Occasion for Structuring: Evidence from Observations of CT Scanners and the Social Order of Radiology Departments', *Administrative Science Quarterly* 31(1): 78–108.

Barley, S.R. and Kunda, K. (1992) 'Design and Devotion: Surges of Rational and Normative Ideologies of Control in Managerial Discourse', *Administrative Science Quarterly* 37(3): 363–99.

Barrett, M., Grant, D. and Wailes, N. (2006) 'ICT and Organizational Change: Introduction to the Special Issue', *The Journal of Applied Behavioral Science* 42(1): 6–22.

Bateson, G. (2000) *Steps to an Ecology of Mind: Collected Essays in Anthropology, Psychiatry, Evolution, and Epistemology*. Chicago: University of Chicago Press.

Bauman, Z. (1993) *Modernity and Ambivalence*. Cambridge: Polity Press.

Bayles Kalman, D. (2003) 'Intranets', *Encyclopedia of Information Systems* 2: 683–92.

Beal, G.M. and Bohlen, J.M. (1981) *The Diffusion Process*. Special Report 24. Ames, Iowa: Agricultural Experiment Station, Iowa State College.

Bechky, B.A. (2003) 'Sharing Meaning Across Occupational Communities: The Transformation of Understanding on a Production Floor', *Organization Science* 14(3): 312–30.

Beck, K., et al. (2001) The Agile Manifesto. Agile Alliance. URL: http://agilema nifesto.org/ (last accessed 25.02.2021).

Becke, G. (2017) 'The Subjectivation of Work and Established-Outsider Figurations', *Historical Social Research* 42(4): 93–113.

Becker, H.S. (1995) 'The Power of Inertia', *Qualitative Sociology* 18(3): 301–9.

Bell, D. (1976) *The Coming Of Post-Industrial Society*. New York: Basic Books.

Beverungen, A., Beyes, T. and Conrad, L. (2019) 'The Organizational Powers of (Digital) Media', *Organization* 26(5): 621–35.

Boltanski, L. and Chiapello, E. (2005) 'The New Spirit of Capitalism', *International Journal of Politics, Culture, and Society* 18(3–4): 161–88.

Bourdieu, P. (1977) *Outline of a Theory of Practice*. Cambridge; New York: Cambridge University Press.

Bröckling, U. (2015) *The Entrepreneurial Self: Fabricating a New Type of Subject*. London: Sage.

Brown, A.D. (2019) 'Identities in Organization Studies', *Organization Studies* 40(1): 7–22.

Brown, J.S. and Duguid, P. (2001) 'Knowledge and Organization: A Social-Practice Perspective', *Organization Science* 12(2): 198–213.

Bruni, A. (2005) 'Shadowing Software and Clinical Records: On the Ethnography of Non-Humans and Heterogeneous Contexts', *Organization* 12(3): 357–78.

Büchner, S. (2018) 'Zum Verhältnis von Digitalisierung und Organisation', *Zeitschrift für Soziologie* 47(5): 332–48.

Buick, F., Blackman, D. and Johnson, S. (2018) 'Enabling Middle Managers as Change Agents: Why Organisational Support Needs to Change', *Australian Journal of Public Administration* 77(2): 222–35.

Buono, A.F. and Bowditch, J.L. (2003) *The Human Side of Mergers and Acquisitions: Managing Collisions Between People, Cultures, and Organizations*. Beard Books.

Burmann, C. and Zeplin, S. (2005) 'Building Brand Commitment: A Behavioural Approach to Internal Brand Management', *Journal of Brand Management* 12(4): 279–300.

Burns, T. (1961) 'Micropolitics: Mechanisms of Institutional Change', *Administrative Science Quarterly* 6(3): 257–81.

Burton-Jones, A. and Hubona, G.S. (2005) 'Individual Differences and Usage Behavior: Revisiting a Technology Acceptance Model Assumption', *SIGMIS Database for Avances in Information Systems* 36(2): 58–77.

Callaghan, J. (2002) *Inside Intranets & Extranets: Knowledge Management and the Struggle for Power*. Palgrave Macmillan.

Cardon, P.W. (2016) 'Community, Culture, and Affordances in Social Collaboration and Communication', *International Journal of Business Communication* 53(2): 141–7.

Cardon, P.W. and Marshall, B. (2015) 'The Hype and Reality of Social Media Use for Work Collaboration and Team Communication', *International Journal of Business Communication* 52(3): 273–93.

Carroll, J. (2003) *HCI Models, Theories, and Frameworks. Toward a Multidisciplinary Science.* Amsterdam: Elsevier.

Carstensen, P.H. and Schmidt, K. (1999) 'Computer Supported Cooperative Work: New Challenges to Systems Design', pp. 619–36 in Itoh, K. (ed.), *Handbook of Human Factors.* Asakura Publishing.

Cartwright, S. and Schoenberg, R. (2006) 'Thirty Years of Mergers and Acquisitions Research: Recent Advances and Future Opportunities', *British Journal of Management* 17(S1): S1–5.

Castells, M. (2003) *The Internet Galaxy: Reflections on the Internet, Business, and Society.* Oxford; New York: Oxford University Press.

Cecez-Kecmanovic, D., Galliers, R., Henfridsson, O., Newell, S. and Vidgen, R. (2014) 'The Sociomateriality of Information Systems: Current Status, Future Directions', *Management Information Systems Quarterly* 38(3): 809–30.

Clark, S.M., Gioia, D.A., Ketchen, D.J. and Thomas, J.B. (2010) 'Transitional Identity as a Facilitator of Organizational Identity Change during a Merger', *Administrative Science Quarterly* 55(3): 397–438.

Clarke, A. (2005) *Situational Analysis: Grounded Theory After the Postmodern Turn.* Thousand Oaks, Calif.: Sage.

Clarke, K. and Preece, D. (2005) 'Constructing and Using a Company Intranet: "It's a Very Cultural Thing"', *New Technology, Work and Employment* 20(2): 150–65.

Clash, J.I., Eccles, R.G., Nohria, N. and Nolan, R. (1994) *Building the Information-Age Organization: Structure, Control, and Information Technologies.* Irwin: Case Book Series in Information Systems Management.

Clemmensen, T., Hertzum, M., Hornbaek, K., Shi, Q. and Yammaiyavar, P. (2009) 'Cultural Cognition in Usability Evaluation', *Interacting with Computers* 21(3): 212–20.

Conrad, L. (2017) *Organisation im soziotechnischen Gemenge - Mediale Umschichtungen durch die Einführung von SAP.* Bielefeld: transcript.

Conrad, L. and Richter, N. (2013) 'Materiality at Work: A Note on Desks', *Ephemera: Theory & Politics in Organization* 13(1): 117–36.

Cooper, R. and Law, J. (1995) 'Organization: Distal and Proximal Views', pp. 237–74 in Bacharach, S.B. (ed.), *Research in the Sociology of Organizations: Studies of Organizations in the European Tradition.* Greenwich, Conn.: Jai Press.

Cooper, R.B. and Zmud, R.W. (1990) 'Information Technology Implementation Research: A Technological Diffusion Approach', *Management Science* 36(2): 123–39.

Corley, K.G. and Gioia, D.A. (2004) 'Identity Ambiguity and Change in the Wake of a Corporate Spin-Off', *Administrative Science Quarterly* 49(2): 173–208.

Costas, J. and Kärreman, D. (2015) 'The Bored Self in Knowledge Work', *Human Relations* 69(1): 61–83.

Crozier, M. and Friedberg, E. (1979) *Die Zwänge Kollektiven Handelns. Über Macht und Organisation.* Sozialwissenschaft und Praxis 3. Königstein: Athenäum-Verlag.

Cushen, J. (2009) 'Branding Employees', *Qualitative Research in Accounting & Management* 6(1/2): 102–14.

Damsgaard, J. and Scheepers, R. (2000) 'Managing the Crises in Intranet Implementation: A Stage Model', *Information Systems Journal* 10(2): 131–49.

Datta, D.K. (1991) 'Organizational Fit and Acquisition Performance: Effects of Post-Acquisition Integration', *Strategic Management Journal* 12(4): 281–97.

Daum, T. (2021) 'Das Agilitäts-Dispositiv. Die Coder-Klasse zwischen Selbstermächtigung und digitalem Taylorismus'. *Berliner Debatte Initial* 32(3): 31-40.

Davies, A.R. and Frink, B.D. (2014) 'The Origins of the Ideal Worker: The Separation of Work and Home in the United States From the Market Revolution to 1950', *Work and Occupations* 41(1): 18–39.

Davis, F.D. (1993) 'User Acceptance of Information Technology: System Characteristics, User Perceptions and Behavioral Impacts', *International Journal of Man-Machine Studies* 38(3): 475–87.

Debono, D., Greenfield, D., Black, D. and Braithwaite, J. (2012) 'Achieving and Resisting Change: Workarounds Straddling and Widening Gaps in Health Care', pp. 177–92 in Dickinson, H. and Mannion, R. (eds.), *The Reform of Health Care. Organizational Behaviour in Health Care Series.* London: Palgrave Macmillan.

de Wit, O., van den Ende, J., Schot, J. and van Oost, E. (2002) 'Innovation Junctions: Office Technologies in the Netherlands, 1880-1980', *Technology and Culture* 43(1): 50–72.

Dillon, A. (2001) 'User Acceptance of Information Technology', in Karwowski, W. (ed.), *Encyclopedia of Human Factors and Ergonomics*. London: Taylor and Francis.

Dörfel, L. and Hirsch, L. (2012) *Social Intranet 2012: Studienergebnisse, Fachbeiträge und Experteninterviews*. Berlin: prismus communications GmbH.

Drucker, P. (2012) *Managing in the Next Society*. London: Routledge.

Einspänner-Pflock, J. and Reichmann, D.W. (2014) '"Digitale Sozialität" und die "synthetische Situation" – Konzeptionen mediatisierter Interaktion', pp. 53–72 in Krotz, F., Despotović, C. and Kruse, M.M. (eds.), *Die Mediatisierung sozialer Welten*. Wiesbaden: Springer Verlag.

El-Mafaalani, A. (2018) *Das Integrationsparadox* (Sonderausgabe für die Bundeszentrale für Politische Bildung.) Bonn: Bundeszentrale für Politische Bildung.

Elsbach, K.D. and Bechky, B.A. (2007) 'It's More Than a Desk: Working Smarter through Leveraged Office Design', *California Management Review* 49(2): 80–101.

Emerson, R.M., Fretz, R.I. and Shaw, L.L. (1995) *Writing Ethnographic Fieldnotes*. Chicago: University of Chicago Press.

Farhoomand, A. (2007) 'Opening up of the Software Industry: The Case of SAP', pp. 1–8 in *Eighth World Congress on the Management of EBusiness*. Communications of the Association for Information Systems.

Farquhar, L. (2013) 'Performing and Interpreting Identity through Facebook Imagery', *Convergence* 19(4): 446–71.

Feldman, M.S., Bell, J. and Berger, M. (2004) *Gaining Access: A Practical and Theoretical Guide for Qualitative Researchers*. Rowman Altamira.

Feldman, M.S. and Orlikowski, W.J. (2011) 'Theorizing Practice and Practicing Theory', *Organization Science* 22(5): 1240–53.

Fenton, C. and Langley, A. (2011) 'Strategy as Practice and the Narrative Turn', *Organization Studies* 32(9): 1171–96.

Flecker, J. (2017) *Arbeit und Beschäftigung: Eine soziologische Einführung*. Wien: Facultas.

Ford, J.D., Ford, L.W. and D'Amelio, A. (2008) 'Resistance to Change: The Rest of the Story', *Academy of Management Review* 33(2): 362-377.

Ford, M.W. and Greer, B.M. (2016) 'Profiling Change: An Empirical Study of Change Process Patterns', *The Journal of Applied Behavioral Science* 42(4): 420–46.

Froschauer, U. (2012) *Organisationen in Bewegung. Beiträge zur interpretativen Organisationsanalyse*. Wien: Facultas.

Garfinkel, H. (1967) *Studies in Ethnomethodology*. Englewood Cliffs, NJ: Prentice-Hall.

Gerlitz, C. (2012) *Brands and Continuous Economies*. London: Goldsmiths College, University of London. Dissertation.

Gerlitz, C. and Helmond, A. (2013) 'The like Economy: Social Buttons and the Data-Intensive Web', *New Media & Society* 15(8): 1348–65.

Gershuny, J. (2001) 'Changing Times: Work and Leisure in Postindustrial Society'. Oxford; New York: Oxford University Press.

Gherardi, S. (2012) *Learning and Knowing in Practice-Based Studies*. Cheltenham, U.K.; Northampton, Mass.: Edward Elgar Publishing.

Giddens, A. (1986) *The Constitution of Society: Outline of the Theory of Structuration*. University of California Press.

Glaser, B.G. and Strauss, A.L. (2009) *The Discovery of Grounded Theory: Strategies for Qualitative Research*. Transaction Publishers.

Goffman, E. (1956) 'Embarrassment and Social Organization', *American Journal of Sociology* 62(3): 264–71.

Goffman, E. (1983) 'The Interaction Order: American Sociological Association, 1982 Presidential Address', *American Sociological Review* 48(1): 1–17.

Goll, M. (2008) 'Arbeitsbeziehungen und Beziehungsarbeiten: Zur Gestaltung arbeitsbezogener und informeller Nachrichten in Unternehmen', pp. 143–64 in Schulz-Schaeffer, I. and Funken, C. (eds.), *Digitalisierung der Arbeitswelt*. Wiesbaden: VS Verlag für Sozialwissenschaften.

Gould, J.D. and Lewis, C. (1985) 'Designing for Usability: Key Principles and What Designers Think', *Communication ACM* 28(3): 300–11.

Haleblian, J., Devers, C.E., McNamara, G., Carpenter, M.A. and Davison, R.B. (2009) 'Taking Stock of What We Know About Mergers and Acquisitions: A Review and Research Agenda', *Journal of Management* 35(3): 469–502.

Henriksen, D. (2002) 'Locating Virtual Field Sites and a Dispersed Object of Research', *Scandinavian Journal of Information Systems* 14(2): 31–45.

Heppner, R.S. (2013) 'The Ideal Worker', pp. 75–91 in Heppner, R.S. (ed.), *The Lost Leaders: How Corporate America Loses Women Leaders*. New York: Palgrave Macmillan.

Heracleous, L. and Barrett, M. (2001) 'Organizational Change as Discourse: Communicative Actions and Deep Structures in the Context of Information Technology Implementation', *Academy of Management Journal* 44(4): 755–78.

Hine, C. (2007) 'Multi-Sited Ethnography as a Middle Range Methodology for Contemporary STS', *Science, Technology & Human Values* 32(6): 652–71.

Hirsch, E. and Silverstone, R. (1994) *Consuming Technologies: Media and Information in Domestic Spaces*. London: Routledge.

Hirschauer, S. (2001) 'Ethnografisches Schreiben und die Schweigsamkeit des Sozialen. Zu einer Methodologie der Beschreibung', *Zeitschrift für Soziologie* 30(6): 429–51.

Hirschauer, S., Hoffmann, A. and Stange, A. (2015) 'Paarinterviews als teilnehmende Beobachtung. Präsente Abwesende und zuschauende DarstellerInnen im Forschungsgespräch', *Forum Qualitative Sozialforschung / Forum Qualitative Social Research* 16(3). URL: https://doi.org/10.17169/fqs-16.3.2357 (last accessed 10.07.2018).

Hughes, J., Randall, D. and Shapiro, D. (1991) 'CSCW: Discipline or Paradigm? A Sociological Perspective', pp. 309–23 in Bannon, L., Robinson, M. and Schmidt, K. (eds.) *Proceedings of the Second European Conference on Computer-Supported Cooperative Work*. Dordrecht: Kluwer Academic Publishers.

Huws, U. (2019) *Labour in Contemporary Capitalism: What Next?*. New York, NY: Palgrave Macmillan.

Jäckel, M. (2008) 'Ein Spiel zwischen Personen. Funktionen und Folgen der elektronischen Kommunikation in Unternehmen', pp. 119–41 in Schulz-Schaeffer, I. and Funken, C. (eds.), *Digitalisierung der Arbeitswelt*. Wiesbaden: VS Verlag für Sozialwissenschaften.

Jacko, J.A. (2012) *Human Computer Interaction Handbook: Fundamentals, Evolving Technologies, and Emerging Applications*. Taylor & Francis.

Jacobs, F.R. and Weston, F.C. (2007) 'Enterprise Resource Planning (ERP)—A Brief History', *Journal of Operations Management* 25(2): 357–63.

Jakobs, E.-M., Ziefle, M. and Lehnen, K. (2008) *Alter und Technik. Studie zu Technikkonzepten, Techniknutzung und Technikbewertung älterer Menschen*. Aachen: Apprimus Verlag.

Jarzabkowski, P. (2004) 'Strategy as Practice: Recursiveness, Adaptation, and Practices-in-Use', *Organization Studies* 25(4): 529–60.

Jarzabkowski, P. (2005) *Strategy as Practice: An Activity Based Approach*. London: Sage.

Jarzabkowski, P., Balogun, J. and Seidl, D. (2007) 'Strategizing: The Challenges of a Practice Perspective', *Human Relations* 60(1): 5–27.

Jarzabkowski, P. and Pinch, T. (2014) 'Sociomateriality Is "the New Black": Accomplishing Repurposing, Reinscripting and Repairing in Context', *M@n@gement* 16(5): 579–92.

Jones, S.L. and van de Ven, A.H. (2016) 'The Changing Nature of Change Resistance: An Examination of the Moderating Impact of Time', *The Journal of Applied Behavioral Science* 52(4): 482–506.

Kansal, S. and Chandani, A. (2014) 'Effective Management of Change During Merger and Acquisition', *Procedia Economics and Finance* 11: 208–17.

Kappelman, L.A. (1995) 'Measuring User Involvement: A Diffusion of Innovation Perspective', *SIGMIS Database* 26(2–3): 65–86.

Kärreman, D. and Alvesson, M. (2004) 'Cages in Tandem: Management Control, Social Identity, and Identification in a Knowledge-Intensive Firm', *Organization* 11(1): 149–75.

Kärreman, D. and Rylander, A. (2008) 'Managing Meaning through Branding — the Case of a Consulting Firm', *Organization Studies* 29(1): 103–25.

Kelly, E.L., Ammons, S.K., Chermack, K. and Moen, P. (2010) 'Gendered Challenge, Gendered Response', *Gender & Society: Official Publication of Sociologists for Women in Society* 24(3): 281–303.

Knoblauch, H. (1996) 'Arbeit als Interaktion: Informationsgesellschaft, Post-Fordismus und Kommunikationsarbeit', *Soziale Welt* 47(3): 344–62.

Knoblauch, H. and Heath, C. (1999) 'Technologie, Interaktion und Organisation: die Workplace Studies', *Schweizerische Zeitschrift für Soziologie* 25(2): 163–81.

Knorr Cetina, K. (1997) 'Sociality with Objects: Social Relations in Postsocial Knowledge Societies', *Theory, Culture & Society* 14(4): 1–30.

Knorr Cetina, K. (1999) *Epistemic Cultures: How the Sciences Make Knowledge*. Harvard University Press.

Knorr Cetina, K. (2001) 'Objectual Practice', pp. 175–88 in Knorr Cetina, K., Schatzki, T.R. and von Savigny, E. (eds.), *The Practice Turn in Contemporary Theory*. London; New York: Routledge.

Knorr Cetina, K. (2009) 'The Synthetic Situation: Interactionism for a Global World', *Symbolic Interaction* 32(1): 61–87.

Knorr Cetina, K., Schatzki, T.R., von Savigny, E. (eds.) (2001) *The Practice Turn in Contemporary Theory*. London; New York: Routledge.

Kornberger, M. (2010) *Brand Society: How Brands Transform Management and Lifestyle*. Cambridge; New York: Cambridge University Press.

Kruse, J. (2004) *Mobilfunk zwischen Wettbewerb und Regulierung*, Hamburger Forum Medienökonomie. München: Fischer.

Kühl, S. (2011) *Organisationen: Eine sehr kurze Einführung*. Wiesbaden: VS Verlag für Sozialwissenschaften.

Kunda, G. (2006) *Engineering Culture: Control and Commitment in a High-Tech Corporation*. Philadelphia, PA: Temple University Press.

Kurz, S. (2012) *Mikropolitik politischer Organisationen*. Wiesbaden: VS Verlag für Sozialwissenschaften.

Lamb, R. (1999) 'Using Intranets: Preliminary Results from a Socio-Technical Field Study', in *Proceedings of the 32nd Annual Hawaii International Conference on Systems Sciences, IEEE Computer*.

Langley, A., Golden-Biddle, K., Reay, T., Denis, J.L., Hébert, Y., Lamothe, L. and Gervais, J. (2012) 'Identity Struggles in Merging Organizations: Renegotiating the Sameness–Difference Dialectic', *The Journal of Applied Behavioral Science* 48(2): 135–67.

Lash, S. and Lury, C. (2007) *Global Culture Industry: The Mediation of Things*. Cambridge: Polity Press.

Lash, S. and Urry, J. (1994) *Economies of Signs and Space*. London: Sage.

Latour, B. (1994) 'On Technical Mediation', *Common Knowledge* 3(2): 29–64.

Latour, B. (2005) *Reassembling the Social: An Introduction to Actor-Network-Theory*. Oxford; New York: Oxford University Press.

Latour, B. (2015) *We Have Never Been Modern*. Cambridge, Mass.: Harvard University Press.

Laube, S. (2012) 'Im Takt des Marktes. Körperliche Praktiken in technologisierten Finanzmärkten', pp. 265–84 in Kalthoff, H. and Vormbusch, U. (eds.), *Soziologie der Finanzmärkte*. Bielefeld: transcript.

Laube, S. (2013) *Nervöse Märkte. Zur Praxis der Marktbeobachtung im Derivatehandel*. Konstanz: Universität Konstanz. Dissertation.

Lauer, T. (2014) *Change Management: Grundlagen und Erfolgsfaktoren*. Springer Gabler.

Lave, J. and Wenger, E. (1991) *Situated Learning: Legitimate Peripheral Participation*. Cambridge; New York: Cambridge University Press.

Law, J. (1992) 'Notes on the Theory of the Actor-Network: Ordering, Strategy, and Heterogeneity', *Systems Practice* 5(4): 379–95.

Law, J. (2004) *After Method: Mess in Social Science Research*. London; New York: Routledge.

Law, J. (2016) 'Comment on Suchman, and Gherardi and Nicolini: Knowing as Displacing', *Organization* 7(2): 349–57.

Law, J. and Urry, J. (2004) 'Enacting the Social', *Economy and Society* 33(3): 390–410.

Lazzarato, M. (2004) 'From Capital-Labour to Capital-Life', *Ephemera: Theory & Politics in Organizaion* 4(3): 187–208.

Lazzarato, M. (2006) 'Immaterial Labour', pp. 133–50 in Virno, P. and Hardt, M. (eds.), *Radical Thought in Italy: A Potential Politics*. University of Minnesota Press.

Lee, S.-J., Park, B.I., and Kim, J.(2015) 'Culture Clashes in Cross-Border Mergers and Acquisitions: A Case Study of Sweden's Volvo and South Korea's Samsung', *International Business Review* 24(4): 580–93.

Lehmuskallio, S. (2006) 'The Uses, Roles, and Contents of Intranets in Multinational Companies in Finland', *Journal of Business and Technical Communication* 20(3): 288–324.

Leimbach, T. (2008) 'The SAP Story: Evolution of SAP within the German Software Industry', *IEEE Annals of the History of Computing* 30(4): 60–76.

Löhndorf, B. and Diamantopoulos, A. (2014) 'Internal Branding: Social Identity and Social Exchange Perspectives on Turning Employees into Brand Champions', *Journal of Service Research* 17(3): 310–25.

Lohr, K. (2003) 'Subjektivierung von Arbeit. Ausgangspunkt einer Neuorientierung der Industrie- und Arbeitssoziologie?', *Berliner Journal für Soziologie* 13(4): 511–29.

Lynch, M. (2001) 'Science and Technology Studies: Ethnomethodology', pp. 13644–7 in Smelser, N.J. and Baltes, P.B. (eds.), *International Encyclopedia of the Social & Behavioral Sciences*. Oxford: Pergamon.

Macdonald, M. (1991) 'Post-Fordism and the Flexibility Debate', *Studies in Political Economy* 36(1): 177–201.

Madsen, D.Ø. (2020) 'The Evolutionary Trajectory of the Agile Concept Viewed from a Management Fashion Perspective', *Social Sciences* 9(5): 69.

Mager, A. (2010) *Mediated Knowledge: Sociotechnical Practices of Communicating Medical Knowledge via the Web and their Epistemic Implications*. Wien: Universität Wien. Dissertation.

Malaurent, J. and Avison, D. (2016) 'Reconciling Global and Local Needs: A Canonical Action Research Project to Deal with Workarounds', *Information Systems Journal* 26(3): 227–57.

Maldonado, T., Vera, D. and Ramos, N. (2018) 'How Humble Is Your Company Culture? And, Why Does It Matter?', *Business Horizons* 61(5): 745–53.

Mangold, C.M. (2007) *Konzepte und Realisierung einer kontextbasierten Intranet-Suchmaschine*. Stuttgart: Universität Stuttgart. Dissertation.

Marcus, G.E. (1995) 'Ethnography in/of the World System: The Emergence of Multi-Sited Ethnography', *Annual Review of Anthropology* 24(1): 95–117.

Martini, A., Corso, M. and Pellegrini, L. (2009) 'An Empirical Roadmap for Intranet Evolution', *International Journal of Information Management* 29(4): 295–308.

Massanari, A.L. (2010) 'Designing for Imaginary Friends: Information Architecture, Personas and the Politics of User-Centered Design', *New Media & Society* 12(3): 401–16.

McGrath, C. (2014) *Reducing Culture Clash in M&A with Social Merger Software.* Thought Farmer / M&A edition.

Mishra, K., Boynton, L. and Mishra, A. (2014) 'Driving Employee Engagement: The Expanded Role of Internal Communications', *International Journal of Business Communication* 51(2): 183–202.

Mol, A. (2002) *The Body Multiple: Ontology in Medical Practice.* Duke University Press.

Morrill, C. (2008) 'Culture and Organization Theory', *The ANNALS of the American Academy of Political and Social Science* 619(1): 15–40.

Mosley, R.W. (2007) 'Customer Experience, Organisational Culture and the Employer Brand', *Journal of Brand Management* 15(2): 123–34.

Mulder, S. and Yaar, Z. (2007) *The User Is Always Right: A Practical Guide to Creating and Using Personas for the Web.* Berkeley, CA: New Riders.

Mullan, K. and Wajcman, J. (2019) 'Have Mobile Devices Changed Working Patterns in the 21st Century? A Time-Diary Analysis of Work Extension in the UK', *Work, Employment and Society* 33(1): 3–20.

Müller, M. (2017) '"Brand-Centred Control": A Study of Internal Branding and Normative Control', *Organization Studies* 38(7): 895–915.

Müller, M. (2018) '"Brandspeak": Metaphors and the Rhetorical Construction of Internal Branding', *Organization* 25(1): 42–68.

Mumby, D.K. (2005) 'Theorizing Resistance in Organization Studies: A Dialectical Approach', *Management Communication Quarterly* 19(1): 19–44.

Nair, N. (2010) 'Identity Regulation: Towards Employee Control?', *International Journal of Organizational Analysis* 18(1): 6–22.

Neil, W.D. and Richard, J.E. (2012) 'Intranet Portals: Marketing and Managing Individuals' Acceptance and Use', *Australasian Marketing Journal (AMJ)* 20(2): 147–57.

Newell, S., Scarbrough, H. and Swan, J. (2001) 'From Global Knowledge Management to Internal Electronic Fences: Contradictory Outcomes of Intranet Development', *British Journal of Management* 12(2): 97–111.

Nicolini, D. (2013) *Practice Theory, Work, and Organization: An Introduction.* Oxford University Press, USA.

Nicolini, D., Gherardi, S. and Yanow, D. (2003) *Knowing in Organizations: A Practice-Based Approach*. M.E. Sharpe.

Nielsen, J. (1999) *Designing Web Usability: The Practice of Simplicity*. Thousand Oaks, Calif.: New Riders Publishing.

Oh, J.-H. and Johnston, W.J. (2020) 'How Post-Merger Integration Duration Affects Merger Outcomes', *Journal of Business & Industrial Marketing* (ahead-of-print).

Olie, R. (1994) 'Shades of Culture and Institutions in International Mergers', *Organization Studies* 15(3): 381–405.

Orlikowski, W.J. (2007) 'Sociomaterial Practices: Exploring Technology at Work', *Organization Studies* 28(9): 1435–48.

Orlikowski, W.J. (2010) 'The Sociomateriality of Organisational Life: Considering Technology in Management Research', *Cambridge Journal of Economics* 34(1): 125–41.

Orlikowski, W.J. and Barley, S.R. (2001) 'Technology and Institutions: What Can Research on Information Technology and Research on Organizations Learn from Each Other?', *MIS Quarterly* 25(2): 145–65.

Orlikowski, W.J. and Iacono, C.S. (2001) 'Research Commentary: Desperately Seeking the "IT" in IT Research - A Call to Theorising the IT Artifact', *Information Systems Research* 12(2): 1–14.

Orlikowski, W.J. and Scott, S.V. (2008) 'Sociomateriality: Challenging the Separation of Technology, Work and Organization', *The Academy of Management Annals* 2(1): 433–74.

Orlikowski, W.J. and Yates, J. (2006) 'ICT and Organizational Change: A Commentary', *The Journal of Applied Behavioral Science* 42(1): 127–34.

Oudshoorn, N. and Pinch, T.J. (2003) 'Introduction: How Users and Non-Users Matter', pp. 1–25 in Oudshoorn, N. and Pinch, T.J. (eds.) *How Users Matter: The Co-Construction of Users and Technologies*. Cambridge, Mass.: MIT Press.

Oudshoorn, N., Rommes, E. and Stienstra, M. (2004) 'Configuring the User as Everybody: Gender and Design Cultures in Information and Communication Technologies', *Science, Technology & Human Values* 29(1): 30–63.

Papasolomou, I. and Vrontis, D. (2006) 'Using Internal Marketing to Ignite the Corporate Brand: The Case of the UK Retail Bank Industry', *Journal of Brand Management* 14(1): 177–95.

Park, S., O'Brien, M.A., Caine, K.E., Rogers, W.A., Fisk, A.D., Ittersum, K.V., Capar, M. and Parsons, L.J. (2006) 'Acceptance of Computer Technology: Understanding the User and the Organizational Characteristics', *Pro-*

ceedings of the Human Factors and Ergonomics Society Annual Meeting 50(15): 1478:82.

Patel, T. (2017) 'Multiparadigmatic Studies of Culture: Needs, Challenges, and Recommendations for Management Scholars', *European Management Review* 14(1): 83–100.

Pellegrino, G. (2012) 'Beyond an IT-Driven Knowledge Society: Knowledge Management as Intertwined Sociotechnical Circulation', *European Review* 20(02): 164–72.

Perlow, L.A. (2012) *Sleeping with Your Smartphone: How to Break the 24/7 Habit and Change the Way You Work.* Harvard Business Press.

Pfeiffer, S. (2021) *Digitalisierung als Distributivkraft.* Bielefeld: transcript. URL: https://www.transcript-verlag.de/978-3-8376-5422-6/digitalisierun g-als-distributivkraft/ (last accessed 22.12.2020).

Pflüger, J. (2004) 'Writing, Building, Growing: Leitvorstellungen der Programmiergeschichte', pp. 275–320 in Hellige, H.D. (ed.), *Geschichten der Informatik.* Berlin; Heidelberg: Springer.

Pollock, N. (2005) 'When Is a Work-Around? Conflict and Negotiation in Computer Systems Development', *Science, Technology & Human Values* 30(4): 496–514.

Pollock, N., Williams, R. and D'Adderio, L. (2007) 'Global Software and Its Provenance. Generification Work in the Production of Organizational Software Packages', *Social Studies of Science* 37(2): 254–80.

Pratt, M.G., Schultz, M., Ashforth, B.E. and Ravasi, D. (2016) *The Oxford Handbook of Organizational Identity.* Oxford; New York: Oxford University Press.

Preece, J. (2001) 'Sociability and Usability in Online Communities: Determining and Measuring Success', *Behaviour & Information Technology* 20(5): 347–56.

Punjaisri, K. and Wilson, A. (2007) 'The Role of Internal Branding in the Delivery of Employee Brand Promise', *Journal of Brand Management* 15(1): 57–70.

Quirmbach, S.M. (2012) *Suchmaschinen: User Experience, Usability und nutzerzentrierte Website-Gestaltung.* Wiesbaden: Springer Verlag.

Reckwitz, A. (2002a) 'The Status of the "Material" in Theories of Culture: From "Social Structure" to "Artefacts"', *Journal for the Theory of Social Behaviour* 32(2): 195–217.

Reckwitz, A. (2002b) 'Toward a Theory of Social Practices: A Development in Culturalist Theorizing', *European Journal of Social Theory* 5(2): 243–63.

Reckwitz, A. (2003) 'Grundelemente einer Theorie Sozialer Praktiken. Eine Sozialtheoretische Perspektive', *Zeitschrift für Soziologie* 32(4): 282–301.

Reckwitz, A. (2005) 'Kulturelle Differenzen aus praxeologischer Perspektive. Kulturelle Globalisierung jenseits von Modernisierungstheorie und Kulturessentialismus', pp. 92–111 in Renn, J., Srubar, I. and Wenzel, U. (eds.), *Kulturen vergleichen: Sozial- und Kulturwissenschaftliche Grundlagen und Kontroversen*. Wiesbaden: VS Verlag für Sozialwissenschaften.

Reckwitz, A. (2008) 'Praktiken und Diskurse. Eine sozialtheoretische und methodologische Relation', pp. 188-209 in Hirschauer, S., Kalthoff, H. and Lindemann, G. (eds.), *Theoretische Empirie: Zur Relevanz qualitativer Forschung*. Frankfurt: Suhrkamp.

Reckwitz, A. (2017) *Die Gesellschaft der Singularitäten: Zum Strukturwandel der Moderne*. Berlin: Suhrkamp.

Reckwitz, A. (2020) *Das Ende Der Illusionen: Politik, Ökonomie und Kultur in der Spätmoderne* (Sonderausgabe für die Bundeszentrale für Politische Bildung.). Bonn: Bundeszentrale für Politische Bildung.

Riad, S. (2005) 'The Power of "Organizational Culture" as a Discursive Formation in Merger Integration', *Organization Studies* 26(10): 1529–54.

Robertson, B.J. (2015) *Holacracy: The New Management System for a Rapidly Changing World*. New York: Henry Holt & Company.

Rohleder, P. (2014) 'Othering', pp. 1306-1308 in Teo, T. (ed.) *Encyclopedia of Critical Psychology*. New York: Springer.

Rogers, E.M. (2003) *Diffusion of Innovations*. New York: Simon and Schuster.

Rose, E. (2015) 'Temporal Flexibility and Its Limits: The Personal Use of ICTs at Work', *Sociology* 49(3): 505–20.

Rottig, D. and Reus, T.H. (2018) 'Research on Culture and International Acquisition Performance: A Critical Evaluation and New Directions', *International Studies of Management & Organization* 48(1): 3–42.

Royer, I. (2020) 'Observing Materiality in Organizations', *M@n@gement* 23(3): 9–27.

Ruppel, C.P. and Harrington, S.J. (2001) 'Sharing Knowledge through Intranets: A Study of Organizational Culture and Intranet Implementation', *IEEE Transactions on Professional Communication* 44(1): 37–52.

Sauer, S. (2021) 'Projektarbeit: Potenziale und Risiken der "schönen neuen Arbeitswelt"'. *Berliner Debatte Initial* 32(3): 19-30.

Schabacher, G. (2017) 'Im Zwischenraum der Lösungen. Reparaturarbeit und Workarounds', in *ilinx – Berliner Beiträge zur Kulturwissenschaft 4: Workarounds. Praktiken des Umwegs*. I-xvi.

Schatzki, T.R. (1996) *Social Practices: A Wittgensteinian Approach to Human Activity and the Social*. Cambridge; New York: Cambridge University Press.

Schatzki, T.R. (2002) *Site of the Social: A Philosophical Account of the Constitution of Social Life and Change*. Penn State Press.

Schatzki, T.R. (2006) 'On Organizations as They Happen', *Organization Studies* 27(12): 1863–73.

Scheffer, T. (2002) 'Das Beobachten als sozialwissenschaftliche Methode – von den Grenzen der Beobachtbarkeit und ihrer methodischen Bearbeitung', pp. 351–74 in Schaeffer, D. and Müller-Mundt, G. (eds.), *Qualitative Gesundheits- und Pflegeforschung*. Bern: Huber Verlag.

Schein, E.H. (2003) *Organisationskultur. 'The Ed Schein Corporate Culture Survival Guide'*. Bergisch Gladbach: EHP Edition Humanistische Psychologie.

Schein, E.H. (2015) 'Some Thoughts About the Uses and Misuses of the Concept of Culture', *Journal of Business Anthropology* 4(1): 106–13.

Schmidt, R. (2008) 'Praktiken Des Programmierens. Zur Morphologie von Wissensarbeit in der Software-Entwicklung', *Zeitschrift für Soziologie* 37(4): 282–300.

Schmidt, R. (2012) *Soziologie der Praktiken: Konzeptionelle Studien und Empirische Analysen*. Berlin: Suhrkamp.

Schönian, K. (2011) 'From "Virtuality" to Practice. Researching the Intranet as a Socio-Material Assemblage', *Graduate Journal of Social Science* 8(3): 142–160.

Schulz-Schaeffer, I. and C. Funken (2008) 'Das Verhältnis von Formalisierung und Informalität betrieblicher Arbeits- und Kommunikationsprozesse und die Rolle der Informationstechnik', pp. 11–39 in Schulz-Schaeffer, I. and Funken, C. (eds.), *Digitalisierung der Arbeitswelt. Zur Neuordnung formaler und informeller Prozesse in Unternehmen*. Wiesbaden: VS Verlag für Sozialwissenschaften.

Scott, J.E. (1998) 'Organizational Knowledge and the Intranet', *Decision Support Systems* 23(1): 3–17.

Seidl, D. and Whittington, R. (2014) 'Enlarging the Strategy-as-Practice Research Agenda: Towards Taller and Flatter Ontologies', *Organization Studies* 35(10): 1–15.

Shapiro, C. and Varian, H.R. (1998) *Information Rules: A Strategic Guide to the Network Economy*. Harvard Business Review Press.

Shove, E., Pantzar, M. and Watson, M. (2012) *The Dynamics of Social Practice: Everyday Life and How It Changes*. London: Sage.

Slater, D. and Barry, A. (2005) *Technological Economy*. London; New York: Routledge.

Slater, D. and Tonkiss, F. (2001) *Market Society: Markets and Modern Social Theory*. Cambridge: Polity Press.

Soeffner, H.-G., Knoblauch, H. and Tänzler, D. (2006) *Zur Kritik der Wissensgesellschaft*. Konstanz: UVK.

Star, S.L. (2002) 'Infrastructure and Ethnographic Practice: Working on the Fringes', *Scandinavian Journal of Information Systems* 14(2): 107–22.

Star, S.L. and Griesemer, J.R. (1989) 'Institutional Ecology, 'Translations' and Boundary Objects: Amateurs and Professionals in Berkeley's Museum of Vertebrate Zoology, 1907-39', *Social Studies of Science* 19(3): 387–420.

Star, S.L. and Ruhleder, K. (1996) 'Steps Toward an Ecology of Infrastructure: Design and Access for Large Information Spaces', *Information Systems Research* 7(1): 111–34.

Stehr, N. (1994) *Knowledge Societies*. London: Sage.

Stehr, N. (2007) 'Societal Transformations, Globalisations and the Knowledge Society', *International Journal of Knowledge and Learning*, 3(2–3): 139–53.

Stenmark, D. (1999) 'A Method for Intranet Search Engine Evaluations', pp. 1–14 in Käkölä, T. (ed.), *Proceedings of IRIS22, Jyväskylä, Finland, 7-10 August 1999*. Presented at the Information Systems Research Seminar in Scandinavia.

Stenmark, D. (2002) 'Standardisation vs Personalisation: An Alternative View'. URL: http://citeseerx.ist.psu.edu/viewdoc/download?doi=10.1.1.19.1343&rep=rep1&type=pdf (last accessed 27.01.2020)

Stenmark, D. (2008) 'Identifying Clusters of User Behavior in Intranet Search Engine Log Files', *Journal of the American Society for Information Science and Technology* 59(14): 2232–43.

Suchman, L. (1995) 'Making Work Visible', *Communications of the ACM* 38(9): 56–64.

Suchman, L. (1997) 'From Interactions to Integrations', pp. 1–3 in Howard, S., Hammond, J. and Lindgaard, G. (eds.), *Human-Computer Interaction INTERACT '97*, IFIP — The International Federation for Information Processing. Springer US.

Suchman, L. (2000) 'Making a Case: 'Knowledge' and 'Routine' Work in Document Production', pp. 29-45 in Heath, C., Hindmarsh, J., Luff, P. and Suchman, L. (eds.) *Workplace Studies: Recovering Work Practice and Informing System Design*. Cambridge; New York: Cambridge University Press.

Suchman, L. (2005) 'Affiliative Objects', *Organization* 12(3): 379–99.

Suchman, L. (2007) *Human-Machine Reconfigurations: Plans and Situated Actions*. Cambridge; New York: Cambridge University Press.

Suchman, L. (2012) 'Configuration', pp. 48–60 in Lury, C. and Wakeford, N. (eds.), *Inventive Methods: The Happening of the Social*. London; New York: Routledge.

Suchman, L., Blomberg, J., Orr, J.E. and Trigg, R. (1999) 'Reconstructing Technologies as Social Practice', *American Behavioral Scientist* 43(3): 392–408.

Suchman, L. and Bishop, L. (2000) 'Problematizing "Innovation" as a Critical Project', *Technology Analysis & Strategic Management* 12(3): 327–333.

Suchman, L., Trigg, R. and Blomberg, J. (2002) 'Working Artefacts: Ethnomethods of the Prototype', *British Journal of Sociology* 53(2).

Tanure, B., Cançado, V., Duarte, R.G. and Muÿlder, C.F. (2009) 'The Role of National Culture in Mergers and Acquisitions', *Latin American Business Review* 10(2–3): 135–59.

Tarhini, A., Hone, K. and Liu, X. (2015) 'A Cross-cultural Examination of the Impact of Social, Organisational and Individual Factors on Educational Technology Acceptance between British and Lebanese University Students', *British Journal of Educational Technology* 46(4): 739–55.

Taylor, F.W. (2001) *The Principles of Scientific Management*. Mineola, N.Y: Dover Publications Inc.

Thrift, N. (2005) *Knowing Capitalism*. London: Sage.

Torres, R.J., Heck, M.P., Rudd, J.R. and Kelley, J.F. (2008) 'Usability Engineering: A Consultant's View of Best Practices and Proven Results', *Ergonomics in Design: The Quarterly of Human Factors Applications* 16(2): 18–23.

Trkman, M. and Trkman, P. (2009) 'A Wiki as Intranet: A Critical Analysis Using the Delone and McLean Model', *Online Information Review*.

Tuckman, A. (1994) 'The Yellow Brick Road: Total Quality Management and the Restructuring of Organizational Culture', *Organization Studies* 15(5): 727–51.

Vaara, E. (2002) 'On the Discursive Construction of Success/Failure in Narratives of Post-Merger Integration', *Organization Studies* 23(2): 211–48.

Vallas, S.P. (1999) 'Rethinking Post-Fordism: The Meaning of Workplace Flexibility', *Sociological Theory* 17(1): 68–101.

Venkatesh, V. and Davis, F.D. (2000) 'A Theoretical Extension of the Technology Acceptance Model: Four Longitudinal Field Studies', *Management Science* 46(2): 186–204.

Vu, T., Willis, A., Kruschwitz, U. and Song, D. (2017) 'Personalised Query Suggestion for Intranet Search with Temporal User Profiling', pp. 265–8 in CHIIR '17: *Proceedings of the 2017 Conference on Conference Human Information Interaction and Retrieval*, New York: Association for Computing Machinery.

van der Waal, K. (2009) 'Getting Going: Organizing Ethnographic Fieldwork', pp. 23–39 in Ybema, S., Yanow, D. and Wels, H. (eds.), *Organizational Ethnography: Studying the Complexity of Everyday Life*. London: Sage.

Wagner, E.L. and Newell, S. (2016) 'Repairing ERP: Producing Social Order to Create a Working Information System', *The Journal of Applied Behavioral Science* 42(1): 40-57.

Wajcman, J. (2002) 'Addressing Technological Change: The Challenge to Social Theory', *Current Sociology* 50(3): 347–63.

Wajcman, J. (2006) 'New Connections: Social Studies of Science and Technology and Studies of Work', *Work, Employment & Society* 20(4): 773–86.

Wajcman, J. and Rose, E. (2011) 'Constant Connectivity: Rethinking Interruptions at Work', *Organization Studies* 32(7): 941–61.

Weick, K.E. (1993) 'The Collapse of Sensemaking in Organizations: The Mann Gulch Disaster', *Administrative Science Quarterly* 38(4): 628–52.

Weick, K.E. (1995) *Der Prozeß des Organisierens*. Frankfurt am Main: Suhrkamp.

Weick, K.E. and Roberts, K.H. (1993) 'Collective Mind in Organizations: Heedful Interrelating on Flight Decks', *Administrative Science Quarterly* 38(3): 357–81.

Weick, K.E., Sutcliffe, K.M. and Obstfeld, D. (2005) 'Organizing and the Process of Sensemaking', *Organization Science* 16(4): 409–21.

Whittington, R. (2006) 'Completing the Practice Turn in Strategy Research', *Organization Studies* 27(5): 613–34.

Wibisono, A., Alhassan, I., Sammon, D., Heavin, C., Kiely, G. and Suryani, E. (2019) 'Understanding Theory of Workarounds in Practice', *Procedia Computer Science* 161: 187–94.

Wilkie, A. and Michael, M. (2009) 'Expectation and Mobilisation: Enacting Future Users', *Science, Technology & Human Values* 34(4): 502–22.

Willmott, H. (1993) 'Strength Is Ignorance; Slavery Is Freedom: Managing Culture in Modern Organizations', *Journal of Management Studies* 30(4): 515–52.

Wilz, S.M. (2015) 'Skizze zur praxistheoretischen Debatte um Organisation', pp. 253–70 in Apelt, M. and U. Wilkesmann (eds.), *Zur Zukunft der Organisationssoziologie*. Wiesbaden: Springer Verlag.

Winner, L. (1980) 'Do Artifacts Have Politics?', *Daedalus* 109(1): 121–36.

Woolgar, S. (1991) 'Configuring the User: The Case of Usability Trials', pp. 57–99 in Law, J. (ed.), *A Sociology of Monsters: Essays on Power, Technology, and Domination*. London; New York: Routledge.

Yanow, D. (1996) *How Does a Policy Mean? Interpreting Policy and Organizational Actions*. Georgetown University Press.

Yanow, D. (2009) 'Dear Author, Dear Reader', pp. 275–302 in Schatz, E. (ed.), *Political Ethnography. What Immersion Contributes to the Study of Power*. University of Chicago Press.

Yanow, D. and Schwartz-Shea, P. (2009) 'Reading and Writing as Method: In Search of Trustworthy Texts', pp. 56–81 in Ybema, S., Yanow, D., Wels, H. and Kamsteeg, F.H. (eds.), *Organizational Ethnography: Studying the Complexity of Everyday Life*. London: Sage.

Yates, J. (1989) *Control through Communication: The Rise of System in American Management*. Baltimore: Johns Hopkins University Press.

Ybema, S. and Horvers, M. (2017) 'Resistance Through Compliance: The Strategic and Subversive Potential of Frontstage and Backstage Resistance', *Organization Studies* 38(9): 1233–51.

Social Sciences

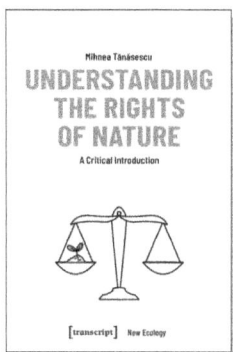

Mihnea Tanasescu
Understanding the Rights of Nature
A Critical Introduction

February 2022, 168 p., pb.
40,00 € (DE), 978-3-8376-5431-8
E-Book: available as free open access publication
PDF: ISBN 978-3-8394-5431-2

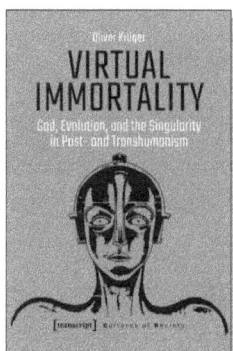

Oliver Krüger
**Virtual Immortality –
God, Evolution, and the Singularity
in Post- and Transhumanism**

2021, 356 p., pb., ill.
35,00 (DE), 978-3-8376-5059-4
E-Book:
PDF: 34,99 (DE), ISBN 978-3-8394-5059-8

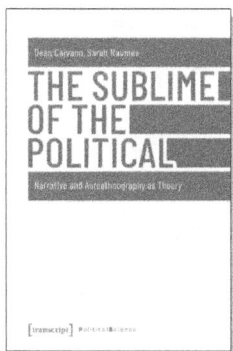

Dean Caivano, Sarah Naumes
The Sublime of the Political
Narrative and Autoethnography as Theory

2021, 162 p., hardcover
100,00 (DE), 978-3-8376-4772-3
E-Book:
PDF: 99,99 (DE), ISBN 978-3-8394-4772-7

**All print, e-book and open access versions of the titles in our list
are available in our online shop www.transcript-publishing.com**

Social Sciences

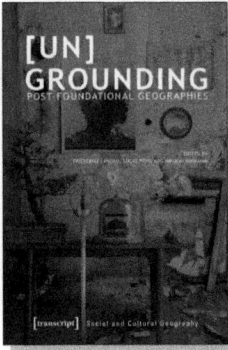

Friederike Landau, Lucas Pohl, Nikolai Roskamm (eds.)
[Un]Grounding
Post-Foundational Geographies

2021, 348 p., pb., col. ill.
50,00 (DE), 978-3-8376-5073-0
E-Book:
PDF: 49,99 (DE), ISBN 978-3-8394-5073-4

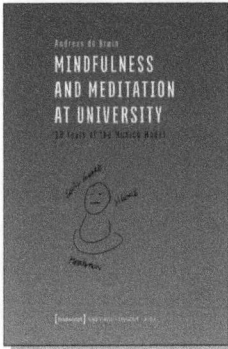

Andreas de Bruin
Mindfulness and Meditation at University
10 Years of the Munich Model

2021, 216 p., pb.
25,00 (DE), 978-3-8376-5696-1
E-Book: available as free open access publication
PDF: ISBN 978-3-8394-5696-5

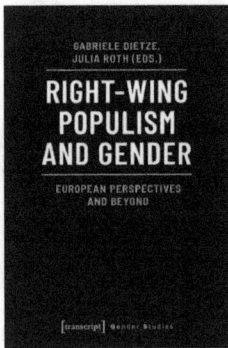

Gabriele Dietze, Julia Roth (eds.)
Right-Wing Populism and Gender
European Perspectives and Beyond

2020, 286 p., pb., ill.
35,00 (DE), 978-3-8376-4980-2
E-Book:
PDF: 34,99 (DE), ISBN 978-3-8394-4980-6

**All print, e-book and open access versions of the titles in our list
are available in our online shop www.transcript-publishing.com**

GPSR Authorized Representative: Easy Access System Europe, Mustamäe tee
50, 10621 Tallinn, Estonia, gpsr.requests@easproject.com